Histories which have been absolutely invaluable include that of *Vickers Ltd* from my ow
kindly loaned by Jack Curwen, and, the real gem, *Golden Years*, the history of the Corne
parent company of *Central Mining and Investment Corporation*, found and loaned to me by my good colleague, and fellow enthusiast from the transport manufacturing industry, Bob Smith who also provided the detailed body production lists to which all the above material was painstakingly linked.

In recent months my good friend Bob Rowe has undertaken the task of assisting in captioning photographs and reading the proofs; Ian Stewart earns my thanks for checking matters relating to his native Glasgow; Keith Barkham and John Davies have ploughed through the proofs, made many useful comments and corrections and gently chivvied me along, for which I thank them. David and Mary Shaw have, as always, cheerfully undertaken the daunting task of overall proof reading. My elder son Mark has tried to keep the computers and I on an even keel and understanding each other – not an easy task I can assure you. Nevertheless, despite all the help I have received, any errors and omissions are down to me.

I offer my sincere thanks to everyone mentioned and apologise if I have inadvertently missed out anyone. I have tried to record one more piece of the history of the British bus manufacturing industry which was once so important in our economy but is now but a distant memory. I hope it will bring back happy recollections and also serve as a record of the achievements of the people who worked there. I wish I could have met more of them, but, above all I hope it will bring pleasure to all those who read it.

The wide selection of photographs used in this book has been gathered from a variety of sources and Author and Publisher would like to thank all those who have assisted. Without their help it would not have been possible to give such extensive coverage.

The basis has been the original Company collection, taken mainly in the factory complex, and recording the vehicles and factory interior scenes. Many of these prints were loaned or given by former employees, or their relatives. In addition John Kaye made available a large quantity of prints from the same original source, but part of the one-time BET Contract Department files. Other operators had file prints which were also made available. The Author's own photographs and those of the Senior Transport Archive – including views from other manufacturer's – supplemented these views. Manufacturer's technical and publicity brochures have also been most useful.

Former employees helped enormously and Bunny Beaver; Brian Burton MBE; Keith Barkham MBE; John Davies; Dave Humphrey and Vic Smith were particularly helpful in loaning material and answering questions.

A number of enthusiast photographers came forward to help and we record our thanks to them – their initials appear, where appropriate, in the captions to the illustrations whilst the identifications are shown below.

If we have missed out anyone we trust they will accept our apologies.

AEJ:	Ted Jones	JAS:	John A Senior
BB:	Bunny Beaver	JD:	John Davies
DC:	David Cole	KWS:	Ken Swallow
DT:	David Toy	MAT:	Dr MA Taylor
GL:	Geoff Lumb	PG:	Peter Gascoine
GMMT:	Manchester Museum of Transport	RM:	Roy Marshall
GW:	Gerage Wedlake	RMC:	Roy Marshall Collection
IGMS:	Ian Stewart	RNH:	Robin Hannay
IGS:	Ian Stubbs	STA:	Senior Transport Archive

Bunny Beaver took many photographs of his colleagues and items in the factory. He was able to describe pre-war days and his determination to make it 'upstairs' to the Author when we met at his home. After the factory closed he went to Frimley, and then having declined the offer to rejoin Bill Shirley at Park Royal, went to London Transport at Chiswick until he finally retired. Without his help it would not have been possible to include so many portraits. Here he poses, front row left, having set his camera on 'timer', in order to join his friends. Brian Burton stands tall behind him.

Two early Newcastle Corporation Weymann bodied Leyland Atlanteans, 230 JVK body number M203 of the first batch, M194-205 delivered in 1962 and behind one of the second batch delivered in 1963, 13-25 JVK body numbers M709-721. Note the inboard fog lamps and wheel spats on the latter.

The British Bus and Truck Heritage

Weymann's Volume 2
A history of the Company and its products from 1942 to 1966

John A Senior

Venture *publications*

© 2012 Venture Publications Ltd

ISBN 978 189 843 2609

All rights reserved. Except for normal review purposes no part of this book maybe reproduced or utilised in any form by any means, electrical or mechanical, including photocopying, recording or by an information storage and retrieval system, without the prior written consent of Venture Publications Ltd, Glossop, Derbyshire, SK13 8EH.

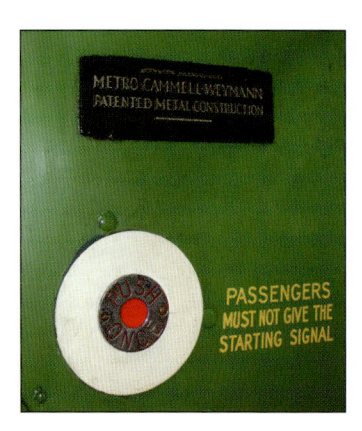

Title Page: Bury took AEC and Leyland double-deckers with the classic Weymann's body of the '40s and '50s. This fine example is now preserved at the Bury Transport Museum in Lancashire and is seen here at a celebratory MCW event at the Manchester Museum of Transport in October 2012. (JAS)

Below: The massive RT project for London Transport, split between Weymann's and Park Royal, required a completely separate factory at Weybridge as described in Chapter 10. RT 3066 was one of the many, seen here at Addlestone after completion in February 1950.

Opposite: The poignant moment as the very last completed vehicle is driven away by a Southdown driver; the SOLD sign confirms that the story is all over now in March 1966. Toddy Bubb and Arthur Mussellwhite see the buses out.

CONTENTS

Acknowledgements	Front end paper
Foreword	4
Introduction	6
The First Twenty Years	9
Chapter 6 – 1942–1946	18
Chapter 7 – Shortages & Production Problems	29
Chapter 8 – 1946-50 Coachbuilding Finale	37
Chapter 9 – 1946-50 Peacetime Production	46
Chapter 10 – 1946-54 The London RT3 Project	78
Chapter 11 – The Early Nineteen-Fifties	90
Chapter 12 – 1956-60	138
Chapter 13 – 1960-62	158
Chapter 14 – 1963-66	174
Chapter 15 – A Question	187
Chapter 16 – An Afterlife Of Sorts	191
Index	Rear end paper

FOREWORD

Looking back, it does not seem possible that Weymann's factory closed over 46 years ago, but, of course, it did. Surely, then, it must be a record that former staff still attend an annual reunion?

When the drawing office was finally disbanded from Frimley, Cecil Fleming, the Chief Draughtsman, proposed that there should be a yearly reunion 'on the first Thursday in May, at *The Otter*, Ottershaw.' It was agreed, and so it has remained, except for just a couple of deviations from this very pleasant hostelry, but now we are back there.

For the last few years these annual get-togethers have taken on a new meaning as John Senior has joined us whilst he has been researching for '*The Weymann Story*'. John has travelled quite widely in his quest to interview former employees and those who have read the first volume will be aware that in addition to those he has met at *The Otter*, he tracked down Gordon Whindle's sister Margaret, the very first Addlestone employee from 1927, and also, amongst others, Beryl Froggatt and June Guarnori, though sadly Norman and Jack, their respective husbands, had both died by that time.

Inevitably, the last few years have seen the passing of other well-known friends – Edna Bubb, Cyril Hutchings, Maurice Bullivant, Ted Gallard, Walter Healy, Vic Smith, Don Arthur, Reg Cox, Reg Allen and doubtless others I am not aware of – all of whom provided considerable information and, of course, are acknowledged in the story.

I was only an impressionable sixteen-year old when I joined Weymann's drawing office at the end of 1962 but very quickly found I had joined a big and mostly happy 'family' as well as a place to work. Most employees had started their careers at the factory and remained there throughout their working lives. John has singled out just a few of those who moved on to even greater things in his look through the personalities, in addition to his pen portraits of others who stayed the course, and this is just a part of the detail which would otherwise have been lost forever.

It should be remembered that the information recorded goes back in some cases over 80 years and the relevant documentation has survived two world wars, a number of changes of ownership of the business, and then been mostly dormant for another 45 years. Because there was such a family atmosphere many people have kept cuttings and photographs to remind them of the happy times they spent at Station Road, and these have been most useful in telling the story, alongside the trade journals which tell the story of the buses themselves without which there would have been no story to tell.

I trust '*The Weymann Story*' will serve as a reminder to transport enthusiasts and historians alike of the quality of workmanship the British coachbuilding industry was capable of producing and which will almost certainly never be repeated. I count myself lucky to have been a part of that industry in those halcyon days.

I have been able to give John some assistance – and encouragement – in his Herculean task and was very pleased when he accepted my offer to produce this Foreword as a tribute to my peers.

Please enjoy this second volume whilst I too think about those happy days at Station Road, Addlestone.

John H Davies
Reigate
Surrey
April 2012

Had things worked out differently, and had the RM contract been split between Weymann's and Park Royal as the RT contract had been, John Davies would have had first hand experience of London Routemaster production. Here he is seen with RM3, the sole Addlestone-built example, now preserved by the London Bus Preservation Group. (JD)

This splendidly-restored example of Weymann's composite construction single-deck output – C9323 from 1950 – was part of a batch of six supplied to Exeter Corporation. It epitomises the Addlestone design of the time and was one of the last to be built before coachbuilt construction finished later that year. An earlier example on an AEC chassis also survives in equally fine restored condition – C9053 from a delivery of 28 to Devon General from 1946. (JAS)

INTRODUCTION

The name Weymann still commands respect amongst the older generation in the transport industry and bus enthusiasts who remember with affection the splendid designs of the Addlestone products, enhanced, of course, by the wonderfully colourful and carefully applied liveries of the 'forties and 'fifties. Those of us who were fortunate to see brand new City of Oxford, Aldershot & District or Eastbourne Corporation vehicles, just to take three examples, will treasure the memories when most front line vehicles in major fleets looked like the surviving examples which today's preservationists are painstakingly recreating.

To have been a part of the team which designed, manufactured, assembled, painted and tested those buses was clearly a very satisfying experience, and their pride in the job has made the production of this book all the more worthwhile.

In this second volume we shall trace the transition from wartime production through the difficulties of obtaining sufficient materials, and of the right quality, with seemingly never-ending Government restrictions, to the heyday of production in 1949 when output reached 972 vehicles in that year.

Our story begins when ownership of the company had just passed to United Molasses, and the final peacetime contracts of the 1930s were being completed. The last patent flexible bus bodies, upon which the company had built its reputation in the car market, had been delivered to City of Oxford in 1940, and, from now, until the end of the hostilities, with only a handful of exceptions, wartime output would be of composite 'utility' double-deckers.

When peacetime manufacture resumed, metal-framed and composite bodies were built alongside each other, but, as the narrative explains, the opportunity was taken to rationalise production and with only a handful of exceptions all composite output was restricted to single-deckers. Metal-framed home-market single-deckers reappeared after the cessation of all composite bodybuilding early in 1950.

The ever-present rumblings of discontent run through the story, side-by-side with the happy-family aspect mentioned in the Foreword by John Davies. It should not be thought that those malcontents on the shop floor who at times brought the

This Karrier E4 trolleybus was one of the second batch supplied to South Shields in May 1937 following inauguration of the town's system in October 1936. Now restored to full operational condition C5083 can be seen – and ridden in – at the Trolleybus Museum at Sandtoft where this photograph was taken. (IGS)

whole enterprise to a grinding halt were typical; rather, from what the old employees I have interviewed tell me, they were the exception. Sadly, as in so many companies, the hotheads tended to make their way into positions of power within the internal trade union hierarchy and so their malevolent influence far outweighed their actual numbers or true importance.

Weymann's should be remembered for what it was, a happy place to work where some gifted designers produced buses whose elegance was a byword in an age when such things still mattered. Sadly, as the need for greater economy took over, commonality of design between the two component MCW factories came in, epitomised by the often-reviled Orion double-decker. We should not forget that what it lacked in elegance it made up for in popularity; examples could be seen in large and small fleets widely scattered throughout the country and on a variety of different chassis makes. Major corporations, the BET fleets and independents all took them. This was the age when products of the two factories – Addlestone and Birmingham – were virtually indistinguishable to all except the very observant.

The huge export business which kept both factories busy brought in much needed foreign exchange in the dark days after the Second World War, while providing variety in terms of customers, vehicle types and liveries. Gradually, however, the once unassailable position of the MCW group was eroded as Leyland and ACV, the only remaining players of any note by the 1960s, merged their interests and produced a combine which for a while could not be beaten. But whereas the acumen and pride of the pre-war companies had fostered competition and innovation, the huge Leyland conglomerate of the 'sixties lost its way and that empire also fell, only a decade or so after Metropolitan-Cammell had finally shut the gates at Addlestone to safeguard jobs in Birmingham.

By 1989 even Birmingham's bus building days had finished and it was all over as far as that part of the MCW organisation was concerned. But that story will have to wait for another day-and another author. Meanwhile, I thank everyone who has helped me in what became something of a marathon, but enjoyable, task, and refer readers to the Acknowledgements.

John A Senior
Glossop
Derbyshire
October 2012

These two buses neatly encapsulate the story told in this volume. AEC and Leyland will be seen as the main source of chassis passing through the factory whilst the change from traditional panel beating to the use of grp (fibreglass) domes is just part of the march of progress. The open-platform rear-entrance design has given way to the safer – and warmer – front entrance version, but the conductor has been retired, requiring the driver to collect the fares on the one-man-operated Aurora body on the left. The prewar design on M1910 continued when peacetime building resumed in 1946 and the 1963 front-entrance model, M563, continued in production to the very end. They are seen at Dunsfold in 2011. (JAS)

A sunny 1946 late summer's day in Eastbourne as newly-delivered AEC Regent II number 19 picks up its passengers. The livery enhances the lines of the body but the small windscreen spoils the effect; the five examples bodied in 1947 on Regent III chassis had the full depth screen which greatly improved the appearance, see page 57. This metal-framed double-decker, a one-off with body number M2884, was among the first post-war double-decker contracts to be built after the Guy Arab utilities of 1943-5 whose body numbers finished at M2692. (STA)

THE FIRST TWENTY YEARS

August 1923 – September 1942: A Recap

We saw in Volume 1 how Weymann Motor Bodies Ltd was founded in August 1923 by a Frenchman, Charles Terres Weymann, and that aircraft technology of the period – the pre-1920s – was used to build high class motor car bodies. Finance came from Charles Weymann and his well-heeled friends who were, largely, from the motoring and racing world. They represented a class of young men seeking adventure and, usually, with money to spend which they could afford to risk losing.

As the business grew, through the licensing of others to build Weymann's patented car bodies, openings were seen for further expansion. The Cunard Motor Company in Putney, a company building high class motor cars and other road vehicles, went into liquidation in 1924 and the assets and premises were acquired allowing Weymann's Motor Bodies (1925) Ltd to come into existence in November 1925. Sadly, it has not been possible to trace the original papers relating to this, for although the PRO at Kew have papers relating to the earlier Company, none appears to have survived from the more important 1925 Company.

Continuing growth, the expectation of even better prospects and the sudden availability of a vacant former aircraft manufacturing facility in Station Road, Addlestone (originally owned by Blériot) prompted the next move and some more, and quite substantial, finance was made available. This was the point at which the Central Mining & Investment Corporation of South Africa entered the story.

In addition to providing capital it also provided the Company with a first class engineer and qualified business specialist, EG Izod. His custodianship as manager, Managing Director and Chairman would last until his death in 1946, through the move to Addlestone, the formative years of manufacture, the change from cars to buses, the introduction, development and rapid growth of metal framed bodywork, the war years and the return to peacetime construction.

Izod joined in late 1927 or early 1928 and quickly pinpointed Bill Black, then still in charge at Vickers' bus building plant in Crayford, as the man to take the company forward. Black recalled being interviewed by Izod and Weymann, and soon afterwards was installed in the new factory in Station Road, Addlestone.

Black was not alone in moving from Vickers, though others who moved may have done so when Vickers were forced out of bus building in 1929. Some – like Moss Nelson – would remain at Weymann's for a good many years; much longer in

Although its bus building had started with the use of the patent flexible frame principle, it was the change to composite, wooden-framed, construction which opened up the market for Weymann's. At Station Road this was always referred to as 'coachbuilt' construction, and, accordingly, the bodies built by this method carried a C prefix, C65 in this instance.

This vehicle, built in 1930, is one from the very first contract, being Green Line's T231 on an AEC Regal chassis. When post-war construction resumed in 1946 the very first contract was for twenty-five T class AEC Regals for London Transport. *Deja vu?*

fact than Bill Black would do. Others again would move on as the company altered direction and the change from building bespoke luxury cars to manufacturing more run-of-the-mill buses took place.

Two examples of men who made the change and eventually became high-fliers in the industry will suffice. Herbert Payne came from Mann, Egerton's in Norwich where he had served his time. He was in Weymann's drawing office from 1928-31, then moving to Vauxhall Motors as Chief Draughtsman. After spending time with Humber Cars he was, by 1945, Chief Engineer of Commer-Karrier. Henry Light was at Vickers from 1924-8 and thus probably joined soon after Black, but before Vickers closed their bus building plant. He was at Weymann's from 1928-32, leaving to join Thrupp and Maberly where, by 1946 in Rootes days, he had become General Manager of the quality car division, later progressing to Director and Managing Director. Time spent at Weymann's was clearly time well spent.

In July 1932 a joint sales organisation was established by Weymann's and Metropolitan-Cammell Carriage and Wagon Co (MCCW) with the creation of Metropolitan-Cammell-Weymann Motor Bodies Ltd. Charles Weymann resigned, and shortly afterwards Weymann's began building metal-framed buses using the Metropolitan-Cammell patents to which it now had access. Output increased rapidly but behind the scenes all was not well. Shortly after the formation of the new joint company Izod wrote a letter to 'the tradesmen' at Addlestone warning that build quality was not acceptable and sackings would result if it did not improve. Soon afterwards, Black went briefly to Beadles, at Dartford, before taking charge at Park Royal in 1934. Engineer Ted Needs joined him from Addlestone to develop that firm's newly introduced metal-framed bodywork, both clearly drawing on their experience of the MCW patents in use at Addlestone.

The introduction of metal-framing meant that there were now three different types of body construction taking place at Addlestone, compared to just one at MCCW's plant in Birmingham. The original Weymann Patented Flexible wooden construction was in use for the select number of customers who preferred it to the

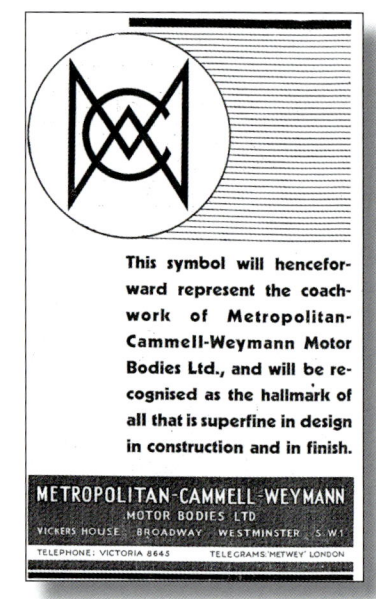

This symbol will henceforward represent the coachwork of Metropolitan-Cammell-Weymann Motor Bodies Ltd., and will be recognised as the hallmark of all that is superfine in design in construction and in finish.

METROPOLITAN-CAMMELL-WEYMANN
MOTOR BODIES LTD
VICKERS HOUSE BROADWAY WESTMINSTER S.W.1
TELEPHONE: VICTORIA 8645   TELEGRAMS 'METWEY' LONDON

When Weymann's started building double-deckers, using MCW patents, the finished result was very similar to an MCCW product. Here Addlestone's M17, an August 1933 example for Lancashire municipality Morecambe & Heysham, awaits delivery. One of these vehicles later skidded off the promenade, falling on to the beach below, and thus provided a graphic demonstration of the strength of the body since the bus was soon returned to service.

This photograph was taken by the Trade Press in 1929 to show the Patented Flexible construction. Body number W588 reflects the amount of car business, not the number of buses built to this time. It was mounted on a Daimler CF6 chassis and is believed to have been supplied to a Manchester operator in 1932 after running with Daimler as a demonstrator.

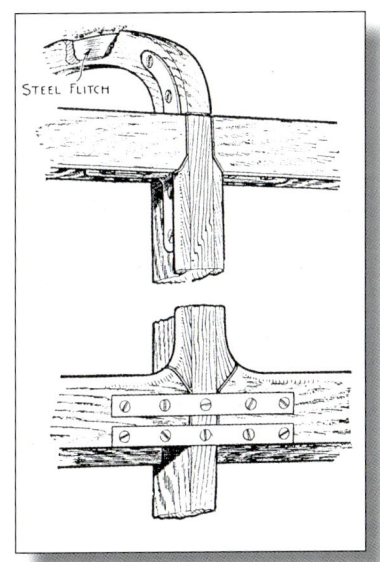

more common Composite or traditional wooden-framed variety as introduced to Station Road in 1930. Now metal framing using the MCW patents and hot riveting brought the immensely strong body which would quickly be recognised throughout the industry for its lasting durability. The hot rivets were used to join the metal sections, tightening up as the rivets quickly cooled, thus making a joint of great strength – and one which did not work loose or rattle. The routine came from heavy engineering in shipbuilding and railway rolling stock construction, both of which were well represented in MCW's antecedents, of course.

In anticipation of the expected increase in business, the first of several extensions to the original factory was now put in hand. The business did indeed materialise, and the MCW group would have substantial contracts with some of the main municipalities, including Manchester, Birmingham, Glasgow, Liverpool and Sheffield, in addition to London Transport and various of the BET company's subsidiaries, with an appreciable proportion passing through Weymann's newly extended plant.

The very different method of producing a rattle-free but flexible frame owed its parentage to CT Weymann's luxury cars and incorporated patented construction using brackets, joiners, spacers and greaseproof paper as shown in the sketch reproduced alongside. It was clearly successful, and operators taking this type of body included City of Oxford and Potteries Motor Traction, both taking examples until the option was withdrawn at the onset of the Second World War.

Just one three-axled chassis received a Patent Flexible body, an AEC Renown demonstrator, and this is it. Body number W1048 (all Flexible bodies were in the W series) was hired by Cumberland Motor Services in 1935/6 and was then sold by AEC to Valiant of Ealing who had operated some of the earliest Flexible bodies built. It was refitted with coach seating for its new role.

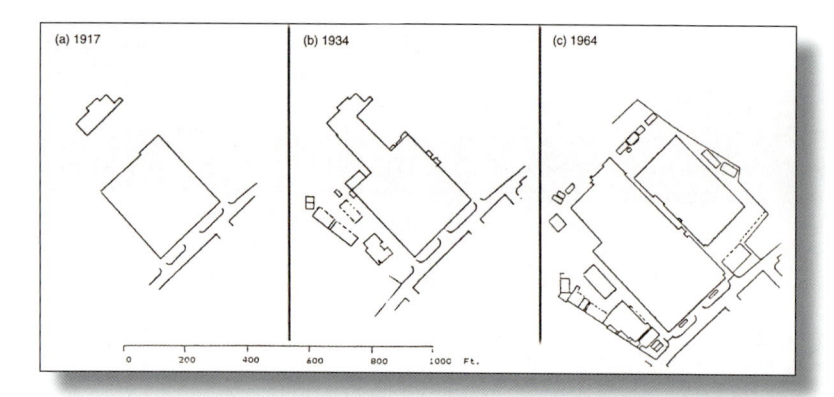

These three sketches show the development of the factory between purchase by Weymann's in 1928, extensions after the creation of MCW, and the final situation prior to closure. The large illustration shows the situation at the outbreak of war, with the additional buildings, including the new paint shop, prominent. The postcard at the foot of the page shows the final situation with the new building to cope with RT finishing being located on the right hand (east) side. The actual construction of RTs was carried out in J Building at Weybridge, of course.

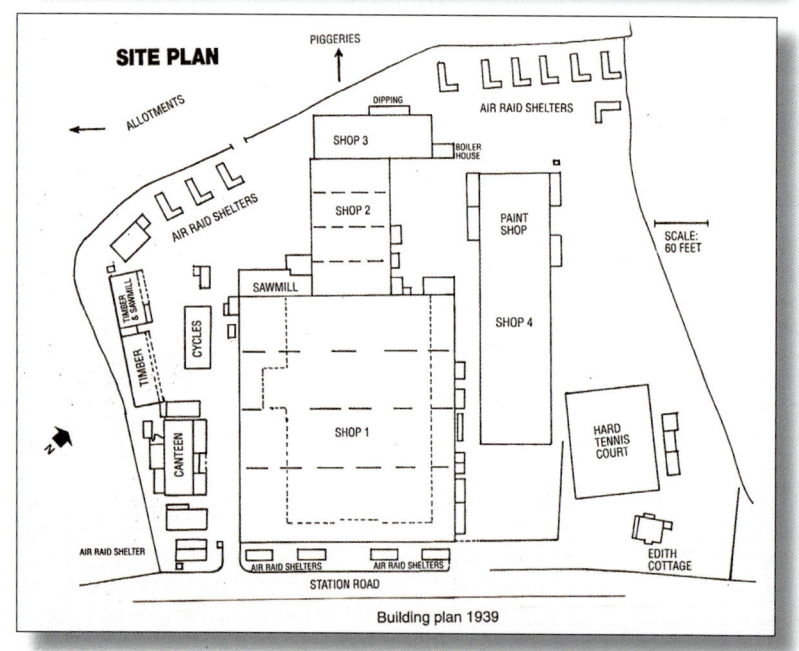

This commercially produced postcard was popular in Addlestone's shops and gives a splendid idea of the now completely changed site where buses and trolleybuses were built by a dedicated workforce whose products were second to none.

Station Road runs across the front of the building and the large glass windows of the various first floor offices and drawing office are clearly visible. Three completed vehicles can be seen awaiting collection on the corner where the tennis court once stood.

12

MODERN TRANSPORT, NOVEMBER 20, 1937.

IN THE CITY.
Transport and Finance.

Weymann's Motor Bodies.

The Central Mining and Investment Corporation is disposing of its interest in Weymann's Motor Bodies (1925), Limited, and other shareholders are made a cash offer of 9s. 6d. for their 5s. shares. The issued capital of Weymann's Motor Bodies is £23,100 in 92,400 5s. shares, and there are outstanding £50,000 6 per cent. debentures, repayable on December 3, 1937, at par, but convertible on or before that date into ordinary shares at par at the rate of 200 shares for every £50 nominal amount secured. Shareholders of the company are informed that the Central Mining Corporation, which holds the whole of these debentures, has given notice of its intention to convert them, and will accordingly be allotted 200,000 ordinary 5s. shares, thus increasing the number of ordinary shares in issue to 292,400. A total of 107,600 shares is reserved for issue against options to apply for shares at par.

Meanwhile a massive financial default on a railway contract in Spain, after the Revolution in that country, eventually caused major problems at the company's bank and, subsequently, ownership of Weymann's to pass to the Prudential Assurance Company after Central Mining announced in November 1937 that 'it was disposing of its interest in Weymann's Motor Bodies (1925) Ltd' but Black and several others had gone by then. Black's departure in 1933 had opened the way for Arthur Froggatt and several of his cohorts to move from Park Royal, and their influence, though not always relished, undoubtedly strengthened the Addlestone company's position. There can be no question that AT Froggatt was the man who made Weymann's the company it then became.

A further change in ownership took place – to United Molasses in September 1942 – and men movements between the two companies continued at all levels and at regular intervals. At the upper end of the companies, Sir Joseph Napier, who had been a Weymann's Director since 1932, was a Park Royal Director by 1948; WH Gray, who had been in the sales department at Park Royal since the company was formed in 1930, moved to MCW in 1943, and as such was based at Weymann's until 1945. And so it went on. In post-war years there were several key people in each organisation who probably knew rather more about costings and quotes than perhaps was good for the other company.

Amongst those who joined at this time and who contributed to the Author's research were Edna Bubb joining in June 1939; Walter Healy, October 1940;

The view below, taken just before the war, shows the progression of the bodies from the beginning of the build routine with floors and outriggers being attached to the chassis in the distance, mounting of the pre-assembled side frames and roofsticks, the construction of the upper-deck floor and then moving forward to the point where the top deck shells, seen in the background, are lifted on and attached. A mobile gantry was used for this purpose. One of Bournemouth's distinctive Leyland TD5s with its sliding roof and front doorway can be seen in the left foreground. In this view the offices are situated on the balcony above the fitters' shop at the top right, and the camera is facing diagonally towards Station Road.

Without doubt, one of the jewels in the ranks of preserved vehicles is this former Brighton Corporation AEC Regent from a batch of ten, body number M1910, but more usually referred to by its registration number FUF 63. Showing the elegance of the pre-war body design, it is seen here at Dunsfold aerodrome in Surrey, in May 2011, on the occasion of the former annual Cobham Rally. (JAS)

Utility bodywork:

Top left, Swindon Guy Arab body number C7905, DHR 192, built in July 1943 and now preserved. Top right, Derby C8014 built 1944, also now preserved. Lower view, South Lancashire Transport FTD 454, C7402, one of four numbered 60-63 and later joined by two more, C8015/6, immediately following the Derby vehicle shown. Photographed leaving Farnworth in 1956/7 shortly before the end of the system's life in 1958. (JAS all)

15

Some operators were still taking delivery of new vehicles from pre-war orders after war broke out. One such example was Cheltenham & District where this Albion, one of five, M2173-7, was delivered in February 1940. Note the wartime headlamp masks, and the finish of the paintwork confirming it has not been in service very long. It will soon lose its shine in the grim days ahead. A further four similar vehicles had been delivered to United Welsh, numbers M2178-81, two months earlier. Both companies were part of the Red & White empire. (RMC)

Wartime exports had included this Albion single-decker for South African Railways. Body number M1964, the penultimate one of a batch of 5, was completed in November 1939 and was photographed at the rear of the factory whilst awaiting its turn to be shipped. It looks much larger than contemporary British vehicles as indeed it was, 30ft long and 8ft wide. It was the use 'at home' of vehicles to these dimensions which were not sent abroad which helped promote the cause for an easing of the Construction & Use Regulations when the war ended. Note the two doors at the front indicating segregated compartments for whites and non-whites.

Maurice Bullivant, January 1941; Ron Barrett, February 1941; Reg Allen, April 1941; Vic Smith. January 1943; Don Arthur, 1944. All stayed at Weymann's until 1965/6, most of them right to the very end. Edna Bubb ended her time as Senior Secretary and went to keep charge of administration at Frimley (page 191) whilst Maurice Bullivant went briefly to Metro-Cammell in Birmingham, (page 190). Downstairs in production, Vic Smith worked in the Body shop but was well known for his enthusiasm in sports and for building the score box, extending the pavilion, and being one of the mainstays of the Ten-Bar-Two darts team for over 50 years (see page 64). Vic and several others are also mentioned on page 77 of Volume 1.

The wartime years meant another change of direction as military production took precedence and buses became a second string, output dropping to one or two per week of the utility double-deckers. Our first Volume finished with the end of wartime build, but for ease of continuity I propose to go back to those grim days and, thus, to cover in this volume roughly a quarter of a century, from the purchase by United Molasses in 1942 up to final closure in March 1966.

November 23, 2000

LETTERS TO THE EDITOR

Wooden guns to guard the factory

I READ with interest a write-up about Weymanns. I hope space can be found to mention the LDV which became Home Guard.

At first it was a joke. We guarded the factory with wooden guns, yes it's true.

But, as time went by, Mr Don Dixon, foreman of the wood mill and Mr George Page, chief inspector, took charge.

We got trained by cigar-smoking French-Canadians. We guarded the factory at night. Some of us had breakfast in the canteen, then into work for eight hours or so.

Many times we crawled about St George's College and also some did fire-watching at night.

We became a top class unit. In fact, Mr Phil Topp, of Eastworth Road, Chertsey, has a picture of us. He is a very active 90-year-old, born in Addlestone. I worked there for 26 years, 1940-66; wonderful people to work with.

The thing that upset us was Mr Page and Mr Dixon went to enrol us in the British Legion. They were turned down flat – excuse, not armed forces. I have never been in their club since.

Mr T WEBSTER
School Lane
Addlestone

● Local Home Guard members pictured in 1944. Mr T Webster remembers guarding the Weymann's factory armed with wooden guns!

The factory's Home Guard platoon, mentioned in the letter above. Chief Inspector Page is in the front row, sporting a moustache. The AFS squad of Firefighters with bow-tied EG Izod centre stage, and AT Froggatt next but one to his right are seen when photographed against the camouflaged factory doors in the view below.

17

CHAPTER 6 – 1942–1946

Under New Management – September 1942

The rather strange set of circumstances which led to United Molasses purchasing Weymann's business are set out in detail in Volume 1; in the event the reason for the purchase – the supposed existence of an electric car and battery – came to naught and Weymann's, like their competitors, found themselves under Government control, but not building the one product which had prompted United Molasses to make the purchase. Sadly, the full story of what actually happened at Station Road during the Second World War will probably never be told; many wartime records were lost or destroyed and those in charge of the factory who knew the full picture are either no longer with us, or have not been traced.

It was quite coincidental that another change of ownership also occurred in 1942, but one which would have quite far-reaching consequences on the Station Road production lines after the end of the war, when Ministry allocation schemes had come to an end. The TBAT (Tilling and British Automobile Traction Company) organisation, holding shares in some large bus companies in both Tilling and BET, decided to rationalise the situation, and by share exchanges to put the ownership of the various companies either into the Tilling camp, or the BET empire.

As with so many schemes, the unintended consequences were perhaps far more significant and when, later in our story, ownership of the Tilling Group passed into State control, and then the electricity industry was nationalised, some of Weymann's customers found themselves on the wrong side of the wire as it were. Although some were then precluded from buying their vehicles from suppliers outside the state conglomerate, others came to Station Road since they were not eligible to buy from within that same monolith. The effects of these swings and roundabouts make for fascinating reading as we shall see.

Buses caught in bomb attacks bore witness to the devastating effect of blast and shrapnel. It was normal practice to evacuate vehicles caught in air raids, and this picture shows exactly why – passengers still inside would have been badly injured or killed.

This Leyland Titan TD4c, with its torque converter header tank clearly visible, had been new in April 1934. The metal-framed body, M300, was one of those completed by Mumfords, and its strength has been severely tested.

Registered CY 5025, No. 107 became a casualty in its home at Plymouth, one of several cities pounded remorselessly by the Luftwaffe. It was photographed at Weymann's in August 1940.

During the wartime period between 1939 and June 1945 Weymann's, like all other manufacturers, had been obliged to divert their attentions to the war effort. Their output was dictated by the requirements of the Ministry of Supply (MoS) through the Ministry of War Transport (MoWT), which had become the organisation responsible for overseeing the procurement and use of essential resources, and, insofar as it affected bus production, the placing of orders and allocations of materials required for construction. The company's new owners, being shippers, were also under the control of the MoS.

From the MoWT's inception Weymann's customers were also routed through that same organisation, and it was now necessary to obtain an instrument so beloved of civil servants, a Permit, before new vehicles could be allocated – by the MoWT – to operators. Shortages of raw materials meant that essential military production came first. Norman Froggatt, son of AT Froggatt and who had joined the company as an estimator in 1936 after his father moved from Park Royal to take charge at Station Road, was a keen recorder of output and noted that some 8,800 military vehicles of various shapes, sizes and uses, ranging from light van bodies,

The wartime bodies clearly were robust, though, ironically, this view is of one of the small number of metal-framed examples built at Addlestone in 1943.

Guy Arab 106, body No. M2664, from Newport and now five years old, has clearly had a major side impact, almost as though someone has tried to drive a railway locomotive through it, but the nearside view demonstrates the localised effect of even such a substantial collision.

The photographs were taken at Weymann's factory before repair work began. The strength of the upper-deck floor has obviously played a major part in the vehicle's survival.

19

Two Weymann official views showing the wartime wooden seating in utility highbridge double-deck bodies, the upper view still having masked lamps whilst in the lower view normal glass shades have been reinstated.

radar vans, decompression chambers, armoured cars and the whole paraphernalia of war, were produced in those days. At that time Norman would have been involved in raising the necessary paperwork to enable Weymann's to be paid by the Government so we may be confident of the accuracy of his figures. The surviving records also show that many contracts for buses, both for home and overseas markets, were cancelled.

Once the need to keep producing buses to move war workers to their places of employment had been recognised, greater awareness began to pervade Government circles. Stopping all bus production was clearly counter-productive to the war effort. Accordingly, as a first move, materials which had been 'frozen' by MoS at the manufacturers were allowed to be completed. Next, plans were made for a unified system of limited production. The wartime austerity bus body designs, usually subsequently referred to as Utilities in line with other austerity products, were then prepared by a committee under the leadership of the Addlestone factory's one-time General Manager, Bill Black, in his capacity as then President of the National Federation of Vehicle Trades.

Nonetheless, bus production, our main interest, quickly became secondary. By 1942 only a small number of such vehicles were being built: the last remnants of pre-war contracts, and, alongside these new-build contracts, the sorry specimens returning to the factory for repair after being caught in the blitz, or victims of the blackout. Some examples are illustrated but no records have been found to show just how many such vehicles were dealt with. There were also export orders, and some vehicles were indeed sent overseas, but the combination of risk of loss through enemy action, need to retain vehicles for use at home and lack of space in ships fully laden with war supplies, meant that they were fewer than would otherwise have been the case.

This cutting-off of supplies to overseas countries would be the catalyst for some of them later to start their own fledgling bus building plants, something which all major British manufacturers would have to address after hostilities finished, by which time the fledglings were maturing and expanding.

The standard wartime utility buses were dealt with in Volume 1 but a recap will doubtless be useful. Originally, it had been intended that Leyland would build the first batch of chassis but military requirements for more tanks quickly caused a change of plan and, instead, Guy Motors were instructed to produce a wartime version of their pre-war Arab chassis and duly did so, apparently using the pre-war Leyland Titan chassis side frame configuration. Daimler also later produced a wartime chassis, though in smaller quantities, and both chassis makes were fitted with the standard wood-framed utility bodies.

C7999 built in 1943 was one of two Daimler CWA6s, 7998/9, with that model's distinctive wire mesh grille supplied to Merthyr Tydfil Corporation. There were also two bodied by Duple which needed to be rebodied by the Corporation, and this Weymann one also shows evidence of some substantial rebuilding. Merthyr, like other operators, would have been busy with workmen's traffic to coal mines and other local industries. (RM)

The MoWT sanctioned 3,000 Guy chassis of Marks I and II to be built, of which just over 2,870 had been produced when peacetime construction resumed with the Mark III. There could have been a potential problem when supplies of the alternative and more powerful, but longer, Gardner 6LW engine became available for installation in what became the Mk II, instead of the up-to-then standard 5LW unit. The overall length for a double-deck bus was at that time 26ft but the bulkhead position in the design of the Guy chassis meant that keeping within that limit with this longer engine some 6ins would be lost from the passenger accommodation. Modifications to the bodywork would have been needed, with the extra work in the drawing offices this entailed, and then changes to material and production requirements. Clearly this was completely unacceptable in what was intended to be a standardised bus.

Black was not a man to be trifled with, and had the ear of Beaverbrook, Churchill's wartime production supremo, through his involvement in London Aircraft Production (see adjacent information panel); we may take it, therefore, that he was instrumental in securing the Ministry decision that from the outset of the utility body programme a concession would be given by the MoWT for Guy Arab Mk II, and, later the Daimler CWA6, utility buses to be 26ft 9ins long. This concession was in force from 1942 until December 1946, with a further period of four months up to 30th March 1947 being allowed for the vehicles to be registered. Thereafter, the existing 26ft length was re-imposed until Construction & Use Regulations were amended in July 1950. The possibility of two lengths of body behind the bulkhead for these marques was thus avoided and Weymann's would not have been alone in being thankful that this scenario did not come about. The AEC-engined CWA6 was also overweight, requiring a further dispensation.

There were, of course, other wartime buses, but Weymann's were not involved in bodying either the normal-control Bedford OWB or the variety of chassis which were bodied or rebodied with the wartime single-deck forward-control type bus body. Thus, by the return to peacetime build at the end of 1945, with only a handful of exceptions like the Bedford articulated trailer vehicles for the Ministry of Supply operated by Mansfield District as described and illustrated in Part One of this history, the Addlestone factory had built only two-axled double-deck buses and trolleybuses to what was in effect one common design; full-sized single-deck utility bus production had been allocated to other body builders, notably Burlingham in Blackpool, Lancashire, where some of Weymann's very first coaches had had their interiors fitted out for Yorkshire Traction in 1932.

After 1943, when the main thrust of the rebodying of war-damaged vehicles and completion of bodies for pre-war orders to peacetime standards is believed to have been accomplished, a remarkably standardised product had emerged from the Station Road gates, as indeed it had from Weymann's competitors' factories. Even the colour was constant at some times, wartime grey irrespective of the customer. Some 500 bodies of highbridge or lowbridge configuration were built on wartime chassis by Weymann's. Guys out-numbered Daimlers over 15:1 with the make being new to Addlestone in motor bus form (there had been some Guy trolleybuses back in 1933) but one with which the bodybuilders would soon become familiar. While the bodies were not always well received, being spartan and using sub-standard timber, the wartime Guy Arab chassis was a robust and reliable piece of machinery and many operators were soon looking to obtain further Arabs in their post-war redevelopment plans. Although the wartime specification for the bodies called for wooden framing there was a smaller number – 23 – of metal-framed bodies built at Addlestone, two apparently being used as prototypes for postwar construction, and those two went to a new-to-Weymann's operator, Southdown Motor Services of Brighton. Southdown also received 22 wooden-framed examples.

Guy's wartime and postwar success with this chassis saved it from a virtually certain death so far as bus production was concerned and it expanded its customer base dramatically; on the back of this, Weymann's were to see orders coming in from customers whose first contact with MCW, or Addlestone's factory, had been brought about by allocations of vehicles over which the customer had had no control.

LONDON AIRCRAFT PRODUCTION (LAP)

Wartime bus production was under the control of the MoWT, as explained. Even more important was the need to increase the output of bomber aircraft and LAP was set up to achieve this. Park Royal were tasked with managing a factory producing wings for the Handley Page Halifax bomber. LAP's constituents were Park Royal, London Transport, Duple, Express Motor & Body Works Ltd and Chrysler Motors Ltd. Bill Black, in charge at Park Royal, and responsible for overseeing the design of the utility bus bodies, now found himself involved with Lord Ashcroft, Chairman of London Transport and also of the co-ordinating committee for LAP, and ultimately repsonsible to Lord Beaverbrook, Prime Minister Winston Churchill's wartime production supremo.

Wartime advertising was all about morale boosting and helping the advertising revenue of the trade journals – orders were by allocation through the Ministry of War Transport of course.

22

Planning for the future

The effects of the Second World War will never be forgotten by those who lived through them, or, worse, went to fight for their country. When, in the early part of 1945, it became apparent that the end of the war could not be far away, thoughts focussed on what would happen when it was all over.

It must have seemed almost impossible to make any plans for future peacetime production with wartime restrictions still in place, many of the workforce still away in the armed forces, all manufacturing subject to Ministry of Supply allocations, many raw materials simply not available and such materials as were to be had available only on allocation against approved orders. There were, additionally, many outstanding orders placed before the war, or during the MoS period but not fulfilled.

Yet Weymann's Ltd, as the company had become with a legal change of registered name on 5th January 1945, were no different from many thousands of companies throughout the land in needing to plan for a return to what would take the place of normality. It was clear that there would be a tremendous backlog of orders for new vehicles; peacetime orders had been curtailed or completed in most factories by 1942 at the latest, (many much sooner) and British wartime production had totalled around 3,500 utility buses between then and 1946. The need to make up this shortfall would keep the manufacturing industry busy for some years to come.

Additionally, there were still 6,200 trams operating throughout the country and many of these would have been scrapped by 1939 had the war not intervened. Major operators including Manchester who had intended to replace their remaining trams with buses found their plans thwarted when bus production was stopped. Now, as operators caught up, by 1950 some 1,500 would be withdrawn, further increasing the demand on bus builders. Clearly there was a huge gap to fill.

The Government was fully aware of this shortfall, but was determined to keep the numbers produced for the home market to a much lower total, electing to allocate sparse resources to what it considered were more pressing socially deserving cases, principally housing.

The directors of the MCW sales company and the two manufacturing organisations thus had to consider the Government's announced intentions (and second-guess the unannounced!) whilst trying to address the future and reassess their sales and production strategies. The pre-war policy of building buses (but not luxury coaches) for large fleet operators would still make economic sense, but the number of options available to customers would have to be reduced.

Government policy regarding allocations of vehicles had been demonstrated as far back as 1940 when, in order to keep money flowing into the country, and to raise funds to help pay for the war, the setting up of the Motor Export Group was announced. Its task was to coordinate export efforts and its target was to generate £12million in the initial 12 months: after the first seven months it was reported that exports of 1,000 vehicles per week had been achieved, and Weymann's would have been required to meet their share. Indeed, they would have had no option, for only vehicles approved by the Ministry of Supply for construction would have qualified for allocations of materials.

Meanwhile, on the other side of the coin, large organisations such as the BET were planning the future as they wanted it to be; orders were announced as they were placed on the chassis builders and very soon there were 1,000 Leyland chassis on order for the BET alone. Clearly, someone was going to have to rethink the whole balance of exports and home production with figures of this magnitude being made available. This was to result in a three-cornered tussle between the MoS, manufacturers and operators which has, perhaps, been underplayed in previous manufacturers' histories. Even allowing for the obvious political leanings of the trade press of the day, it has become apparent in the research for this book that restrictions and shortages would hold back output and freedom of action or choice for well over five years. These restrictions, and their manifestations, will became obvious as the tale unfolds in both the text and the illustrations shown in the next chapter.

The TRANSPORT WORLD

FIFTY-FIRST YEAR OF PUBLICATION

Founded in 1892 as The Tramway and Railway World

Editor: JAMES FINLAY

Publishers
TRAMWAY AND RAILWAY WORLD PUBLISHING CO. LTD.
82 Tankerville Road, London, S.W.16.
Telephone: Pollards 4153.
Telegrams: Tramgro, Streath, London

Directors
A. M. WILLCOX (Chairman)
J. FINLAY (Managing)
H. E. TOWNELL
W. M. WILLCOX

LONDON, AUGUST 13, 1942   No. 2939 (Vol. XCI)

Wide Trolleybuses for Bradford and Nottingham

SUNBEAM-B.T.H. JOHANNESBURG CHASSIS FITTED WITH M.C.W. BODIES

Near side front view of one of the eight-foot wide trolleybuses

When it became too risky, or impossible, to export vehicles to South Africa and elsewhere due to the very real danger of merchant ships being sunk by enemy action, the opportunity was taken to divert some to UK customers. Fifteen trolleybuses ordered by Johannesburg fell into this category and in 1942 ten were diverted to Bradford, as one seen here, body numbers C7318-27, whilst the remaining five, C7328-32 went to Nottingham. The bodies were clearly to the utility specification, but of greater significance, were 8ft wide. Dispensation was necessary to allow them to be operated in the UK but clearly this was not a problem in the prevailing circumstances. Their ability to operate in the streets of Bradford and Nottingham without difficulty became important in the post-war arguments for the relaxing of vehicle lengths and widths.

Eight single-deck metal-framed 39-seat Daimler buses, built in 1941/2, for Salisbury, Southern Rhodesia, were similarly affected. One, body number M2523, was diverted to West Monmouth where it was fitted with a driver's door and emergency exit, neither being part of the original specification, before entering service as seen later in the photograph by Roy Marshall below. The other seven, M2524-30, were diverted to Potteries Motor Traction after being similarly modified. All eight were 30ft long and 8ft wide, needing dispensation as had the trolleybuses.

24

The Hard Times Get No Better

During 1945 some wartime restrictions began to be eased and thereafter utility bodywork incorporated more opening windows and a return to upholstered seats. These vehicles were usually known as the relaxed utilities. The utility body had been designed as a wooden-framed product but, as mentioned, Weymann's had been authorised to build 23 metal-framed examples between 1943 and 1945, some as prototypes for post-war production methods. The last two metal-framed utilities, M2691/2, went to Southdown Motor Services, along with many composite examples, including the last four of the wartime composite body numbers – C8904-7.

Amongst the chassis manufacturers Bristol were allowed to resume limited bus building in February 1945, joining Guy and Daimler who had shouldered the task throughout the war, along with Bedford who built single-deck chassis. By June other manufacturers, including Crossley Motors in Manchester, were allowed to resume civilian production. Crossleys were one of the few major manufacturers whose chassis never carried Weymann's bodies from new, and so this particular change made no difference in Addlestone. The Government next faced pleas for easing of restrictions on materials, and non-availability of good quality paint quickly became a major issue.

Victory in Europe, when Germany finally capitulated in May 1945, was duly followed by an unconditional surrender by Japan in August. Some of the fighting men were quickly on their way home, ready to return to their former employment, and some of Weymann's workforce were amongst them. Sadly, the world would be a very different place even though hostilities were largely over, and the costs both in human and financial terms were staggering; an estimated 55 million people had died. The financial cost would be incalculable.

We can only try to imagine the feelings of men who had seen the horror of war, who had travelled the world and seen countries and life styles which until then would have been virtually unknown to most. In an age when travel abroad was by ocean liner, or, perhaps, by one of the few long-distance sea planes (the original air-liners), but in either case only for the rich, they had visited continents which would remain inaccessible to most people for another two decades. Not everyone would have relished the experience; MCW's Bon Cole, for example, had been a PoW in the Far East after seeing active service in North Africa.

Other examples of relaxation of restrictions by May 1945 included the removal of anti-blast netting from vehicle windows and a return to normal lighting for buses, except those in coastal areas. On the very day the war in Europe was officially declared over, 7th May, the MCW Sales Office left Addlestone and returned to Vickers House, Broadway, Westminster in central London.

The Vickers headquarters building, opened in May 1931, was home to over 20 of the companies within the group, split into three main categories, and providing a convenient

A post-war view of an East Kent Guy, BJG 419, body number C8746, clearly showing the extended radiator to allow fitment of either 5 or 6-cylinder Gardner engine. Built in February 1945 to the relaxed specification the increase in opening windows in each deck will be noted. The destination display would have been modified by the operator and the quality of the paintwork is clearly not the original. (RNH)

and central location for Government officials, customers and others to see the range of products which the group members manufactured in factories throughout Great Britain. These covered armaments and shipping under Vickers-Armstrongs; various steel manufacture under the English Steel Corporation aegis; bus, tram and trolleybus, railway carriage and wagon building under Metropolitan-Cammell Carriage and Wagon and MCW; and lastly Vickers (Aviation) Ltd together with other miscellaneous items. The building housed offices, showrooms and other facilities, and there were displays of components, models, drawings etc.

Back at Station Road in spring 1945, the Addlestone management was virtually the same as it had been in pre-war days. EG Izod, although no longer a well man, was still Chairman and Managing Director, jointly with Homfray Davies. Arthur Froggatt MBE was General Manager, Francis Webb was Company Secretary and all four were Directors of Weymann's along with James Don, the United Molasses appointee since January 1943, UM having purchased Weymann's from the Prudential Assurance Company in September 1942 as previously recorded. Hilda Nash as Secretary of the Sports Club, and living at The Bungalow, was a close confidant of Izod. WCS Chatfield was looking after sales in the absence of Bon Cole, still recovering from his wartime experiences.

In the Drawing Office Moss Nelson was Chief Designer, with Freddie Maddocks as Chief Draughtsman, Cecil Fleming his assistant, and then Joe Allen, Bunny Beaver, John Biden, John Carman, Gordon Whindle and former BET inspector Frank Wright, amongst other stalwarts. Gordon Whindle's sister had been in charge of the switchboard from 1927 until she left to start a family in 1942. In the mid-1950s the switchboard/reception was in the hands of sisters Betty and Marcelle Penton. A third sister, Carole, worked in the contracts department. Marcelle later married Walter Healy. This gives a very small indication of the family connections which were part of the strength of the company. The long service of this team also gives some clues as to the general continuity of the Weymann's body designs and why they were so recognisable – until the Orion period when commonality with Metro-Cammell became MCW policy.

On the upstairs balcony Fred Smith looked after the print room and Brenda and Millie were the tracers. Joe Allen, already mentioned, was the nephew of Freddy Rayer who had developed the MCW metal framing, and Joe had worked at Metro-Cammell and later Midland Red with Hugh Wooton before a spell out of work in the depression in the early 1930s. He joined Weymann's in 1933, the same year as the young Norman (Bunny) Beaver. Bunny later went to London Transport after a spell at Frimley and was interviewed by Bill Shirley to work at Park Royal, but not surprisingly declined the offer. Once was enough, as readers may remember from tales in the first volume.

Jack Guarnori had joined in 1934, some three years after Homfray Davis joined from Park Royal (he had been there in Hall, Lewis days). Each was to make his mark, Homfray as salesman *par excellence* and Jack as engineer *extraordinaire*. It would fall to Jack to organise and manage the production of London's RT buses for Weymann's as described later.

Harold Cook was now Chief Engineer, and he together with Moss Nelson, George Biggs and Miss Sanson (who later married Bill Shirley) had all come with Bill Black in 1928. There were others whose names have escaped us, but one who must be mentioned was Tim Healy who had been mechanic to racing driver and Director Henry Segrave, record breaker in Golden Arrow who was killed making another record attempt in 1928. Tim became chauffeur to Izod when the latter joined, remaining in that position until an injudicious comment saw him demoted to factory lorry driver after the war when Izod was no longer a well man. Tim's son Walter joined the wages office in 1940 before call-up and joined the buying office on his return. He became a stalwart of the darts team and worked his way up the management team. Norman Froggatt was the Estimator, becoming Chief Estimator in 1946, Walter Dodsworth was the Buyer and Bill Lawrence was the Contracts Manager.

Downstairs George Biggs was in charge of the erecting shop, Monty Ellis was the bodyshop foreman, with Fred Osborne, Jim Knight, Jim Lindon and Cyril Hutchins in charge of the Panel Shop, Finishing Dept, Trimming Dept, and Paint Shop respectively. Tom Bradbury was in charge of the sawmill until he retired, when Don Dixon took his place. Interviewed when he was 92 Don still had clear memories of the early 'thirties.

Some of the people returning from active service had worked for British manufacturers such as Leyland and AEC, then amongst our principal heavy goods

Jack Guarnori, a talented engineer, model maker, organiser and family man whose talents were wasted by MCCW when he was moved there after Weymann's closed. (BB)

George Biggs, Weymann's General Foreman. (BB)

and passenger chassis builders, and were able to seize the opportunities which would be on offer when they were demobbed. With the end of the fighting in Europe the Government began to sell off some of the shadow factories it had been using for wartime production and many found further use in car or aircraft engineering and manufacture.

At home the widespread shortages led to increasing unrest, culminating in a far-reaching change when, in a surprise move after Labour withdrew from the wartime coalition administration to allow for return to normal elections, the vote was for a new Government and Winston Churchill was shown the door in the first post-war contest.

Despite its large majority Attlee's labour administration of July 1945 never really stood a chance when faced with the task of trying to get a virtually bankrupt country back on track, and saddled itself with policies including public ownership and social reform which, with hindsight, only made the job more difficult. Lack of money, foreign exchange and raw materials, meant that every move they tried to make was thwarted. Pragmatism was needed as never before, but hard-line political dogma ruled the day. Sadly, red tape then became the one commodity of which there was no shortage.

Attlee spelled out the difficulties to Parliament a few weeks later when he warned that peace was going to bring even greater austerity than the war had done. Imports were going to have to be drastically restricted because there was no money to pay for them. His warning came true sooner than even he could have expected when, just a few weeks later and with great irony, 43,000 militant dockers went on strike for seven weeks seeking a national minimum wage and troops had to unload vital cargoes of food. With friends like that . . .?

At a time when many of the country's entrepreneurs were straining at the leash to get things moving, restrictions of every sort held them back. The editorials of the trade press such as *Bus and Coach* and *Transport World* reveal their frustrations and also record the alarm and anger as the true cost of rebuilding Europe, destroyed by our forces as the war had progressed, now fell largely to us. The victim was recompensing the aggressor. One piece of good news, however, appeared in August 1945 when it was announced that from the end of 1945 the restrictions controlling operators' right to choose who bodied their chassis would be withdrawn. In 1946, although the MoS would still control output and allocation of chassis, body makes would be the choice of the operator. If he could find one with capacity and material allocations! It was at least a step in the right direction.

Overriding this new found freedom, exports became even more vital, to earn currency to pay our debts and also to allow us to purchase goods and raw materials from overseas. One of the first large MCW export orders in 1946, shared between Addlestone and Birmingham, was for 300 buses and trolleybuses for South Africa, some complete, some as upper and lower decks separately, and some as sections

PASSENGER VEHICLES

Bodies Decontrolled in 1946

PRODUCTION programmes for buses in 1946 are necessarily somewhat fluid owing to reduced or changed war requirements, but the Ministry of War Transport, in conjunction with the Ministry of Supply, has arranged for the following makes of public service vehicle chassis:

Double and single-deck (heavy p.s.v. chassis):
A.E.C., Albion, Bristol, B.M.M.O., Crossley, Daimler, Dennis, Foden, Guy, Leyland, Thornycroft and Tilling-Stevens.

Single-deck coach (heavy p.s.v. chassis):
Maudslay.

Single-deck only (light p.s.v. chassis):
Vauxhall (Bedford) and Commer.

After the end of this year the Ministry of Supply does not intend to continue the direction of bus chassis manufacturers to particular bodybuilders. The Ministry of War Transport will be concerned only with the allocation of chassis. In order that arrangements can be made with Ministry of Supply for the increased production programme, and to enable bodybuilders to make their plans sufficiently in advance so as to provide for the needs of operators requiring specialised bodies, the Regional Transport Commissioners will press for details of all operators' requirements for new public service vehicles in 1946 without further delay. Applications at present at the Ministry are being held in suspense until all the applications are received, in order that the demand may be balanced against the anticipated supply.

This Lancashire United vehicle, C8222 from a batch numbered 8219-26 built in 1944, is looking very smart in this 1956 view, but shortages of paint had been a serious issue being raised with the Government after the end of the war as imports – including colour pigments – were still very closely controlled. Unless the operator was able to provide paint from its own stock Weymann's and other manufacturers would have had to use what they could get, very often battleship grey. (JAS)

for assembly in South Africa. In part this was unfinished business from pre-war orders which had been cancelled or put on hold when shipping space was needed for other commodities. Galling though it was, it was also necessary to make provision to export some of the very items we desperately needed at home into Europe in order to build the peace.

Adding fuel to these fires was the new Labour Government backing the Unions in their fight for greater power, and the policy of widespread nationalisation which would create power bases of huge size. Weymann's, and many other London area based organisations, notably the docks and Fleet Street, would have the side effects of this millstone around their neck until they moved away from the capital, or went out of business. Many contended that the communists had come to stay, and to try to see capitalism defeated. Strikes now took the place of guns and bombs.

Plans to nationalise transport and steel had the most effect on the progression of Weymann's future; they caused unease, unrest, and an understandable reluctance to invest when the terms of future recompense were unclear. At a time when entrepreneurial flair was most needed it was shackled beyond hope. Challenged by MPs, industrialists and economists about the damage their policies were causing, Attlee's ministers would only say that "the people voted for them".

The bumpy road to recovery was going to be a very long one indeed.

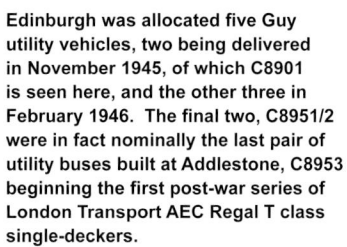

Edinburgh was allocated five Guy utility vehicles, two being delivered in November 1945, of which C8901 is seen here, and the other three in February 1946. The final two, C8951/2 were in fact nominally the last pair of utility buses built at Addlestone, C8953 beginning the first post-war series of London Transport AEC Regal T class single-deckers.

Southdown Motor Services Ltd had not been a Weymann's customer until the wartime allocation of utility-bodied Guy Arabs began. It was to receive the last two Addlestone metal-framed bodies to carry utility bodywork, body numbers M2691/2, delivered in March 1945.

The first of the pair is seen after the war, on a hot day, when the increased number of opening windows, which the relaxation in wartime regulations had permitted, was being put to good use.

CHAPTER 7 – SHORTAGES & PRODUCTION PROBLEMS

Shattered Dreams and Sad Realisations

It came as a bitter pill to many that, after the war was over, the chronic shortages which had been accepted whilst the fighting was going on actually became far, far worse. Everything was in short supply: raw materials, coal, electricity and, crucially for many forms of manufacturing, steel. Almost everything was on ration and the ration book was an essential tool of everyday life for items not available from 'under the counter' to favoured customers. Discontent was widespread and when the miners went on strike in 1946, affecting electricity and coal supplies, and creating widespread misery for people who could not keep warm or light their homes, they further exacerbated the difficulties of the steel-makers to produce what was required.

If 1939/40 was the time of the phoney war, then 1946 might be considered a time of phoney peace. Although the fighting was over, the restrictions which were imposed, affecting every walk of life, were making everyday living even more miserable for many people than the wartime days themselves. Shortage of food and coal were probably the most misery-making; throughout the war there had always been sufficient food but in 1946-7 catastrophic shortages were evident and even bread was put on ration – for many people that was indeed the last straw. The freak winter of 1947 with record snow falls and the great freeze-up just compounded the situation.

Raw materials of every description were in short supply, often because there was no money available to pay for them. The financial assistance we had received from America during the time of conflict had come to an end, and now the day of reckoning had arrived. How was the huge debt to be repaid? Only by a massive export drive could we raise the cash to pay our debts and then try to pay our way.

The domestic timber problem with the lack of quality seasoned timber has been referred to, while hard woods from the far east were simply unavailable. The patent-flexible body needed good quality well-seasoned timber, and it was no surprise that it was discontinued in 1940. It was perhaps a surprise that with so few being produced – just 400 in the years 1928-40 – it should have lasted so long. Another puzzle is why such a limited-output product, and one making such a minimal contribution to turnover, should have warranted a place on the MCW stands at each Motor Show – 1931/33/35/37 and with a vehicle allocated for the aborted 1939 Show.

Wartime experience of building composite double-deckers with unseasoned wood convinced MCW that post-war production should, where possible, be confined to metal-framed vehicles, using the successful pre-war routines – hot riveted construction and separate upper and lower deck assembly – which had created long-lasting and extremely sound vehicles whose pedigree was now clear to see. Unfortunately, their hands were tied by what was available and so the decision was taken to continue with composite construction for single-deckers until sufficient steel was available to switch. No one could have foreseen at this time just how long it would be before the shortage of steel would eventually be resolved; by the time it had been resolved the demand for new buses had peaked and many large orders had been cancelled.

The problems were industry wide, of course. Leyland and Metro-Cammell, building only in metal, would be able to avoid the sub-standard timber problems, only to be caught by shortages of steel. Leyland Motors, mindful of limitations on permitted output, and material shortages, restricted its production solely to double-decker bodies – 'all-metal' – until 1950 and had only re-introduced single-decker bus and coach bodies when its new underfloor engined chassis came on stream . Eastern Coach Works, wanting to build in aluminium, had to accept the need to use timber until sufficient aluminium became available. Park Royal, like Weymann's, found themselves caught in the problems of both wood and metal. Other coachbuilders would have faced all these and many other problems. The legacy of this period is clear to see; by the early 'fifties many operators were involved in major rebuilding of composite bodies from the 1946-9 period. In many cases they gave up and ordered replacement bodywork to be fitted to the existing chassis.

When looking at this gloomy scene we should not forget that great as our problems were, many throughout the world were very much worse off after the devastating bombing, burning, looting and what we now call ethnic cleansing. There was a general recognition by the major powers that only a concerted and coordinated effort would avert worldwide repercussions whose long term effects were unthinkable. Accordingly, in December 1945, the International Monetary Fund and the World Bank came into being, to provide a means of financing the necessary reconstruction and future redevelopments. In this area, at least, working for a better future was taking place.

At home, housing was seen as the greatest priority, with transport coming much lower down the list. A further complication was the restriction on the chassis makers, whereby, for example, only a minority of single-deck chassis could be built for the home market. Weymann's could take orders, and hopefully obtain approval to build. But could they then get the materials to execute the orders? Clearly, it was going to be a very different way of working compared to pre-war when orders were obtained, materials purchased, vehicles built and delivered, and invoices were then paid.

The MCW sales team had doubtless been in discussion throughout the war with the group's major customers, in particular BET and the large municipalities, together with the MoS, to discuss how manufacturing capacity might best be used to meet customer's requirements. Government export requirements now meant that single-deck chassis would be in shortest supply, whilst the lack of good timber would clearly delay matters because of the time required to season new wood. Since Metropolitan-Cammell built no composite bodies in its Birmingham factory this latter problem would only affect Addlestone.

Weymann's, therefore, prepared to gear itself to concentrate its main output

Weymann's composite body construction from 1946 was to be exclusively devoted to single-deck vehicles with the exception of 15 trolleybuses for Hastings Tramways which had been ordered in 1939 and were completed and delivered in September 1947. Trolleybuses were subject to additional Construction & Use Regulations, the salient one here being that where interior lighting used traction voltage, the bulbs being wired in series and taking 110volts, metal framing was not permitted. Hence, this one batch of composite double-deckers became the exception to the single-deck only building plan. C9157 is shown in its distinctive livery.

on metal-framed bodies using the MCW patented structure as it had before the war. Composite (wooden-framed) bodywork – 'coachbuilt' at Station Road as previously mentioned – would be produced for single-deck vehicles only, except for an incomplete order for Hastings Tramways for a handful of trolleybuses where the traction wiring arrangements meant that metal-framing was not permissible.

In 1938, the last full year of peacetime production, Addlestone's output of metal-framed bodies had been almost eight times that of composites. If peacetime requirements followed the same pattern MCW's directors could clearly be confident that they were taking the right decision.

Doubtless the signing of an agreement to build quantities of the new post-war metal-framed London Transport RT3 bus (see later) must have helped to clarify their thinking. It also caused the acquisition of the lease on a building in Weybridge, an aircraft hangar which was redundant now the war was drawing to a close. Thus J-Building was acquired, the factory which would shortly be used exclusively for RT production as we shall see in Chapter 10.

First signs of return to normality

When the first chassis arrived from AEC in late 1945 it was a clear sign that some things, at least, were getting back to normal. The first Regents down the line included some for London Transport, using the same construction methods that, with the exception of the 23 utility metal-framed vehicles culminating in the two for Southdown, already mentioned, had ceased around 1943. The last wartime Guy Arab had taken the body number series to M2695, and the first Regent II for London took the next number in the sequence. As before, the bottom deck was assembled as a complete box directly on the chassis, using the pre-assembled side frames, and then the top deck was constructed onto it. Curved front and rear domes reappeared as the skilled panel beaters resumed their occupation. Although there was a short

Brighton had replaced its trams in 1939 and the brand new bus and trolleybus intake had created a surplus of vehicles, thanks to the war, with some trolleybuses being loaned to Newcastle, though perhaps more surprising was the allocation of a brand new Brighton bus to the Royal Navy by the Ministry of War Transport as seen in this cutting.

transitional period the photographs show that the distinctive Weymann's body was back in business. The origin of that design is worth considering.

At the beginning of that year, on New Year's Day 1945, Brighton Hove & District had finally opened the Company portion of its trolleybus system, it having been sidelined due to the war. Weymann's had built 65 buses and trolleybuses for Brighton Corporation in 1939, and at least one of these Corporation buses had been commandeered by the Royal Navy and fitted out as a classroom for training naval personnel. However, the eight trolleybuses for the Company had not been put into service, and were stored until 1945. Incidentally, they were re-registered with then-current marks before entering service and one, CPM 61, has survived – in the Science Museum's overspill collection and now at Wroughton (see page 74). The vehicles were significant in the evolution of Weymann's double-deck design and it is worth digressing for a moment to consider their pedigree.

When Winston Robinson was appointed as General Manager of Brighton Corporation Transport in July 1937, following a spell looking after the council's other municipal vehicles, he was able to start with a clean sheet, so to speak, where road vehicles were concerned since his order for vehicles to replace the trams would be the first placed by the Corporation for buses and trolleybuses. Maybe, because of this, he made considerable input into the detail design and finish of the buses and trolleybuses in this contract. In addition to working with AEC on the specification of the trolleybus chassis, he wanted the appearance of all three types of vehicle's bodywork (composite-framed and metal-framed motor buses, and the trolleybuses) to match each other as closely as possible, particularly where window glasses were concerned. Robinson knew what he wanted, but, more importantly, his background enabled him to talk to both AEC and Moss Nelson and the rest of Weymann's drawing office design team in their own language.

Robinson had joined Brighton from Hull Corporation Transport, where he had been chief engineer for three years, during which time Hull had been taking Weymann's bodies. Previously, and also not without some relevance, he had been assistant engineer and rolling stock engineer with Midland Red.

Clearly, he made a better impression at Weymann's than the last Midland Red man, the unliked Hugh Wooton who had been superintendent at Carlyle Works before briefly taking charge at Addlestone after the demise of Bill Black in 1933. The outcome was just as Robinson had wanted and the writer is convinced that his input, translated by the Weymann's design team, was partly responsible for the superb pre-war Weymann's classic double-decker which, of course, would reappear as post-war production began.

Weymann's trolleybus body, in particular, by now had evolved into a very sleek,

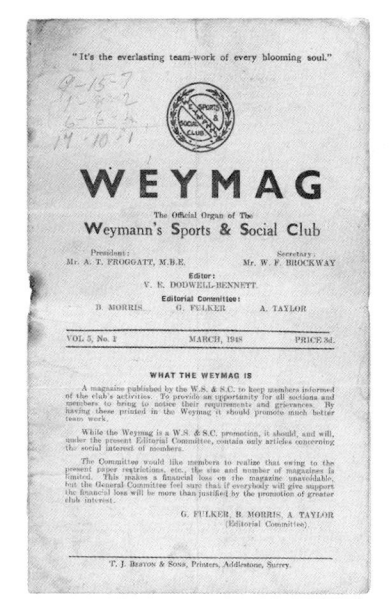

The early Weymag was produced to keep members of the Sports and Social Club abreast of progress, outings and results of competitions.

In addition to the mass exodus of the workforce for the annual works outing, with up to two trainloads of participants, the Sports and Social Club also organised outings for its members and one of the first post-war trips is shown below. All these activities were intended to maintain the family relationship within the firm.

smooth, outline and Robinson wanted the new buses to be every bit as handsome. This insistence on commonality of design almost certainly explains why Harringtons, who were originally awarded a contract for ten of these 65 vehicles, withdrew, leaving Weymann's to complete the full order although lack of headroom in the Harrington factory would have created problems.

By 1946 peacetime build was under way, although the last Guy utility double-deckers were actually built in March of that year. Now, in April, a batch of 50 AEC Regal single-deckers for London Transport heralded the start of peacetime-standard, composite bodies, with body number C8908 marking the changeover. (The corresponding change in metal-framed bodies was marked when M2696 became numerically the first peacetime double-decker, being built for Mansfield District early in 1946.)

It was perhaps no surprise that London Transport received the first post-war Regals from Southall, nor that London Transport also received some of the very first Regent II double-deckers. Delivery of the London Regals took until November, with similar composite bodies on the same chassis marque being built in that period for East Midland, Hebble, Rhondda and Devon General.

Clearly, the great need, however, was to produce the maximum number of double-deckers, and these would initially be mainly on the AEC Regent II and Leyland PD1 chassis. Thus, as a further part of the post-war rationalisation, no metal-bodied single-deckers were produced at Addlestone for the home market until late 1949, after the announcement of the cessation of composite bodybuilding. The industry would have been relieved that Leyland Motors were to resume bodybuilding at their famous South Works, easing the overall shortages, but more of this later.

Strengthening the export drive, alongside the composite vehicles mentioned above, were six single-deck vehicles for Lisbon, and twelve for a selection of operators in South Africa, part of the order for 300 vehicles mentioned alongside. No more metal-framed single-

The most obvious sign of a return to peacetime output was the reappearance of single-deck buses coming off the production lines and out of the factory gates, none having been built since eight Daimlers intended for Southern Rhodesia in 1942, one of which is shown on page 24.

This example, body number C8959 of May 1946, fleet number T725, HGF815, was one of 50 on AEC chassis for London Transport, and is typical of the immediate post-war design, being a composite-bodied vehicle – as were all single-deckers from 1946 until 1950. Note the builders' plate on the riser in the entrance. The destination arrangement, to suit London's deep display, gives a frowning aspect to the front canopy.

List of Contracts

The operators to receive buses with M.C.W. bodies in the near future include the undermentioned; for the sake of completeness the order described above is included in the total of 300 bodies from the Metropolitan-Cammell and Weymann factories.

WEYMANNS LIMITED, ADDLESTONE, SURREY
(1) 12 double-deck bus bodies through the Ministry of Supply.
    (a) 6 completely assembled.
    (b) 6 with lower decks mounted on chassis and upper decks shipped separately.
(2) 30 ditto for Cape Town or Port Elizabeth companies, shipped as (b) above for Cape Electric Tramways, Limited, on Daimler chassis.
(3) 50 ditto as (2) for the Cape Electric Tramways, but these may be shipped in sections for final assembly and finishing in the M.C.W. Port Elizabeth factory. The bodies are for Daimler chassis.
(4) 25 66-seat double-deck trolleybus bodies for the Cape Electric Tramways, on Sunbeam six-wheeled chassis, shipped as (1) (b).

deckers were built until a further 42 Regals for Portugal (illustrated in the later view of the bodyshop on page 75) and an export AEC demonstrator for Africa followed in 1948, with 27 single-deckers for East London and Salisbury, both in South Africa, in 1948/9.

The world was still rumbling with discontent in various places, and Jerusalem and Palestine were in and out of the news in 1946, both places where export business was available but under difficult conditions.

At Weymann's, in July 1946 there were a series of staff promotions. AT Cheesley, HN Edwards and WH Gray joined the MCW board, whilst WCS Chatfield was appointed Sales Manager and RM Cole was appointed assistant to the Managing Director. William Gray had joined MCW from Park Royal Coachworks in 1943, having been with that concern since Arthur Froggatt's days when the company was formed after the collapse of Hall, Lewis in 1930. Jack Davies became Weymann's Director and Commercial Manager, Harold Cook became Director and Chief Engineer, Walter Dodsworth became Director and Production Manager, CR Ward became Chief Buyer and Norman Froggatt, ATF's son who had joined in 1936, became Chief Estimator.

A move outside the organisation which would later impinge on matters at Addlestone took place in May when CH Davies left Charles Roe's Cross Gates Coachworks in Leeds to move to Mumford coachbuilders in Plymouth as General Manager. In that same month *Essential Works Orders* ceased to apply to the bus industry as a small ghost of normality returned to the country. Another event which would later have a huge impact on Weymann's future occurred early in 1946, but probably passed most people by. The national press reported that test civilian flights had taken place from an airfield outside London – Heath Row as it was then known – somewhere which in later

London Transport, like all operators, faced a huge problem with worn out vehicles and shortages of men and materials to repair and renew them when the war finished. The LPTB had already committed themselves to a replacement plan which would see the new AEC RT3 bus sweeping away thousands of pre-war vehicles but, in 1946, it was necessary to employ short term stopgap measures until the RTs came on stream.

The standard Weymann's highbridge body on AEC Regent II chassis was a logical choice, extending the numbers of STL class buses. This as yet unnumbered example is believed to have been the first of the 20, STL2682, built in early 1946. There were some 44 vehicles in the Weymann's batch, with examples being delivered to Liverpool, Newcastle, Mansfield District and Leicester to whet customer's appetites. The last of the London batch was withdrawn in 1955 and all 20 were sold for further service in Dundee, Grimsby and Widnes.

The extracts from the weekly trade journal *Modern Transport*, below, record progress with international harmonisation of road traffic standards, and dimensions, as far back as October 1949.

> **The New International Standards**
>
> IT is the first time that approval has been given to a convention on road transport which includes permissible maximum weights and dimensions for vehicles in international traffic. The new standards ensure that all vehicles complying with them will, on technical grounds, be accepted by contracting states on international highways. Delegates attending the conference believed that this fact will create a certainty which in turn will encourage road transport. Larger dimensions and heavier weights may be allowed under regional agreements, but the world standards may now serve as a guide in future road and vehicle construction.

> **Road Passenger Vehicle Dimensions**
>
> THE need for a more enlightened attitude by the authorities with a view to the running of coaches 30 ft. in length on two axles—curiously enough, they can be that length if on three axles—and 8 ft. in width, has frequently been expressed in this journal. Only on "authorised routes" can 8-ft. wide vehicles be used, and the difficulty is to secure such a route. The present procedure of mapping the routes for 8-ft. wide vehicles is complicated and cumbersome both to operators and licensing authorities, and there is room for more generous interpretation. Meanwhile we commend the Passenger Vehicle Operators' Association for compiling and circulating a schedule of routes over which 8-ft. wide p.s. vehicles have already been authorised. This should assist members in considering projected applications to the licensing authorities, and they are recommended to contest refusals where they can supply useful additional particulars regarding the general state and width of the road and the use made of it by other vehicles. The advantages to both user and operator of an increase of only 6 in. in the present normal width of 7 ft. 6 in. are so considerable that the situation ought to be met by prescribing the roads on which such vehicles cannot pass one another, and the use of the wider vehicles then be made a rule rather than an exception. The new Convention on Road Traffic confirms in this respect a generally accepted view contrary to official policy in this country which must necessarily have regard to safety considerations. But our own view —and it is shared by manufacturers and operators—is that in the light of the generally high standard of coach driving in Britain authorisation would be reasonable and feasible.

The transport press gave good coverage to the big MCW order for South Africa as would indeed be expected. One of the 2-axle Daimler double-deckers from the batch M4075-9 is seen here and there were also single-deckers with body numbers M4048-62.

years would drain Weymann's, and most other London manufacturers, of labour as it became almost a city in own right, offering better terms and conditions for those who chose to join its rapidly expanding and well-paid workforce.

There would be many events over the coming months which would highlight the growth and importance of the aircraft industry, and also the use of materials and innovations from wartime which were now finding their way into civilian life. Plastics, electronics and communications were all to assume much greater importance and at this time an announcement by IBM that it had produced a domestic machine from a wartime gunnery calculator seemed to be of no immediate interest, yet this invention would eventually lead to the now universal electronic calculator. The words *transistors* and *programming* were beginning to enter the language. Only a matter of months later the US announced one of its planes had broken the sound barrier whilst soon afterwards another broke the altitude record by climbing almost into space at 63,000 feet. It was as though the world was getting smaller.

However, if the world was getting smaller, buses were certainly getting bigger, for in July 1946 the maximum permissible width of psvs for operation in Britain was increased from 7ft 6ins to 8ft subject to local authorisation. Brian Burton, by now working in the drawing office, was pleased to see that one of his relatives was in the forefront here. His cousin Jackson Hoggard, GM at Southport, took the first Leyland-bodied example whilst his uncle, Richard Hoggard, was still recalling having taken the first original lowbridge Titan under the Stonebow at Lincoln. Name dropping was useful in the office, especially when said cousin later came to inspect his Weymann's buses and Brian was also taken out to lunch with the bosses!

This increase in dimensions was part of the harmonisation of standards with Europe, something which had been ongoing since a conference in September 1949 . Length, width, height, gross vehicle weights, axle loadings, road signs and a host of other matters were also being considered. The change to 8ft wide vehicles did not affect Weymann's single-deck composite production, all such post-war vehicles having been built to 27ft 6ins x 7ft 6ins except for the PMT diverted export Titan OPD2s seen on page 43.

Although harmonisation was on some people's agendas, others had more pressing matters to consider. In July 1946 food shortages became even more critical, and allowances, already meagre, were further cut. Quite simply we did not have the money to import the food we needed. Shortage of manpower was also a problem throughout Britain at this time. Although one million men had been demobbed by Christmas 1945, and another million released from munitions work, output in most industries was still restricted because vacancies could not be filled. In a move to ease this problem United Molasses Board Minutes record that Weymann's management attempted in July 1946 to employ non-union labour but were refused by the shop-stewards. Here, perhaps, was the first real post-war trial of strength, and the management lost. It was not a good omen.

Another loss was that of EG Izod who, after a long illness, died on 2nd October. His death marked the last link with the original Weymann company, and also with Central Mining & Investment Corporation who had owned the 1925 company from the late 'twenties until 1937, and for whom he had earlier worked as a mining engineer in South Africa.

Following Izod's death, AT Froggatt was appointed Chairman in November 1946, also becoming Joint Managing Director, rotating with Homfray Davies. Harold Cook was appointed acting Managing Director of MCW at this time, relieving pressure on Bon Cole who was suffering from persistent ill-health, no doubt related to his dreadful wartime experience as a PoW in the far East.

Norman Froggatt recorded that in this year a collective bonus scheme was introduced, and ran until 1959, when it was scrapped. Those earning bonuses might have welcomed the news that Government restrictions on the manufacture of television sets were lifted that same month, though in truth there would have been little to watch in those days.

More significantly, the UM Minutes record that Weymann's were given approval to spend £60,000 on jigs, tools, a new paint shop and various alterations in preparation for expansion in connection with the new RT3 bus production line described in Chapter 10. This was clearly a very major investment and boded well for the future.

Production for the year totalled 389 buses plus 61 assorted Ministry of Supply vehicles.

Events in the industry which made the news were the formation in October of Park Royal Vehicles Ltd, formerly Park Royal Coachworks; the creation of British United Traction Ltd (BUT) as a joint Leyland-AEC organisation for producing and selling trolleybuses and, later, diesel railcars; and the creation of SEAS (Saunders Roe) as a bus builder using the premises and staff at Beaumaris in Anglesey where previously they had been repairing sea planes.

The man who took charge as Managing Director at SEAS was WP Kemp, who had previously been with Short Bros before being seconded to Anglesey when the planemakers were placed under Government control. Kemp held his own and also joint Short's patents for aluminium bus construction; he and these patents, and their application, became a key component in the huge Leyland export story in which MCW would also be heavily involved.

There was another reminder that the Labour administration was not giving up on its plans, whether Britain was broke or not. In December 1946 the nation was given a rather dubious Christmas present in the form of the announcement that transport was to be nationalised. There seemed little jubilation outside the party faithful.

The MCW organisation commissioned a series of paintings, including water colours of the two assembly halls – Weymann's and Metro-Cammell's – and also high-quality accurately coloured versions of official black and white original official photographs. These were used in advertising and also formed the basis of a booklet to be given to visitors at the 1950 Commercial Motor Show. A selection is included in the following pages.

Below is the Show model for Maidstone & District incorporating the new form of glazing, using aluminium window pans. This would not be available for the home market until restrictions on the use of aluminium were lifted.

At the foot is a 56-seat export model on Daimler chassis for Cape Town, delivered in 1947 as part of the big African order for 300 MCW vehicles.

36

CHAPTER 8 – 1946-50

COACHBUILDING FINALE

The story of the output up to 1940 stressed the value of the metal-framed bodies, and in particular the double-deckers. Now, in post-war times the renowned metal body output would be crucial to Weymann's success, but, of course, single-deckers were just as important to many of Weymann's customers, especially the BET subsidiaries.

Once chassis were available the Station Road sawmill became busy cutting and machining timber for coachbuilt bodywork, and BET and municipal orders were soon being completed. During the first six months of 1946, single-deck output totalled only 31 bodies, all AEC Regals for London Transport. Output would gradually increase as the workforce numbers rose, but all to one basic design with either front or rear entrance according to customer preference. MoS allocations were adjusted to take the enhanced capacity into account.

At the beginning of 1947 further management changes took place following Izod's death. Jack Davies now became Director and General Manager; Harold Cook, also now a Director, became his Deputy. Walter Dodsworth, previously Director and Production Manager became Director and Works Manager. Perhaps to their joint relief the SMMT announced that it had decided not to hold a Commercial Motor Show in London that year 'because it would interfere with production'. Here was the break with tradition which saw the Show move from the 'odd' years of pre-war to the 'even' years of the post-war period.

Shortly afterwards Crossley and Guy were amongst the first companies in the bus industry to adopt the five-day week – Weymann's were not ready to take that step just yet for this was going to be a busy year and overtime working, made easier if the factory was routinely open six days, would be crucial.

However, it was an announcement from Leyland Motors that took the headlines – they had secured an order for bus chassis for Poland worth £200,000. Some people wondered if we could ever deliver them even if they were built since the

This spectacular view was almost certainly taken in early 1947, a year which saw high winds and heavy falls of snow throughout the country. Here HTT 490, C9056, one of a batch of 28 AEC Regals supplied to Devon General – C9046-73 – poses in a manner which most definitely would not be allowed today. The order followed the large first post-war contract for London Transport Regals, the vehicles being built between July and November 1946.

37

Variations on a theme

The Devon General vehicles already mentioned and illustrated on page 37 incorporated front entrances with a porch doorway, having a hinged door at the top of the steps. HTT 487 is preserved in full working order and here C9048, HTT 482, is seen before leaving Addlestone in July 1946.

Rhondda vehicles used a rear entrance, and the same porch arrangement can be seen with a door at the top of the short staircase. C9088 delivered in autumn 1946 was one of six, C9086-91.

East Midland Motor Services, based in Chesterfield, Derbyshire, preferred a rear entrance/exit layout, with a folding door at the foot of the steps, as shown on C9024. The batch of 12 Regals, C9024-35, was built alongside the Devon General vehicles from July 1946.

38

dockers were once again on strike, and food shortages were rife throughout the country. Never mind the unrest though, think of the greater good, and in February came the announcement that put even Leyland's Polish order into the shade: the mines were to be nationalised.

It was in March 1947 that Arthur Froggatt was elected President of the Institute of British Carriage and Automobile Manufacturers, a position he held for three years. It must have given him enormous pride in that position to hand over to London Transport Weymann's first RT, RT 402, in April, and to see it enter service just ahead of Park Royal's first delivery on 12th May. The RT story overlaps this portion of our narrative and, accordingly, has been given a chapter in its own right from page 78.

If, as is likely, Bill Black was put out by being pipped to the post, his comments have not survived but he was probably mollified soon afterwards by the purchase by Park Royal of CH Roe in July. He would also be waiting to see who was going to body the 1,000 chassis which Leyland had just announced that BET had ordered from the Lancashire factory. In addition to that he was also no doubt digesting the news that UK production had reached 1,319 buses in September, 388 of them for overseas in line with Government export percentage directives. Of less direct interest to him was the news that a Captain Formby had been appointed a Weymann's Director from that same month, but he would have no doubt welcomed the award of the Military Cross to Bon Cole. Cole had finally been forced by ill-health to resign his directorship and his position as Managing Director of MCW in February, and the long-serving Harold Cook had been promoted from acting to Managing Director.

By early 1947 London Transport was able to complete its hat-trick when the first post-war Leyland single-deck chassis at Station Road were coming down the line as part of an order for 31 of London Transport's TD class, in addition to examples for East Yorkshire Motor Services, Sheffield and Devon General. A couple of Daimler single-deck chassis for Dundee added a touch of variety. Greater variety was introduced when Weymann's built two batches of bodies to the BEF 'Federation' design, one for Western Welsh and the other for Yorkshire Traction. As the photographs on page 40 show, they were markedly different in appearance from the contemporary Addlestone product. The new paint shop was being built, ready for the RTs, and the 44 hour week had now been introduced, though still with Saturday morning working.

Although this all boded well for the future, everyday life was far from settled at that time. Many commodities were still on ration, including meat, sugar, soap, clothing, petrol and sweets. Government plans for more nationalisation were being formulated and overall there was a sense of frustration that things were getting no better, even though the war was now behind us. And this was before the cost to everyone in Britain of the National Coal Board had become apparent. One James Callaghan MP, later Prime Minister of course ("Crisis? What Crisis?"), was at this time in the news regarding Government allocations and total predicted bus output – the figures were challenged, never believed, and not reached. They epitomised the confusion being created by muddle-headed thinking and policies.

In the autumn of 1947, however, the last of the composite-bodied double-deck vehicles were built, the Sunbeam W4 models for Hastings Tramways mentioned previously. From now on all composite production would be of single-deckers until it finished in late 1949: 455 single-deckers and the 15 Hastings double-deck trolleybuses had been produced in the period from April 1946. When metal-framed single-deck production for the home market resumed at this point in late 1949, 1,200 double-deck metal-framed bodies had been built in the same period. Of these, 25 were trolleybuses, 118 lowbridge motor buses, and the rest 56-seat highbridge motor buses for a variety of customers.

East Midland's buses were painted in a distinctive and very attractive brown, biscuit and cream livery, shown here in this offside view of one of the 1946 batch of Regals as also seen on the facing page. HR Lambert, its Manager, was a well known stalwart of the industry having begun his career with Scottish General Transport, then worked his way up the National Omnibus Co Ltd before moving to East Midland as General Manager in 1938. He would move to North Western just as these vehicles were being delivered and North Western began taking Weymann's vehicles in 1949, including the very last Addlestone composite single-deckers, and a wide selection of other single- and double-deckers. Mr Lambert retired in 1952. (AEJ colln.)

The 18 Leyland Tiger PS1 vehicles supplied to Western Welsh in early 1947, body numbers C9092-9109, were built to the BEF Federation design, as shown. Together with 23 similar buses for Yorkshire Traction, C9110-32, they were the only examples of this body style produced at Addlestone. Brush and Roe were among other bodybuilders also manufacturing to this design and a Brush-bodied example from the former Yorkshire Woollen District fleet survives in preservation. Note the single, forward-facing, seats alongside the rear wheel arches instead of the inward facing style bench of the Weymann's design though both designs seated 32 passengers.

This 1940-built composite body for East Yorkshire Motor Services, C9135, shows the small oval window which Weymann's still used at that time. After the war it was replaced by the larger and more modern looking design below right on body C9135, delivered to the operator in May 1947 and one of a batch of five, C9133-7. Another view of the same vehicle is included at the page foot. The earlier EYMS Tiger had provision for a spare wheel but some vehicles, including the Exeter one below, C9323, incorporated a luggage boot. This may be compared with the Federation design opposite, which incorporated a rear emergency exit. (JAS colour)

41

Hebble was another of the Yorkshire area BET fleets which took some of its purchases from Station Road. Here C9142, ACP 723, delivered in May 1948, poses in its dull red livery before collection by its driver. A Leyland Tiger PS1, it was one of a batch of three.

In the early post-war when single-deck chassis – particularly Leylands and AECs because of the export drive – were in short supply, BET placed some substantial orders for bodies to be fitted to pre-war chassis and Weymann's examples from two of its fleets, Yorkshire Traction of Barnsley and Potteries Motor Traction of Stoke on Trent, are seen here. Yorkshire Traction took twelve such bodies, centre left, and they were fitted to pre-war Leyland Tigers. One has survived in preservation.

In addition to rebodying prewar single-deck Leylands (see overleaf) North Western took 20 bodies on new Bristol L5G chassis, body numbers C9287-9306 in September 1949.

Potteries took 20 bodies, also for fitting to Leyland Tigers, with body numbers C9364-83, and C9370 is shown. This batch followed on from 14 for North Western as part of the same BET contract. PMT have already implemented the change in livery to mainly red in the cost-cutting exercises appertaining at the time.

Potteries Motor Traction of Stoke also took some Leyland double-deck OPD2/1 chassis from a cancelled export order. The chassis dimensions were to the longer overseas standard and, as such, could only be fitted with single-deck bodywork for use in the UK until the Construction and Use Regulations were changed, in 1950. NEH 450, body number C9410, is seen below when new. It was rebodied by Northern Counties of Wigan with a double-deck body after the change in Regulations and survives in preservation with one of its fellows as recorded in the *Northern Counties* and *PMT* books published by Venture.

43

Kingston upon Hull took six of the Regal III chassis with 35-seat front entrance bodies in 1949, C9329-34. They were the last composite bodies taken by Hull and one has been preserved, as shown. (AEJ)

Hastings Tramways composite trolleybuses have already been mentioned and here BDY 813, C9153, one of the final batch of 15 is seen, this time on the Sunbeam W4 chassis. They were introduced in 1947/8 and all were sold for further service when the system closed in 1959. (KWS)

Lancashire United took five of these Dennis Lancets during 1949, body numbers C9384-8. The operator normally took its single-deckers from CH Roe, with BET Federation style bodies as seen on page 40, and so these were somewhat of a surprise when they were delivered. Weymann also supplied double-deckers to the company in that year as seen later. LUT favoured the porch doorway, with the door at the top of the steps as seen here, on its single-decker buses. (JAS)

North Western also took new bodies for pre-war vehicles and C9350-9363 from the BET block order found themselves on a mix of TS6/7/8 chassis. NWRC were prolific body swappers at this time and when the Tigers had finally expired the bodies were transferred to 1938 vintage Bristol J chassis, one being shown here. This routine swapping of bodies was, of necessity, common in many fleets at that time and goes a long way to explaining the operating industry's reluctance to embrace integral (chassisless) vehicles. (KWS)

North Western took the final batch of composite bodies, C9433-60, in 1950 and had them fitted to Bristol L5G chassis as those in the previous year. C9442 is shown below. Of the 28, the final seven were classed as dual-purpose vehicles, and had 32 instead of 35 seats, thus providing additional luggage accommodation. These were the last half cab single-deckers delivered to the Stockport company and their next Addlestone buses were the underfloor-engined Leyland Olympic and Atkinson vehicles, all from Weymann"s metal-framed M series as shown in later pages. (AEJ)

45

CHAPTER 9 – 1946-50
PEACETIME PRODUCTION

The problems in getting back to anything like normality must have seemed overwhelming as 1946, the first full year of what was going to pass for peace, opened. There was, however, a very full order book, with vehicles being needed in large quantities for both home and overseas customers. Meeting export percentage requirements would present no difficulty. That was the good news: the bad news, as we saw in Chapter 6, was the lack of the wherewithal to handle those orders and AT Froggatt and his team would have to tread a four-way balancing act through pressing orders, shortage of materials, shortage of manpower and outside influences completely beyond their control.

Some positive steps had already been taken: the decision to rationalise post-war production which resulted in single-deck output being very standardised, but double-deck design would be slightly more varied, with highbridge and lowbridge models being built, though the latter were initially very much in the minority. The standard post-war double-decker was either a five-bay highbridge 56-seat rear entrance open-platform model, or the lowbridge 53-seat equivalent; both metal-framed and weighing around 7tons 3cwts. Dimensions had not yet been relaxed to allow wider vehicles to be operated and so everything going down the lines for the home market, single or double-deck, metal or composite was 7ft 6ins wide.

Municipal and BET customers were taking these vehicles in large quantities and most were on the AEC Regent II chassis, largely because the MoS initial sanction for AEC production of 80 such chassis were earmarked to be bodied by Weymann's (60) and the balance by Park Royal. Aberdeen, Brighton, Burnley, Eastbourne, Glasgow, Hull, Leicester, Liverpool, Luton, Newcastle, Plymouth, Portsmouth, Rochdale and Sheffield were among the municipal customers with a selection of BET company fleets for good measure. The first lowbridge examples were those supplied to Chesterfield in 1946 on Leyland Titan chassis; further similar bodies on Titan PD1As were built for Plymouth, with those built on Dennis Lances going to Lancashire United. Plymouth came back for more PD1s in 1947 but, as with some earlier contracts, they were to be finished by local bodybuilder Mumford in similar manner to Liverpool, and later Glasgow, or some overseas contracts.

The first post-war Weymann's lowbridge buses to be delivered went to Chesterfield who took a mixture of seven Leyland Titan PD1 and eight PD1As. One of the former, M3003, JRA 638, is seen in November 1946 and it was to be January 1947 before the contract was completed. The half drop windows and lining out give a pleasant continuity with pre-war design and standards. The small windscreen is necessitated by Leyland supplying the dash panel attached to the chassis and including the instrumentation (sparse as it was) in that panel.

Chesterfield had taken MCW products before the war and would remain a regular and loyal Weymann's customer to the end, taking eight front-engined Daimler double-deckers in October 1965. (KWS)

The full height 7ft 6ins double-deckers look somewhat tall and gaunt by today's standards. Here a January 1946 delivery, this time for Newcastle Corporation, is seen in service when quite new. The small windscreen on the Regent II models is particularly noticeable in this view, but the vehicle looks smart in its then traditional dark blue municipal livery. Number 28, JVK 628, body number M2718, was the first of seven bodied by Weymann's; a further seven chassis from the order were bodied by Park Royal, but with composite bodywork. Newcastle's trams have not yet all been withdrawn, the mix of tram and trolleybus overhead creating an interesting pattern in the skyline, especially where the live tram wire crosses the neutral of the trolleybuses' supply.

Liverpool Corporation continued its pre-war practice of taking chassis with Weymann frames and completing the bodies in its Edge Lane workshops.

It had been able to place an order for 100 AEC Regent chassis during 1942, for delivery after hostilities ended. These were delivered in three batches, during 1945/6, one completed example being shown.

47

The second contract for post-war lowbridge double-deckers was for 25 Leyland Titan PD1As delivered to Plymouth between August 1947 and September 1948. The batch was numbered M3135-59 and M3136, seen here, survives in preservation. (JAS)

Leyland Titan PD1s began to appear down the lines around May 1946 with examples for Portsmouth, Plymouth and, above, Lancashire United Transport. GTC 352, number 325, with body M2998 delivered in the autumn of 1946, was the second of four in this contract; a further eight were bodied by Leyland. Top sliding windows are apparent in this view taken by the author on a hot sunny summer afternoon in Bolton in 1956; the overhead wires belong to sister company South Lancashire Transport, some of whose trolleybuses also came from Addlestone. (JAS)

By the time the Regent III chassis became available in 1947, Weymann's had fitted some 245 double-deck bodies onto its predecessor, the Regent II chassis, since peacetime production had resumed.

The bus industry, generally speaking, was carrying on much where it had left off in September 1939, but there was one small but significant exception. Midland Red, the huge Birmingham-based operator which built its own vehicles, chassis and bodies, had just launched a new single-deck model with the engine located under the floor, allowing the whole interior apart from the driver's cab to be available for fare-paying passengers. Once this concept became available on the open market, through Leyland, and later AEC, the shape of the single-deck bus at Weymann's and every other bodybuilder would change quite dramatically, as we shall shortly see.

A choice of design is offered

London Transport's new RT3 design, prepared in the Chiswick drawing office and exclusively for LT's own use, has been mentioned briefly, on page 31. It will be covered in detail in Chapter 10 but suffice to say at this point that it incorporated a four-bay structure whereas Weymann's and most other bodybuilders were still working with a five-bay design. In 1946, however, a series of events caused the Addlestone factory to be in a position to offer an alternative. The impending RT bus had now brought an awareness of four-bay design into the forefront of fashion, and Weymann's and others were not slow to take advantage of this.

This elegant four-bay Regent III, M3191, KRH 474 was delivered to Hull as part of a batch of 50 vehicles, M3170-3219, during 1947. When the contract was completed in June, Hull had taken almost 200 MCW bodies and would continue its purchases until 1960. The body seated 58 passengers.

From Weymann's, and all other bodybuilders' points of view, both the RT, and, when it became available, the Regent III chassis, differed in one important respect from the Regent II; their front bulkheads were located some 6ins further back relative to the radiator line than they had been on the previous Regent model. This meant that the upper deck first bay was longer, and where a five-bay design was used the remaining windows would be shorter, giving an unbalanced and cramped appearance. It was this revised dimension which offered the opportunity for the drawing office to produce their own design,

49

Shortages of materials and components, often bought-in products, sometimes meant that vehicles had to be sent to their owners with items missing, as here. Such was the need to get replacement buses into fleets ravaged by wartime neglect that these were minor problems in the overall situation. In some cases operators would be recovering components from withdrawn vehicles, or using spares they still held in stock. Tynemouth placed this Regent II, M2836, into service in June 1946 and it was one of 13 in the batch. Either the equipment or the roller blinds for the destination display was evidently not available and a metal plate covers the missing section. Note that the five-bay body still incorporates half-drop windows; sliding windows have yet to make their appearance.

The interior views show a clean and tidy appearance with traditional upholstery of the familiar style which looked good, wore well, and above all was comfortable. Just visible on the original print are the raised letters MCW on the flywheel housing, a feature of Addlestone-built buses with this component.

Addlestone-built vehicles carried MCW on the flywheel housing of front-engined vehicles, as seen here on a preserved Rochdale AEC Weymann's bus in the Manchester Museum of Transport. (JAS)

50

Devon General's Regent III M3794, KOD 582, was delivered to the operator in March 1950. This was some three years after the 23 RT chassis mentioned in the text made their way to Weymann's factory and were fitted with similar 56-seat highbridge bodies but it is included here to allow the comparison between the Regent III and the RT front ends to be made; the latter with its lower bonnet line, can be clearly seen. Eight of the vehicles went to Devon General, and another five to Rhondda as shown, in addition to the balance of ten to Aberdeen. Delivery of the RTs took place between November 1946 and March 1947.

similar in appearance but completely different in manufacture, from the RT with its LPTB patents and registered design. Accordingly, Weymann's lost no time in introducing their own, new, four-bay design, whereby the front upper deck bay and the four bays between the bulkheads were more evenly matched in length, greatly improving the appearance as the photographs in this section of the book show.

There had been some 4-bay single-deckers from Addlestone before the war when Midland General took a batch of 22 express vehicles on Regal chassis, but whereas that appeared to be a bespoke commission the new design was generally available. Conversely, design-wise, the 1940 wartime RT Weymann's-bodied demonstrator which entered service in Glasgow had a five-bay body.

Harold Cook's promotion to Director and Chief Engineer in the appointments following Izod's death in autumn 1946 is almost certainly significant at this time but, undoubtedly, the most important factor was the decision by AEC, in conjunction with the MoS, to release onto the open market some of London Transport's RT chassis which were accumulating at the Windmill Lane premises and elsewhere due to the longer-than-planned lead time before completed bodies were to be available for fitting to these chassis, either by Weymann's or Park Royal. Twenty-three of these chassis found their way to Weymann's, through Government allocation, to be finished for customers other than London Transport. The first to be bodied at Station Road were ten – M3033-42 – for Aberdeen Corporation, six in November and December 1946, with the remaining four delivered to the Scottish operator by April of the following year, and thus carrying the first of Weymann's new four-bay bodies. Their body numbers followed a batch of Regent IIs for Liverpool and they formed an impressive sight when they entered service in the Granite City.

The next five RT chassis were bodied for Rhondda in December 1946 as body numbers M3043-47, with eight for Devon General – M3048-55 – being completed in February, just ahead of the final four for Aberdeen. All these RT chassis carried the new body design and the finished buses could be instantly recognised by the low bonnet line of the RT chassis made possible by London's decision to dispense with the top-mounted air cleaner. Mindful that only a small number of these chassis were coming to them, Weymann's made no attempt to alter their bulkhead design to provide a deeper front lower deck passenger window, which the RT body would incorporate, and which many believed enhanced that body design enormously, since the Regent III, which was imminent and would shortly carry this new body of theirs, unfortunately did not incorporate the lower bonnet line.

The undoubted improvement in appearance first seen on the Aberdeen RTs was soon recognised, and when the Regent III model became available in 1947, Eastbourne, Hull, Rochdale and Sheffield were amongst the first municipal customers to take the four-bay body on that chassis.

Some BET customers began taking the four-bay design in 1947 with Devon General and Tynemouth among the first, whilst others continued to take the five-bay version, though that now looked quite dated. Highbridge and lowbridge versions of both designs were produced.

Lancashire United took nine Dennis Lance lowbridge double-deckers in September 1947 and they were soon put to work on a wide variety of duties including local stage carriage, workmen's specials and express services such as Manchester to Blackpool. In later years Ribble would use some of its toilet-equipped Atlanteans on that same service – some contrast. M3079 from the batch M3076-84 is seen here glistening before entering service. (STA)

In the days when most municipal vehicles were smartly presented, reflecting local pride, Eastbourne's were perhaps in the top league. The blue and cream colour scheme always seemed to enhance the body design. M3223, JK 9652, one of five delivered in September 1947, is seen here. The body is of the four-bay construction, possible on the Regent III model. Note that half-drop windows are still being used. (STA)

Overseas the dominance of the British Empire was over and developing countries wanted work for their own people instead of importing completed products such as buses and trolleybuses. All the major manufacturers were obliged to address this situation and most began to set up factories to assemble, and later manufacture, vehicles in Africa, India and elsewhere. Weymann's (Bus Bodies [SA] Ltd), Park Royal (BMS Ltd) and Brush (Brush SA Ltd) were three of those which set up production units in southern Africa. RH Morter, by then Assistant Works Manager, but one of Arthur Froggatt's protégés from Hall, Lewis days, left Weymann's in February 1947 after a send off from the Company and trade press to take charge of what became Bus Bodies (SA) Ltd in Johannesburg.

By this time, some 18 months after the end of the war, the trade journals were reporting the widespread travels of key men from several important British manufacturers including, of particular relevance to this story, Leyland and AEC. Amongst others Africa, South America, the Caribbean, Ceylon, India, Portugal and Spain all offered significant potential sales opportunities but involved lengthy journeys by sea to reach them – civilian air travel over these distances was still some time away and three-month sales tours were quite common. A visit to southern Africa by Major Chapple, the Chairman of the Bristol manufacturing company, taking convalescent leave, was put to good use and his observations were quoted in the trade press. He noted that many countries were building new factories, to become manufacturers and assemblers (not just of transport-related products), and that there would shortly be opportunities for transporting the employees of these new organisations to and from their places of work. Other former serving officers, in particular Commander Hare RN and his colleagues in the Overseas Motor Transport Company, noticed the same trends as did those at 88 Kingsway in the BET's London headquarters, and Weymann's would supply vehicles to these new African companies or subsidiaries before many months had passed. There would also be a steady procession of British BET managers heading out to Africa and the Caribbean to take charge of that organisation's new undertakings.

Of greater eventual significance to Weymann's future, Henry Spurrier and Donald Stokes, both of Leyland, spent many months in South America and the West Indies; Leyland's field engineers were active in Africa and elsewhere and sales and engineering were being brought together as never before. Britain needed food and raw materials whilst the developing and expanding countries needed buses and trucks. Deals were done and the Government would have acted as broker in negotiations which brought, for example, beef from Argentina, in return for buses for

M3073 delivered to Cheltenham District in November 1947 also had a four-bay body but the combination of top sliding windows and rain louvres is not a happy one as can be seen. There were three vehicles in the contract, M3073-5, and they were finished by Lydney Coachworks. Dowty, based at Ashchurch, were manufacturers of railway wagon braking systems for marshalling yards throughout the world, using friction pads between the rails to bear on the wagon wheels for retardation. (KWS)

53

Buenos Aires. Metal ores and timber were also no doubt traded against the supply of buses with Chile, Uruguay, Montevideo and others. Cuba would have traded sugar and tobacco against its enormous contract for Leyland single-deckers. The size of the forthcoming orders, and their value, would be colossal; time and again the press would report another order which out-stripped all previous records in size and value. If there was ever a golden age of British bus manufacturing, then in terms of output against the odds this was to be it. In retrospect, perhaps one of the strangest, though not in that instance involving Weymann's, was Leyland Motors deal with Poland where payment was made in live geese!

At the end of 1947 Weymann's recorded production of 468 vehicles, and probably felt they had done a good job. In the boardroom, back in the City of London, United Molasses probably thought so too, and were talking to Metro-Cammell to try to arrange a merger between the two bus building concerns. The coming year, 1948, would see some changes, but with surprises for both Weymann's and UM.

Metro-Cammell quickly decided that mergers with Weymann's, and perhaps anyone else, were not on their agenda. Accordingly, UM turned their attentions to Park Royal and began discussions with Bill Black to consider an amalgamation. Black was equally disinclined, though it took until May before negotiations were abandoned. Park Royal at this time were building over 20 vehicles per week (just over twice Weymann's output), with their share of the RT contract averaging eight bodies weekly. Over the duration of the contract production ran 3:2 in favour of Park Royal – co-incidentally the same split as MCW had originally created between Birmingham and Addlestone, of course.

A factor which many people would not have been aware of at this time was the need for the British Government to adhere to the terms of the *European Recovery Programme*, designed to assist in the rebuilding of economies and infrastructure, and to avoid the pitfalls created after the First World War. It was this programme which also influenced the percentage of manufactured goods to be exported, and it was closely monitored. *Bus and Coach* and other trade papers commented ruefully on its detrimental effect at home.

When post-war production resumed in 1948 the 1939 designs which had been produced for Brighton formed the basis of many contracts. Amongst forthcoming trolleybus deliveries, none of which had been made since the wartime Utilities on Karrier W chassis, were examples for Notts & Derby Traction Co in 1949, and Bournemouth and Bradford Corporations, both in 1950.

In this post-war Brighton view we see just how well the bus and trolleybus designs had been harmonised. (STA)

54

A New Year brings some excitement at last

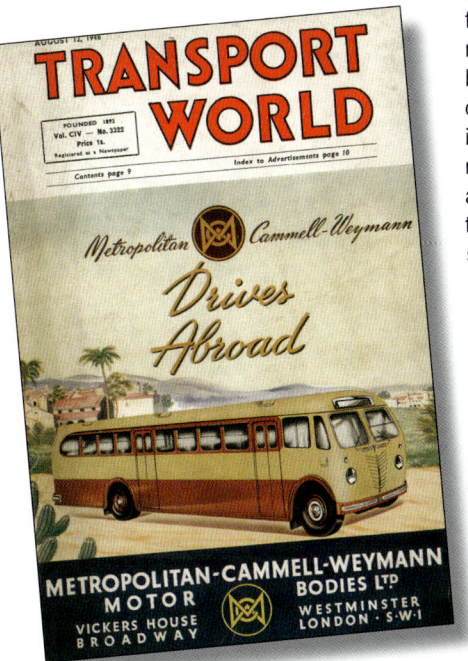

In 1948 the Olympic Games ('The Austerity Games') were held in London, and finding sufficient vehicles to move athletes and spectators was taxing everyone's mind. The Government, helpful as always, and seeking to increase bus output, had just imposed a ban on the production of luxury coaches, though it struggled to define what such a vehicle actually was. It seemed to turn on such matters as the inclusion of radios or the type of seating. The ban was almost impossible to apply or monitor, and was apparently widely ignored. Weymann's, as bus builders, were not affected, of course. By January 1949 it was being recognised that the income from tourism was more important than the perceived advantages and possible small savings the MoS was looking for, and the idea was about to be quietly dropped.

More serious, and much more confusing, was the 'allocation' of new buses for 1949 – in other words what the MoS was prepared to allow to be built. At the time of the Motor Show in October 1948 – the first such post-war event – the official figure was said to be 4,000 vehicles. After the show GR Strauss, the Minister of Supply, gave the figure as 7,700. The Ministry of Transport told the MPTA that the figure would be 9,000. Small wonder that the industry was sick and tired of red tape and ineptitude when all it wanted was to get on with the job of planning man-hours against available materials and fulfilling orders. This bumbling bureaucracy provided plenty of ammunition for the Leader writers in the trade press.

Cover and inside double-page spread for the 1948 Commercial Motor Show with MCW advertising to the fore, and only Maidstone & District representing the home market. (STA)

Much more appeared in the Press concerning a far more immediate topic, for, notwithstanding all the uncertainties about allocations, availability of materials and output, troubles in parts of the world where we would hope to sell our goods, and dockers on strike, the 1948 Earls Court Show, deferred from 1947 as explained earlier, was opened by Earl Mountbatten on Friday 1st October, and ran until Saturday 9th October – it was judged to have been a great success. With its emphasis on exports, 47 vehicle manufacturers were displaying 450 assorted types of trucks, vans, ambulances, buses, trolleybuses, coaches, tractors, trailers and special municipal vehicles, powered by diesel, petrol and battery electric sources. Had things gone as intended by UM, Weymann's would have been taking orders for their new electric car, of course. Open from 10am until 9pm each day except Sunday, it breathed life into a struggling industry, allowed old friends to meet and discuss new trends, and makers to show off their wares.

Reading through the list of exhibitors is a sad reminder of just how the once-mighty and world-respected bus industry has collapsed in Great Britain. The announcement in the trade press just three weeks earlier that the Tilling group had sold out to the BTC for £24.8million would render the Bristol and Eastern Coach Works respective stands superfluous since they would in future be limited to supplying their products to the Nationalised concerns only. Another announcement in the same issue confirmed that there was to be an Extraordinary General Meeting of the AEC organisation to consider changing its name to ACV in view of the

Newport had taken pre-war and wartime buses from Weymann's, but this was the last post-war order. General Manager Charles Baroth moved away after some two years in the post – 1944-46 – and was followed by Lee Wilkes who had been at Darwen and then Chester. Newport then took Guys, Wilkes preferred choice at Chester and Weymann's also lost out. M3367 seen here was one of nine, M3367-75, Leyland Titan PD1As delivered in 1947. There were also eight Daimler CVG6 double-deckers bodied at Station Road, M2961-8, in that same year. The Leyland shows signs of having had attention to the body, with rubber mounted glazing replacing the original window arrangements. (AEJ)

This Titan PD1 was one of 23, M2974-96, delivered in January 1946. However, it was clearly a hot day in Portsmouth when M2976, DTP 814, was photographed some years later, with driver's windscreen wide open and saloon windows dropped down. (AEJ)

M3241, one of a batch of 30 for Sheffield, was photographed in front of the office block at AEC's Windmill Lane plant in June 1948. The four-bay body confirms it is a Regent III, and KWE 260 was one from M3225-54. Deeper sliding windows now present a much neater – and surely more effective – appearance.

The main Great Western railway line on the embankment in the background runs into London's Paddington Station, crossing the famous iron bridge over the busy road outside the factory.

Rochdale Corporation's striking livery immediately confirms it as owner and M3261, delivered in February 1948, was one of a batch of 13, M3255-67, following on from the Sheffield vehicles above. Rochdale would be a regular customer of Weymann's with vehicles appearing at the Motor Shows and, as below, in advertising material.

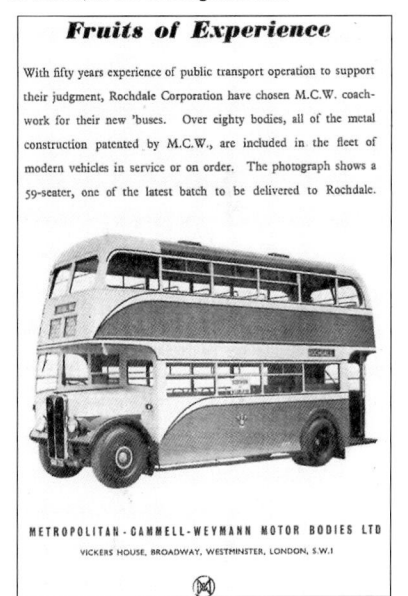

Fruits of Experience

With fifty years experience of public transport operation to support their judgment, Rochdale Corporation have chosen M.C.W. coachwork for their new 'buses. Over eighty bodies, all of the metal construction patented by M.C.W., are included in the fleet of modern vehicles in service or on order. The photograph shows a 59-seater, one of the latest batch to be delivered to Rochdale.

METROPOLITAN-CAMMELL-WEYMANN MOTOR BODIES LTD
VICKERS HOUSE, BROADWAY, WESTMINSTER, LONDON, S.W.1

---

recent acquisition of over 90% of the shareholding of Crossley Motors Ltd and the Maudslay Motor Co Ltd. Clearly there would be some interesting changes before the 1950 Show took place. But now, in 1948, there were 430 stands covering a quarter of a million square feet. Admission to this wonderful event cost just half a crown (12½p), or one shilling (5p) after 5pm.

Wartime commitments and current material shortages combined to create a situation resulting in the comment that there was nothing revolutionary at the show. John Ferguson of *Passenger Transport*, looking for trends, considered that the only really new venture was the presentation of the Commer two-stroke engine, whilst petrol engined exhibits 'could be counted on one hand'.

MCW had adjoining stands, numbers 22 and 23, one for each company. On the Birmingham stand was a single-deck BUT trolleybus for Auckland, New Zealand, 35ft 6ins long and 8ft 6ins wide, together with a 33ft 5ins long single-deck demonstrator on a Leyland chassis and designed for the South American or other overseas markets. These and many other similarly large exhibits fuelled the arguments for an increase in the UK dimensions. It may be appropriate to mention here that whilst Weymann's used the unique body numbers quoted as a means of identifying each vehicle built, Metro-Cammell used the standard railway builders convention whereby orders were allocated a build or 'sanction' number, meaning that individual vehicles were not so delineated.

South Lancashire Transport had been allocated Weymann's utility trolleybuses as seen on page 15, and ordered Karrier 3-axle trolleybuses for delivery after hostilities finished. M3164-69, fleet numbers 66-71, were delivered in 1947/48 and number 71 was the last SLT trolleybus in 1958. The upper view shows one working the service between Bolton and Leigh whilst the lower one shows Leigh's Spinning Jenny Street trolleybus terminus. The name reflects the activities of the nearby cotton mills. Subsidiary company LUT was, of course, a regular customer for motor buses at this time as we have seen. (JAS above; KWS left)

Right and Facing: Three examples from the exhibits on the MCCW portion of the MCW display at the 1948 Commercial Motor Show.

This dual-door trolleybus on an export BUT chassis for Sao Paulo, Brazil was apparently run on demonstration in London in August 1948 before the Motor Show. One of four in the contract, M3160-3, it featured a dual-door body seating 43 with standing capacity for a further 29 passengers. The body was 35ft 6in x 8ft 6in, outside the UK dimensions at that time.

Another of the export exhibits was M4104, this dual-door 37-seat demonstrator model for South America on an AEC Regal chassis. At 32ft 3in x 8ft it was slightly shorter than the Sao Paulo trolleybus and was a single-vehicle contract.

Facing page: MCW showed this Newcastle 70-seat double-deck trolleybus at the 1948 Commercial Motor Show and proudly announced that 200 MCW bodies of all types would have been supplied to Newcastle on completion of this contract. LTN 484, fleet number 484, had been built by Metro-Cammell in Birmingham to the London Q1 design. It was another one of the vehicles illustrated in the Motor Show souvenir book.

Bradford Corporation had taken vehicles with Weymann's bodywork before the war but this was their first success in the early postwar years, a batch of 40, M3973-4012 including FKY 7, seen below, supplied in late 1949/early 1950. Bradford's purchasing policy meant that bodies from Barnard, Brush, Crossley, East Lancashire Coachbuilders, Leyland, Neepsend, Northern Coachbuilders and Roe were also represented in the fleet – a veritable who's who (or who-was-who). There were to be no more from Station Road, however, although two batches of Regent Vs were early casualties of the 'build-them-in-Elmdon' policy very soon indeed after the 1963 takeover of Weymann's. (AEJ)

59

On the actual stands, significantly but probably not then generally recognised, both Weymann's exhibits were metal-framed – one of the AEC Regal single-deckers for Lisbon Tramways, M3556, and a Bristol K6A double-decker for Maidstone & District Motor Services Ltd, M3595. Soon the MCW group would only manufacture public service vehicles which were metal-framed and so there would be no more Weymann's composite-framed vehicles at the forthcoming motor shows. As previously noted the last patent flexible bodies had been produced in 1940, the last one to be exhibited at a Commercial Motor Show having appeared back in 1937, though once again one had actually been earmarked for the aborted 1939 Show.

The Lisbon single-decker seated 45, with large standing areas at the front and rear, and in acceptance of expected regular overloading, the vehicles incorporated dual main cross bearers. The Mark III chassis had a drop frame extension, was of left-hand drive configuration, and 7ft 6ins wide with an 8ft wide body.

The Maidstone & District vehicle was a very handsome production as the official photograph opposite shows. It featured a new form of interior and exterior panel fixing, but also, and more noticeable, a revised form of glazing giving a very neat appearance which immediately made the previous form of window mounting look out-dated. Bespoke aluminium extrusions were used as fixings, riveted to the main pillars on this body, and their use confirms that this scarce commodity was at last becoming available again, even if only in restricted quantities at this time. Photographic evidence appears to confirm that the show model was the only one to incorporate these new features.

These were the only double-decker Bristol chassis bodied by Weymann's in the post-war period, with North Western's Ls as the only Bristol single-deckers. Further MCW group vehicles appeared elsewhere throughout the show. There was a Metro-Cammell-bodied luxury coach on the Albion stand, for South African Railways, and thus, being for export, able to make quite extensive use of aluminium in its construction and finish. This vehicle was 8ft wide, but its length at 35ft 9ins was rather more impressive, as were its interior appointments incorporating air conditioning, aircraft type reclining seats, fluorescent lighting, radio and public address system and so on. Elsewhere in the Show, two Metro-Cammell-bodied trolleybuses could be seen, a 70-seat export example for Durban together with a home market example of the London Q1 class type but actually destined for Newcastle-on-Tyne and seen on page 58.

By the time of this show in 1948 only a handful of trolleybuses had been bodied at Station Road since the war. Government directives had precluded the building of any three-axled vehicles in the 'utility' period and it was not until now that they reappeared. The 15 composite-bodied Hastings vehicles had been built on the wartime Karrier W4 chassis, but the first peacetime contract was for Sao Paulo, Brazil on chassis from the newly formed BUT company (see also page 59). Allocated body numbers M3160-3, these were integrally constructed and expected to carry 90 or more passengers, and were fitted with an English Electric 150hp traction motor and control gear, the contactor equipment being located under the rear seat and accessed from external doors in 'luggage boot' fashion. At least one of the four was tested under London Transport's wires and then demonstrated between Fulwell and Hampton Court before being exported in 1948. Sao Paulo was at that time one of the greatest industrial areas of South America and the vehicles, similar to those being built for New Zealand, were believed at the time to be the first all-British trolleybuses to operate in South America although in fact there had earlier been some Roe-bodied examples for Lima, Peru, built in Leeds in the 'twenties, which everyone seemed to have forgotten about.

Immediately following these jumbo Brazilians, numerically, were six three-axle Karrier MS2 double-deckers for South Lancashire Transport, but there had in fact been nine BUTs for Brighton Corporation and BH&D, delivered earlier in 1948. Interest in electric traction was, unfortunately, now in decline largely because the cost of electricity had risen sharply following Nationalisation of the industry, and it was no longer permissible for undertakings to generate their own power and use it for traction purposes at less than the National Grid rates, or to obtain substantial concessionary terms; in Cardiff, as one example, this was quoted as resulting in power becoming one third more expensive. Thus operating costs rose, without the ability to recover the increase, other than by seeking to raise fares which, even if allowed, was likely to discourage passengers.

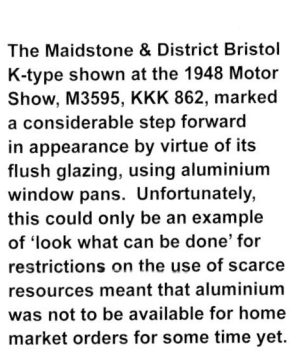

The Maidstone & District Bristol K-type shown at the 1948 Motor Show, M3595, **KKK** 862, marked a considerable step forward in appearance by virtue of its flush glazing, using aluminium window pans. Unfortunately, this could only be an example of 'look what can be done' for restrictions on the use of scarce resources meant that aluminium was not to be available for home market orders for some time yet.

The difference is immediately apparent when looking at the view of the other vehicle, M3591, **KKK** 871 from the same batch, shown on the right. (AEJ)

Bury Corporation took a batch of 20 Leyland Titan PD1A models in 1949 as it prepared to withdraw the last of its trams. Here the first of the contract, M3376, is seen at work in the town. A further batch of 20 similar bodies but on PD2 chassis were delivered in 1949/50. Bury would also take AEC Regent III models, and Titan PD2s, with 4-bay bodywork, in 1953.

Midland General obviously enjoyed a more mellow climate than Bury to judge by the upper deck front ventilation arrangements. NDT on the radiator refers to Notts and Derby Traction, the Balfour Beatty organisation which owned Midland General and Mansfield District. Regent III JVO 947 of December 1948 came from the batch M3679-711. (KWS)

A general view over the fitter's and blacksmith's area in 1949, underneath the offices and not conducive to a quiet life upstairs – especially when some people made a habit of leaving the drawing office door open to annoy those within . . .

62

By 1950, when tramcar replacement was proceeding at an ever-increasing rate, Liverpool Corporation had taken 240 AEC Regents bodied by Weymann's, though they were supplied as framed chassis only. Most, as in these examples, would be finished by the Corporation's craftsmen in the Edge Lane car works where many of the trams had been built. (KWS)

Below: HKF 820, body number M3515, was the penultimate one of a batch of 100 delivered as framed chassis from 1947 and completed between January 1948 and April 1949. It passed into preservation after withdrawal and is seen here in 1972. (JAS)

The works canteen provided the ideal setting for the annual Christmas Party for children of the workforce. With so many children having fathers, uncles, grandfathers, mothers, aunts and older sisters working in the factory it really was a family event and another opportunity for the management and Social Club to get together to make the event one the children would remember – and their parents would appreciate when money was tight and food was in short supply. The canteen staff are seen in the adjoining picture.

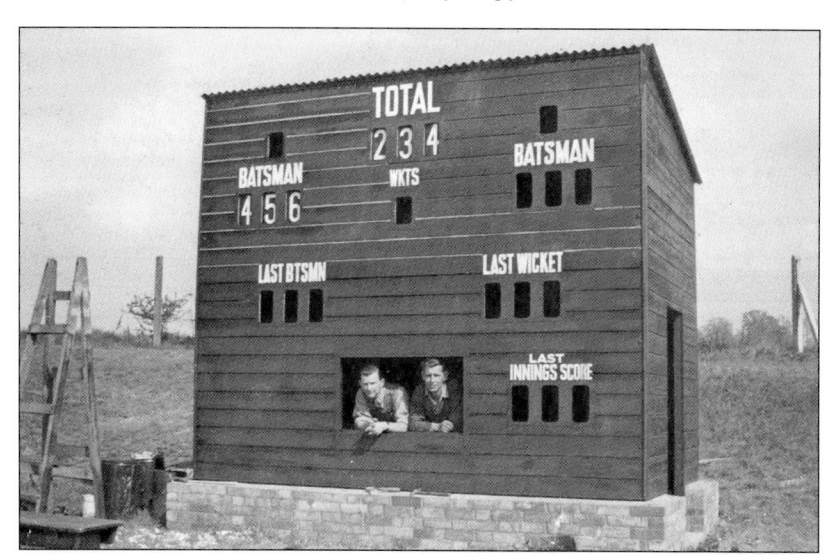

When Vic Smith joined Weymann's during the war EG Izod was quick to see that his enthusiasm for sport, and his woodworking capabilities, could be put to good use. Vic soon became involved in the darts team – Ten-Bar-Two – and served as its Secretary for over 50 years. He remained with the players until his death in January 2009 and practised once a week with them almost to then. He was involved in many other activities and after Izod's death AT Froggatt was keen to continue to assist matters, and materials for anything to do with sporting and social activities were made freely available after suitable requests. The scorebox, left, was one example built by members in their own time and extensions to the pavilion was another. In the picture below Vic Smith, second from left on the front row, holds the shield after another winning event. In the other view the team celebrate the Golden Anniversary.

> MEMBERS of the Weymann's Works Band travelled to Reading in order to compete in an open contest organised by the Berkshire and Neighbouring Counties Band Festival Guild. Against greater opposition than in past years they were awarded second prize from an entry of nine parties in the septet section. The band also came fourth from an entry of 14 parties in the senior quartet section.

The Annual Outings were a much anticipated event and when Brighton hosted the event it was always particularly well appreciated since the good relationship between town and company, as customer and supplier, was acknowledged with a particularly fine spread. The speeches provided an opportunity for pep talks for the workforce.

> **SPORTS AND SOCIAL CLUB'S ANNUAL OUTING**
>
> The Club's Annual Outing was held this year on June 17th and a visit to Brighton was arranged — a popular choice in view of the amenities afforded by the Town, and also owing to the firm's very friendly association with the Corporation's Transport Department, for whom we have built all the 'buses they have required since 1939.
>
> Just over 300 members went on the outing, but we were particularly sorry that owing to illness, Mr. Nelson Knight, who has been associated with the Club since its inception, was unable to be with us. This is the first time he has missed an outing of this nature.
>
> A special train had been arranged from Addlestone which, unlike most special trains, kept a commendable schedule and arrived at Brighton shortly after 10-0 a.m.
>
> Lunch had been arranged at King Alfred's Restaurant in Hove and 315 members and guests sat down in the large Dining Room. We were delighted to have as our guests—
>
> Councillor Alfred Rostance, Chairman of the Brighton Corporation Transport Committee;
> Mr. Winston Robinson, General Manager of the Transport Department;
> Mr. Arthur Brown, Deputy Gen. Manager.
> Mr. G. T. Gibson, Traffic Manager;
> Mr. W. Docwra, Rolling Stock Superintendent;
> Miss Frampton, Mr. Robinson's Secretary, and Mr. Bon Cole from M.C.W.
>
> An excellent luncheon was provided by the Restaurant and during the meal we were entertained with popular music from the band.
>
> Our thanks are particularly due to Mr. Gibson who was largely responsible for the arrangements for the luncheon and also to Mr. Pozzi the Manager of the Restaurant and his staff who catered so well for such a large number.
>
> Informal speeches by Mr. Froggatt, Mr. Jack Davies, Mr. Cousens, Mr. Cole and the officials of the Brighton Corporation concluded the luncheon and the kind references to the Company which were made by Councillor Rostance in a felicitous speech were loudly applauded.
>
> During the afternoon members took full advantage of the amenities of the Town and,

The reason for this increase from the CEGB was spelled out in *Passenger Transport*, when considering the implications. The cost of coal needed to be raised appreciably, to stem the huge losses the newly formed National Coal Board was making. Suddenly, trolleybuses and trams, at a stroke, would face a huge hike in their operating 'pence-per-car-mile' costs and their previous cost advantage was eliminated. This was just one example of an underestimated knock-on effect having devastating consequences.

Another major factor now mitigating against the trolleybus was London Transport's decision to replace its remaining trams with buses, instead of the expected trolleybuses, thus reducing demand on the electrical suppliers and putting up their unit costs. Of the UK trolleybus vehicle total of around 2,500 units, some 1,000 or 40% were owned by London Transport. The newly formed BUT company would seemingly need to look elsewhere for its future, and successfully turned its attention to diesel railcars. Before the war Weymann's had built 271 trolleybuses for 12 UK systems. Between 1947-63, when the final examples were built for Bournemouth, only 158 vehicles were bodied for 10 systems, 25 of these being for export contracts.

Immediately prior to the Motor Show there had been a revision to the Joint Sales Agreement between Weymann's and Metro-Cammell, with United Molasses continuing to seek further improvement in the arrangements. Now came a crucial change when the ratio of order allocations was changed from the original 60:40, being the ratio of the 1932 shareholdings, to 55:45, still in MCCW's favour, effective from January 1949. The division of the cost of the sales office remained a bone of contention, however. Homfray Davies now became Managing Director of MCW in the annual rotation between Weymann's and Metro-Cammell and must have been pleased that progress was being made in this contentious area.

Although the emphasis in this narrative is focussed on work and sales, it should not be forgotten that Weymann's had a wide variety of sporting and other social activities. The monthly *Weymag* recorded the progress of members playing cricket, football, rugby, hockey, tennis, darts, billiards and snooker, enjoying gardening, belonging to the male voice choir or the works band whilst even the works fire brigade found time to partake and succeed in various Surrey area competitions of the British Fire Services Association. The restoration of the allotments after the land had been partially commandeered for air raid shelters during the war was also naturally welcomed.

Sadly, despite all the goodwill and camaraderie generated by these wide-ranging activities which were always actively encouraged by the management, a sign of continuing unrest was a strike at Station Road in 1948 and, sadly, such strikes were to be an unwanted fact of life throughout the last two decades of Weymann's existence. At one stage AT Froggatt, thoroughly fed up with the whole situation, arranged for a police presence outside the factory one morning and refused to open the gates – thus creating a lock-out. He then decided who he was prepared to re-employ, and therefore who would be allowed in, subject to their signing an agreement not to cause any further disruption, and who would be refused employment. Even this action secured only a relatively short period of stability.

In the City, economists and other observers wondered if the world had at last gone completely mad. While Britons were desperate for food, and the army had been brought in to unload ships held up at the docks, over in Berlin we were flying round the clock to beat a communist blockade – a manifestation of the Cold War – preventing food being moved over land. Happily the Berlin airlift was a resounding success – but once again the victims were helping out the former aggressors.

Despite the unrest, at the end of 1948 production had risen to 719 vehicles. Plans for the forthcoming year included the cessation of composite body building as steel supplies improved; from the end of 1949 all bus production would be of metal-framed models, with only MoS contracts and Beardmore taxis using wooden framing and coachbuilding until final closure of Weymann's factory.

The main event at the end of the year, however, in terms of future overseas potential was the announcement of the forthcoming Leyland Olympic integral bus, though its impact was not yet capable of being assessed, of course. This was the outcome of the time spent by Leyland's engineers and salesmen around the world and once full production began it became a resounding export success. Initially, the vehicles ordered through MCW were produced in Birmingham, and this project would mark a new phase in Leyland Motors' relationship with Metropolitan Cammell Carriage and Wagon and the MCW organisation.

The ACV Group makes its appearance

The catalyst for this new relationship between MCW and Leyland Motors had been the Lancashire company's awareness of the huge potential overseas markets which it could penetrate if it had the right product, at the right price, and sufficient manufacturing capacity. Its engineers were looking to produce an underfloor-engined integral bus in large quantities, but Leyland did not have the capacity to handle such a project alone. Accordingly, it then looked to Metropolitan-Cammell as a logical partner and joint manufacturer, the two organisations having worked together before the war. The outcome, and the model produced for those markets, was the Olympic integral bus.

The exact timing of the start of this particular collaboration is uncertain but it can safely be assumed that matters must have been in hand for many months before the announcement of the forthcoming Olympic bus was made. It can also be safely assumed that AEC were aware of at least the bare bones of the concept and strategy, since both they and Leyland were looking to sell into the same markets, but, of course, as staunch competitors.

AEC must have felt some concern that its arch-rival was strengthening its position in the industry by its enhanced relationship with Metro-Cammell, and took steps to improve its own standing by acquiring two of its competitors, Crossley Motors Ltd and the Maudslay Motor Co Ltd, as previously stated. The announcement of the acquisition of over 90% of each of those company's shares was made just before the Motor Show in October 1948, and it was also announced that an Extraordinary General Meeting had been called to reconstruct the company as ACV – Associated Commercial Vehicles – with AEC as a subsidiary.

This move must have caused some concern at Leyland's headquarters but within twelve months worse was to come with the announcement also mentioned earlier that the newly formed ACV group had purchased Park Royal Vehicles Ltd, and with them, of course, their wholly owned subsidiary Charles H Roe Coachbuilders Ltd of Leeds. Park Royal by this time were achieving an output of 27 vehicles some weeks; their total output for this year would be some 1,145 against Weymann's 972.

Leyland Motors now found itself facing a group with resources and facilities, including as it did AEC, Crossley, Maudslay, Park Royal and Charles Roe, at least as extensive as its own, and when these new constituent companies were fully integrated, with far greater bodybuilding capacity.

Weymann's too would have had good reason to be apprehensive of the effects of the ACV group's potential. In the first four post-war years, *ie* up to the purchase of Park Royal, the majority of chassis passing down the lines at Station Road were of AEC manufacture. The new group would be in a position to offer a complete package to customers, with AEC chassis being bodied by any one of the three well-known and respected bodymakers within the group and whose combined capacity would have been roughly double that of the Addlestone company. If such a package was offered, and with a price advantage, then Weymann's would certainly lose business. Many years later, in a reversal of roles, Leyland would find itself the subject of questions in Parliament, raised by Alexander's Managing Director Ray Braithwaite, on just this very subject.

Meanwhile in 1949, in a further world campaign, Leyland's Export Manager, Donald Stokes, went to the Far East whilst CB Nixon, Leyland's Chairman no less, went to South America. The results would be to take MCW products across the world and Weymann's workforce would be involved in orders for a great many new customers. The first Olympic buses, single-deck integrals (*ie* without a separate chassis), were produced in Birmingham and therefore it would not be until 1950 that Weymann's started to build this model. On a much smaller scale there were some interesting exports for Portugal and Israel during 1949, in both cases LHD double-deck vehicles with mirror image bodywork as shown on page 75.

During 1949 a sad note was recorded with the death of Director and Company Secretary Francis C Webb. Mr Webb was one of the longest-serving employees, having been with the company from the earliest Addlestone days, if not before. His place as Secretary was taken by PH Gimson. Another death, that of Sir Malcolm Campbell, killed in Bluebird at Daytona whilst attempting to beat the world land

Left to right, Bill Shirley, Deputy General Manager, Stanley Kennedy, Chairman of the Tilling Group Management Board, and Sir William Black, Director and General Manager of Park Royal at the time of the creation of ACV in 1948.

Bill Black had left Weymann's in 1933 to go briefly to Beadles before taking charge at Park Royal in 1934.

Bill Shirley left Weymann's around the time the Park Royal men arrived at Addlestone, in 1934, moving to Eastern Counties at Lowestoft as Foreman of the Coach Fitting department. In 1935 he moved to Leyland Motors to become Body Assembly Shop Superintendent under Colin Bailey who had joined the Lancashire company from Metropolitan Cammell. Shirley returned to Lowestoft in 1938 as Works Manager of the by then ECW under Bill Bramham who in 1948 moved to Northern Coachbuilders. Bill Shirley left ECW in late 1947, becoming Deputy General Manager (Production) at Park Royal Vehicles. Later in 1948 he moved back to ECW as General Manager, becoming Director and General Manager during 1949. In 1953 he returned once more to PRV as Director and General Manager, staying there until he retired in 1975.

He had interviewed at least one, possibly more, of the Frimley team after Weymann's closure but his offer of work at Park Royal was declined. Some old memories of working with him were best left undisturbed.

Probably the most famous Weymann's individual, Henry (later Sir Henry) Segrave was the first person to simultaneously hold both land and water speed records. The first to travel at over 200mph in a land vehicle he gained the world record of 231.46 mph at Daytona Beach on 11th March 1929. He broke the water speed record on Lake Windermere at 98.76mph and died the same day trying to better this. His significant financial input and shareholding in Weymann's is believed to have caused problems for the company when his estate was being settled. His mechanic, Tim Healy, became EG Izod's chauffeur after the tragic accident.

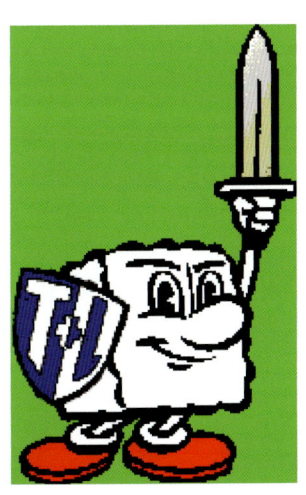

United Molasses and Tate & Lyle ran a widespread and vociferous campaign against the Nationalisation of sugar, including posters, newspaper adverts and advertising on public transport, with the help of the sugar cube logo. (Tate & Lyle)

speed record, reminded some of the older hands that in 1927 Henry Segrave, Weymann's then Sales Director, and Campbell's brother-in-law, had raced along that same stretch of sand in Golden Arrow and attained the record speed of 231.46 mph before losing his life on Lake Windermere trying to beat the water speed record. Most employees would probably also mourn comedian Tommy Handley's passing, having listened to his ITMA programmes in the works canteen and at home on the radio. Mrs Mopp was out of work now, along with Fumf, Hotch and the rest of the gang.

Prime Minister Attlee's Government was still busy with plans for more nationalisation, despite the desperate currency problems. Having given a sweetener to the country by ending clothes rationing in March they then announced that the gas industry would be taken over in May, following on from the Iron and Steel Bill of November 1948. Shipping and sugar were intended to be next and the dockers – who could be expected to have been staunch Labour supporters – mounted a three week long strike to demonstrate their feelings against the proposal. Tate and Lyle took the sugar issue on board and mounted a spectacular campaign to bring their case to the public. United Molasses would have been caught in either of these nets, and their Addlestone subsidiary would then have been a bed-fellow of Bristol and Eastern Coach Works, a fascinating prospect . . . Sugar was certainly a problem and sweets were on and off ration as an indication of attempts to balance supply and demand. Milk was restricted to two pints per person per week now.

In July, Sir Stafford Cripps, the Chancellor, finally conceded that there was indeed a dollar balance-of-payments crisis. What took everyone by surprise was the outcome; on September 18th Sterling was devalued by 30% against the dollar. The pound dropped overnight from being worth $4.03 to $2.80. Whilst this helped exports, including for example Olympic buses, it made imports even more expensive. In the aftermath, many of Labour's wilder dreams were quietly buried. Mr Cube breathed a sigh of relief.

There was, however, one huge boost for British morale when, in October 1949, the mammoth Bristol Brabazon aeroplane made its maiden flight from Filton, where it had been built in the giant hangar which in later years would see Concorde pre-production aircraft being assembled. It was named after the Minister of Transport, Lord Brabazon, famous amongst other things for his eye-catching car registration number, FLY 1, recognising that he held the first pilot's licence to be issued in this country.

There were other developments during 1949, some more obvious, some more mundane, but most of them undoubtedly less contentious. As predicted, coachbuilt bodywork, using wooden framing, was finally phased out at Station Road at the end of this year. From now on both Birmingham and Addlestone would be able to produce a common product, though how long it would take before the external appearance was commonised will remain to be seen. The first steps in this direction were now taken, however, as new metal-framed designs were prepared.

The final months of the composite contracts had seen a variety of examples for BET customers, always a substantial source of Weymann's business, of course. There had been some 64 pre-war single-deck AEC and Leyland chassis rebodied for Devon General, Yorkshire Traction, Potteries Motor Traction and North Western Road Car. The latter Stockport-based company – a very longtime Lowestoft supporter – had only recently become a Weymann's customer, taking as its opening order a batch of ten lowbridge Leyland PD2s, but the doubtful honour of being the last composite contract fell to a batch of Bristol L models, again for North Western. These bodies were to have a varied life, being transferred to early 1930s Leyland Tiger chassis, and then when those chassis were finally worn out, on to earlier Bristol L chassis before being sold on by a dealer. As stated previously, the patent flexible option had finished with Oxford's Leyland TS8s in 1940; now ten years later the composite option had also been withdrawn.

The penultimate contract was for Potteries who, in addition to their rebodies, also took a batch of frustrated export double-deck Leyland chassis, which were 8ft wide but of long-wheelbase, and had them bodied as single-deckers. After the regulations were amended to allow 27ft long double-deckers to be operated they were rebodied by Northern Counties of Wigan as double-deckers and the Weymann's single-deck bodies were placed onto second-hand Guy single-deck

A Weymann's body from the batch C9409-32, now on the Guy chassis from an independent operator taken over by PMT in 1951, although the chassis had been new to Milton Bus Service in 1947. The 'new' ensemble was photographed standing in Whitworth Street West below the then Central Railway Station waiting its turn to move across to Lower Mosley Street bus station via the curiously named Trumpet Street. (AEJ)

chassis by the operator. Two of the rebodied Leyland double-deckers have survived into preservation.

By the end of composite construction some 5,179 vehicles had been built using this method of framing in routines little changed from 1930 when the first Green Line buses were built. Production since 1945, when peacetime build resumed, totalled 468, all being single-deckers except 15 which were trolleybuses for Hastings. The corresponding figure for metal bodies from the start of peacetime build to the end of 1949 was around 1,484, of which 47 had been single-deckers. This is, therefore, an appropriate point to look at the numbering system, opposite.

A significant number of buses had been driven away from Station Road as framed chassis for finishing elsewhere. Liverpool Corporation took 225 such vehicles and finished most of them in the Edge Lane Works where its craftsmen had built many of the tramcars the new buses were being bought to replace.

Other orders to be completed by the operator included Plymouth Corporation, where three complete vehicles were accompanied by twelve to be finished by the Corporation and ten by Mumfords, where CH Davies had moved from Charles H Roe coachbuilders at Crossgates in Leeds. Cheltenham & District took three partially completed vehicles to be completed by Lydney Coachworks.

Some redeployment of staff and machinery would no doubt have taken place as the importance of the saw mill diminished and the type of work passing through the mill would have been down-graded from accurately machined pillar sections to mundane items such as floorboards and fillets. A similar change at Duple's coachworks in Hendon in the same period resulted in a strike lasting several months, becoming a major factor in the eventual move out of London to Blackpool.

During 1949 another large export contract was handled, with 56 assorted single- and double-deck vehicles being completed, plus an AEC Regal demonstrator for South America. These vehicles carried body numbers M4048-104.

In anticipation of the imminent cessation of composite construction, metal-framed single-deck bodybuilding was now resumed for the home market, with a batch of 24 Regal III dual-purpose buses for Mansfield District following on from the African order, with body numbers M4105-28. A further 35 similar bodies, but mounted on Leyland PS1 chassis, were also built. Both these companies had become State-owned following the recent Nationalisation of the Balfour Beatty Group's electricity interests, and they would have felt the effects sooner than they might have wished when the Midland General Leyland Tigers were diverted to another BTC fleet, Crosville Motor Services of Chester. Although classed as dual-purpose their seating, in line with the directive forbidding the building of luxury coaches, was decidedly basic, a point Crosville's General Manager later made in his memoirs. Midland General probably thought he was an ungrateful so-and-so, especially as he made a great fuss when some of *his* buses were diverted from Eastern Coach Works at Lowestoft straight to London Transport before eventually entering the Chester company's fleet!

Access to the factory was controlled from the gatehouse but Peter Gascoine formed a strong friendship with gatekeeper and security man Stan Carter, seen here around 1965, and was allowed to go round 'out of hours' on Saturday mornings, photographing the vehicles ready for delivery, and later, in build. At the end this access allowed a full record to be created as to which vehicles were finished at which factory and when they left Addlestone. (PG)

BODY NUMBERING

Although this book is principally concerned with bus production, and the relatively small number of coaches produced in the last few years of the Company's existence, there had earlier been high quality motor cars and in the period covered by this volume there were also taxis, fire engines and other ministry contracts between 1952 and 1954. Some of these were allocated numbers in the bus series and these have been quoted where they are known. Unfortunately few details exist of the majority of the MoS contracts handled between 1952-4. Space considerations preclude listing all the body numbers allocated to the Station Road products which have, in any case, been well covered by the PSV Circle whose publications are available from them, or from our associate company MDS Booksales, at 128 Pikes Lane Glossop.

The Body Numbers carried by the vehicles were allocated when the order was placed. There were at least six series of numbers, and their origins go back, retrospectively, to the very beginning. It appears that when Norman Froggatt joined in 1936 he decided to try to make more sense of the overlapping series. The early production run of cars and the small number of Flexible Patent buses and coaches was allocated a W prefix, indicating a Weymann Patent body structure. From 1930 when conventional Coachbuilt bodies began to be constructed a C series was used, and this remained in use until coachbuilt construction ceased around 1950. This series had reached 763 in 1936 but then jumped to C5000 following Mr Froggatt's rationalisation.

There was a separate (third) series with prefix M for metal-framed bodywork and this was used from 1933 to the end. The series reached M9753 but reverted to M1 after the fire in 1961 as explained in the text. Integral Olympics and Olympians used an L or LW prefix. Finally the W series was re-used for the RT and RTL vehicles built in J-Building, in addition to the solitary Routemaster.

In 1958 work began on building Beardmore taxis (see picture below) with the first 40 being numbered in the bus series (M8685-8724) but they later had a separate series with a D prefix.

Although M1966 is the highest-known Weymann-built body number, other higher numbers had been allocated for work in progress in the drawing office for vehicles not subsequently built at Addlestone. These had certainly reached over 2,010.

Vehicles built by Metropolitan Cammell Carriage & Wagon did not carry individual body numbers which is why no numbers are quoted against their vehicles where they appear in this book.

This book has been put together using a combination of the surviving information compiled by Bob Smith, friend and fellow enthusiast of the Author, using chassis manufacturers' records and operator data, John Carman had the foresight to preserve the original production records and deserves a special mention. Martin Ingles gave Bob considerable assistance, particularly with non-psv activities. Norman Froggatt's final summary, together with the PSV Circle lists, and notes and observations from people in the factory either as employees, or, in the case of Peter Gascoine, enthusiasts who were granted regular access have all been invaluable. Without the efforts of all the above the production of this book could not have been accomplished.

Tiger Cubs for Edinburgh and Beadmore taxis in build side-by-side in the body assembly hall. (Courtesy David Hunt)

Lancashire United took three post-war batches of lowbridge bodies, starting with nine Dennis Lance lowbridge double-deckers in 1947. Then in 1949 they took ten Guy Arab III chassis with similar bodywork, M3823-32. A further ten, again on Dennis Lances would follow later in 1949. The company, like many others, had been impressed with its wartime Arab I and II models and would shortly standardise on Guys for its double-deck requirements for some years. Here, the last of the batch has the extended bonnet signifying that the vehicle, like the others, is powered by a Gardner 6LW engine. (GL)

Market Share and Share Exchanges

The trolleybus boom was now almost over, and in the five years in question – 1946-50 – only seven British operators took such vehicles from Addlestone, six with BUT chassis and the seventh, South Lancashire Transport, on Karriers. The Hastings Tramways order was divided between Weymann's and Park Royal with near identical products from the two factories.

Although the Atherton-based SLT company was now buying Karrier trolleybuses it still provided facilities for nearby Leyland Motors to test trolleybus built in that organisation's famous works. Sometimes these were bare chassis, adding variety to the passengers' view through the windows! The new SLT Weymann-bodied Karriers were very much at home at Atherton, where sister company Lancashire United had a good many MCW products in the fleet including one of the prototype metal-framed Metro-Cammell double-deckers from the very start of collaboration between Addlestone and Birmingham, and delivered in 1933.

The reasons for the decline in the market for UK trolleybuses has already been touched on, with London's decision to design a new model of diesel bus – the soon to become famous Routemaster – the sharp increase in the cost of traction electricity

Below left: M3820 had been delivered to Brighton in 1962 although the chassis, one of a pair, had been built in 1947 and stored in the meantime. When the Brighton system closed in 1959 both were sold to Maidstone Corporation and LCD 52 passed into preservation. It is seen here during a spell at the Carlton Colville museum in East Anglia. (STA)

Other trolleybuses sold when the Brighton system closed went to Bournemouth and here M3402, new to Brighton, Hove & District in March 1948, is seen below with its new owner in 1960, soon after refurbishment and repainting. There were three in the batch, M3402-4, immediately following five similar examples for the Corporation, M3397-3401, and the three BH&D vehicles duly passed to Bournemouth in 1959. (JAS)

70

Notts & Derby took 15 BUT trolleybuses with Weymann's bodies, M4033-47, as seen in this depot lineup in May 1949 when they replaced a like number of MCCW-bodied AECs, seen facing them here, with their unusual bonnetted front end design and dating from 1933. From this point the whole fleet carried Weymann's bodywork, but not for long for the system closed completely only four years later. (STA)

The heyday of the trolleybus was far from over in Bradford in 1953 and the whole of the Notts & Derby fleet of 32 vehicles was quickly snapped up. M4038, dating from May 1949 and thus only four years old when it changed hands, was photographed in 1956 still very much as it had left Station Road except for a change of colour scheme. These fifteen BUT trolleybuses were withdrawn between 1965 and 1967. The other 17, older vehicles, were rebodied whilst with Bradford, extending their lives until 1958 or 1968 depending on their age. (JAS)

following the nationalisation of the electricity supply (the CEGB) and the decision by some operators to avoid the high cost of replacing worn out expensive overhead and traction poles. Another factor involved the road planners who were having to face the need to cater for ever-increasing volumes of traffic, though the boom years of the private motor car were still some time away. All these factors combined to reduce the number of trolleybuses being ordered, and Weymann's, through their MCW sales office, were not alone in seeing the decline in this sector of their order book. By the law of averages it should not have made too much difference since diesel buses would replace the electric ones on a seat-for-seat basis, and so it proved.

There were other factors at work, however, and these did make a significant impact on the order book. In 1942, as already mentioned, a share exchange between Tilling and BET took some companies from one empire to the other. The main impact was to come after the Tilling Group sold out to the State in 1948, and Bristol and Eastern Coach Works found that their products were not to be available on the open market any longer.

To take two examples, Crosville Motor Services of Chester had long been staunch Leyland users, and now found themselves obliged – like all Tilling companies – to buy Bristols. Whilst this had little or no impact on Weymann's, a change in the other direction had a profound effect. North Western Road Car of Stockport had settled on Bristol chassis and Eastern Coach Works bodies from the late 'thirties, and had built up a modern and very standardised fleet. Now, at a stroke, as a BET company, it was precluded from buying either. In this case, however, Addlestone did become the beneficiary, and to some tune. The first non-Lowestoft bodies arrived in 1948, 14 from Leyland

One of Weymann's bodies finished by Liverpool Corporation is lowered onto its Daimler chassis in the giant Edge Lane workshops where the skeletal frame seen on page 63 would have been completed. This is a scene which the Station Road craftsmen did not see, for they built the body framing in two halves, and the lower deck was built up from the chassis. They would not see the completed body off its chassis. This view, taken after a major 7-year overhaul, demonstrates that for many operators lifting bodies from their chassis at major overhaul time was routine. This was why integral construction of buses would be an uphill struggle. Note the overhead crane and, in the foreground, the traverser, both part of the major facilities provided in what was once one of Britain's major tramcar building emporia. (STA)

Motors fitted to that manufacturer's Titan PD2 chassis, and ten from Weymann's on the same chassis type. All were lowbridge models since the entire double-deck North Western fleet was of that rather awkward layout at that time.

The Addlestone bodies clearly found greater favour, possibly because the price through the BET buying regime was advantageous, partly because Leyland could not offer a single-deck body for front engined chassis, but also probably because the product was judged to be superior. Between 1949 and 1958 North Western took 220 bodies from Weymann's, many on Leyland chassis of various types.

Although in this instance Weymann's were clearly the beneficiaries of the change of ownership of the Stockport company it does illustrate how easily outside factors could change the market, and the ensuing orders. Changes in engineering policy also played their part and a decision by BET to purchase cheaper vehicles for a shorter life would affect all the major body manufacturers, Weymann's included.

North Western took its last ECW bodies in 1948, a batch of twelve Bristol L5Gs and ten Leyland Titans. It then turned to Leyland and Weymann's for its requirements and the first contract from Station Road was for a batch of composite bodies on Bristol chassis still outstanding (see page 45). There then followed the first metal-framed examples, ten lowbridge bodies on Leyland PD2 chassis in 1949, M4017-26, with M4024 being shown before delivery and M4023 in service.

Crosland cutting machinery and guillotines were used widely throughout the printing industry at that time and North Western would have carried many of their skilled workforce to and from this factory in Bredbury, Stockport. (AEJ)

73

Bournemouth bought four former Brighton Corporation and three Brighton, Hove & District Weymann-bodied BUT 9611T trolleybuses when they became redundant in 1959. One of the ex-Brighton Corporation vehicles, HUF 45, new in May 1948 with body number M3399, is seen in its new home in 1960. (JAS)

When the Brighton trolleybus system was closed one of the BH&D vehicles was chosen to become part of the national collection and was taken to the then new Museum of Transport at Clapham, London. Located in a former bus depot it housed a wide selection of vehicles and railway artefacts. Here CPM 61, M2095, one of the vehicles completed in September 1939 but stored until after WW2 had ended, and then re-registered (from BPN 340) before entering service in January 1945, is seen outside the rear of the museum premises in 1963. It is now stored at the Science Museum overspill site at Wroughton, near Swindon. (JAS)

This excellent shot in the body shop neatly shows the wider framing for the 8ft Lisbon single-deckers; the gap beyond the dash panel clearly indicates the extra width. When interviewed by the Author, Cyril Smith, the man working on the cantrail, described filling the curved portions of the body with horsehair on the last of the Weymann's cars when he joined the company in 1933. He also remembered working for Mr Black – or rather keeping out of his way, for Mr Black's temper was legendary.

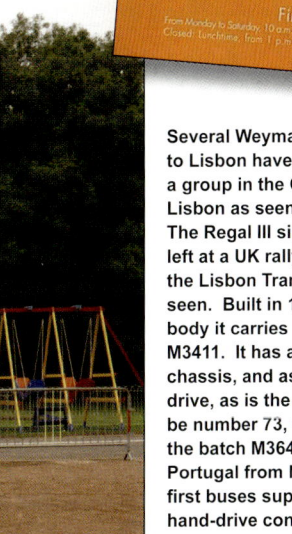

Several Weymann-bodied AECs supplied to Lisbon have been preserved including a group in the Carris transport museum in Lisbon as seen above.

The Regal III single-decker shown to the left at a UK rally was formerly number 17 in the Lisbon Tramways fleet, and later 141 as seen. Built in 1948 with a dual-door 20-seat body it carries Weymann's body number M3411. It has an 8ft wide body on a 7ft 6in chassis, and as can be seen is left-hand-drive, as is the example above, believed to be number 73, the 1948 Show Model from the batch M3649-78 which were shipped to Portugal from Newport, South Wales. The first buses supplied to Lisbon were of right-hand-drive configuration, with doors on the 'wrong side' but all were built for anticipated severe crush loading operation.

75

The first single-deckers, as stated, had right-hand drive chassis with left hand configuration bodies, as seen above left. Later contracts were able to use the left-hand drive Regal chassis, resulting in the body style seen above right. Note the more upright rear, allowing for greater standing capacity at the rear. They served the city well, their livery changing over the years as the transport fleet moved from more green through to orange and white.

Standing in front of the spectacular display hangar at the Imperial War Museum, Duxford, at a ShowBus event is this beautifully restored AEC Regent III, Lisbon's 255, originally registered 68 21 07 and built at Addlestone in 1955 with body number M6652. One of a batch of 16, its mirror image body seats 56 passengers. (DC)

76

One of the B.U.T.-English Electric trolley buses on a London Transport route. Gangways are spacious in the 8ft. 6in. wide vehicle and there is ample space for standing passengers. On the right is shown the accessible contactor panel at the rear.

A contemporary cutting from the trade press before the 1948 Commercial Motor Show concerning the demonstration running of one of the four dual-door trolleybuses for Sao Paulo shown earlier in colour on page 59 but included here as part of the export story. One of four in the contract, M3160-63, its body was 35ft 6in x 8ft 6in, outside the UK dimensions at that time, and dispensation must have been obtained before it could run.

Cape Town was another good customer for Weymann's bodywork, and had taken buses and trolleybuses before the Second World War as seen in Volume One. In 1949 they took 20 of these three-axle Daimler CVG6/6 models with 64-seat bodywork, M4080-99. There were also 27 single-deckers, Daimler CVG5SD and AEC Regal models, in the same contract, split between East London, M4048-62, and Salisbury United, M4063-74, all with 39-seat bodies. East London also took five AEC Regent 56-seat double-deckers, M4075-79.

77

CHAPTER 10 – 1946-54
THE LONDON RT3 PROJECT

We have seen in the previous chapter how Weymann's coped with the transition from wartime to peacetime conditions and how, as far as they were concerned, this change concluded early in 1950 with the end of construction methods using timber framing. Now we need to return to the end of the war, when British Industry generally was desperate to make up for the lost years after production had been concentrated on the war effort, in order to see specifically how Britain's largest bus operator, the London Passenger Transport Board, dealt with this situation, and the impact it had on the Weymann story. LPTB was in virtually the same situation as most other bus operators; the war years had seen the double effect of lack of deliveries combined with limited maintenance on those vehicles that were in the fleet, which meant that when peace returned there was a significant amount of catching up to do. It was also the Board's avowed intent to replace the remaining trams, but the incidence of war had seen a change of direction, for the post-war replacements were to be buses, not trolleybuses.

In April 1944, long before peace in Europe had been on the horizon, London Transport (as the LPTB was conveniently abbreviated), had therefore reached agreement with the Associated Equipment Company of Southall for the delivery of 1,000 chassis, of a type that would follow on from the 151 RT's that had been delivered up to 1940 and whose further addition in numbers had temporarily been held up by the hostilities. London Transport's original intention had been to build the bodies themselves, the initial pre-war RTs having had bodies built at Chiswick, but the circumstances now prevailing, not the least of which was the tremendous backlog of repairs needed to be carried out at the works, meant that at this stage London Transport approached two outside contractors with a view to them providing the bodies. The two concerns were Park Royal Coachworks (later Park Royal Vehicles) and Metro-Cammell-Weymann, both of whom had supplied metal framed bodies to the board before the war, a factor which doubtlessly influenced the decision. They agreed in March 1945, subject to Ministry of Supply approval, to

Weymann's RT factory was established in a redundant aircraft hangar on what later became the Weybridge Trading Estate. The building was originally one of several on the site, and in wartime had been designated 'J-Building' – the name by which it continued to be known.

Left to right in this photograph can be seen an RT chassis, staging and stocks of components, an upper-deck structure, a partly-completed lower deck on its chassis, and various framing items.

Materials and in-house manufactured items were brought here from the Station Road factory by the works' lorries.

each supply 450 bodies per annum up to September 1950. On this occasion it was Homfray Davies who represented the joint sales organisation, and MCW allocated its share to Weymann's; it was agreed that the other part of the sales organisation, Metropolitan Cammell Carriage & Wagon could also be allocated work if Addlestone became overloaded. As mentioned in the previous chapter, it was in May 1945 that the MCW sales office had returned to Broadway in Westminster, conveniently just across the road from London Transport's HQ.

The reason for the choice of metal framing for the bodies was based partly on London's pre-war experience of the method of construction, but also on what could perhaps be described as one of the positives to come out of the wartime effort. Both the works at Park Royal and Chiswick had been part of the London Aircraft Production network, both having built many wing assemblies for the Halifax bomber. By their very nature, these had been jig built to ensure total interchangeability, and had clearly demonstrated the advantage of such structures. The RT3 body (as it became known) was approved by the Ministry of Supply in June 1945, and the very first stage in construction, the production of office drawings, was a joint Chiswick/Addlestone/Park Royal undertaking.

The Ministry of War Transport gave permission to LPTB to order bodies for half the chassis on order (*ie* 500 bodies) in January 1946. With such bureaucracy to be navigated, it is perhaps remarkable that production got under way as quickly as it did! Whilst RT 152-401 were to be built by Park Royal, RT 402-651 were to be Weymann built. This equal split of production was not to be repeated; thereafter orders were to be 60:40 in favour of Park Royal. Both companies had to agree a definitive commitment to London Transport until September 1950; in Weymann's case this represented an undertaking to ensure that never less than 35% of total production was for London (the figure for Park Royal was 40%). Such a large contract, whilst it represented a tremendous opportunity for Weymann's, was nevertheless potentially fraught with danger if the calculations concerning labour, materials and the availability of factory space were not exactly right. The company elected to deal with the latter aspect — that of space — by leasing a disused aircraft hanger (yet another!) at Weybridge, within ten minutes or so walking distance of the main Station Road complex. The man they put in charge was Jack Guarnori who we met in Volume One as being in charge of the bending of the metal sections way back in 1933 when Bunny Beaver joined Weymann's and the MCW metal-framed bodies were starting to go down the lines.

This photograph clearly shows that whereas Weymann's normal method of construction was to build the lower-deck directly on to the chassis, the RT bodies were assembled on blocks or dollies, and each part-finished unit was then lifted on to its chassis. Similarly, the upper-deck shell was later lifted on to the lower deck/chassis structure.

It is important to remember that London Transport's policy was geared to lifting the bodies from the chassis at Aldenham at overhaul time, and that with the different timescale for chassis and body overhauls, a body would not normally return to its original chassis.

It was for this reason that absolute interchangeability of all the bodies – and chassis – was essential.

79

Guarnori had a talent which perhaps would have been unknown to most except his closest friends. He was a skilled model engineer, interested in model railways, and regularly exhibited at the Model Engineering exhibition in Central London where the quality of his work earned him several prizes, diplomas and recommendations. The author has been privileged to see some of his work, including matching models of an LMS Royal Scot locomotive from the late twenties built in 4mm and also 7mm scale. Here was a man who understood precisely what working to thousandths of an inch meant and he was able to build full size buses to the same exacting tolerances without difficulty. He also had to lead, and his self-contained team were able to meet the very exacting schedules and tolerances and satisfy London Transport's requirements.

The first chassis was, in fact, delivered to Addlestone in May 1946, and it had initially been hoped that the first complete vehicle would have been available in July that year. In the event that proved impossible, and a revised date of October 1946 was targeted, which was again revised to February 1947. These delays were not entirely the fault of the bodybuilder. Jig built construction on this scale was an entirely new concept for bus bodies and required exceptional tolerances as mentioned above. This had required, as previously indicated, an expenditure of £60,000 which had been agreed by the United Molasses Board for machine tools, jigs, gauges and an additional paintshop, a not inconsiderable sum at the time. Coupled with this Park Royal too had set aside separate buildings for the production of the RT3 body — in Weymann's case this was the 'J' building (as the newly leased hangar continued to be known). The supply of raw materials as has been seen in Chapter 7 was by no means easy. Some components such as side lights and switches were provided by LT whilst other items were provided by authorised suppliers. In some cases these were purchased with London Transport authority and delivered direct to the bodybuilder. Such was the delay in producing the end product that AEC was actually forced to suspend RT chassis building from Christmas 1946 until May 1947, space simply having run out to store the completed units. These delays to the delivery of the first completed RT to the capital ironically resulted in the earlier entry into service of RT chassis elsewhere, but as we have seen Weymann's were still very much involved.

The four parallel production lines at Station Road stretched almost the full extent of the building, starting just beyond the fitter's area as seen in the photographs on pages 13 and 62. This view in the 300ft long paint shop, taken in 1948, shows RT3s from the initial batch, including RT562, being finished. Note the prominent roof-mounted number indicator box on these early red-liveried examples.

To the left can be seen Regent IIIs for Sheffield Transport, also with a four-bay style body, though a very different one from the London RT class.

The gantry planks the men are working on look precarious to today's eyes, but were typical of the type used throughout the industry at that time and since the beginning of double-deck bodybuilding.

However, before considering this, it is perhaps interesting to appreciate how cooperation between the chassis and body builders resulted in entirely new concepts appearing. The RT chassis, for example, was supplied without front mudguards, cab floor, dash or bonnet, as these items were, contrary to normal practice, incorporated as part of the body construction. The chassis was fitted with low profile high pressure 9.00-20 tyres, rather than the more usual 11.00-20 type, one result of which was that the overall body height came out at 14ft 3ins. Given this, the perceptive St Helens Manager Edgley Cox was later able to put a batch of highbridge RT buses under a low bridge in that town. Because of the extremely tight tolerances, necessary to ensure complete interchangeability of the bodies, the use of jigs throughout manufacture was essential. Whilst this was time consuming initially as has been seen, ultimately it made for speedier production and the whole body was put together in the form of one large Meccano set. By its nature all metal construction was slightly heavier than a comparable composite design. The very first RT, RT 1 in 1939 could seat only 55 in order to meet the construction and use weight requirements, and 56 seats were only able to be fitted in RT 2-151 because of the reversion to composite construction. The post war RTs, which were heavier than their predecessors at 7tons 10cwt, were able to seat 56 thanks to amendments to the C & U regulations during the war in respect of overall weight. By comparison a Leeds AEC Regent III bus with Weymann's 4-bay highbridge body weighed just over 7tons 14cwts.

As indicated above, the Ministry of Supply were very much involved in the allocation of new vehicles to operators. At the same time as agreeing to London Transport's initial deliveries, they were also allocating buses to the provinces in the same way as they had allocated utility buses during the war. During 1946 the MoS also allocated a total of 72 RT-type chassis to provincial operators for early delivery, subject to bodybuilders being able to obtain the necessary consent from the Ministry of Transport. After this initial distribution, no further chassis of this type were allocated outside London. The first nine were bodied by Charles Roe with centre entrance twin staircase bodies and entered service with the West Riding company in May to August 1946. A further eleven Roe bodies, but this time with conventional rear entrances were delivered to Grimsby (3) and Halifax (8) by December of that year. It seems that the bodybuilder had some problems with the front end design, not being used to chassis being delivered without bonnet or front wings!

Of more relevance to our story, however, were the Weymann-bodied RT's delivered to Aberdeen (10, between November 1946 and March 1947) and Rhondda (5, also in December) and Devon General (8, in February 1947). Whilst

There were two parallel lines of RT body completion, the finished buses coming out into the yard at the back of the Station Road building. This photograph was taken to show the mix of vehicles in autumn 1948, at the time of the Motor Show, with two of the single-deck Regal IIIs for Lisbon, a Regal II for Devon General, and a completed RT in central area red. Inside can be seen further RTs, and a four bay Sheffield Regent III.

the Aberdeen examples had straight side skirt panels, the examples delivered to the BET subsidiaries had the classic outswept skirt panels. For the record, the remaining provincial RTs were delivered to Birmingham Corporation, 25 with Park Royal bodies, Douglas Corporation, 2 with Northern Counties bodies, the Ebor Bus Co of Mansfield, a solitary example with Brush bodywork, and finally the unique RT delivered to Coventry Corporation, with the only Metro-Cammell RTL-type body fitted to an RT. In fleets such as Devon General where these vehicles operated alongside normal AEC Regent IIIs, the RT chassis were always conspicuous by their lower bonnet line, caused as a result of London Transport's decision to dispense with the fitting of an external air cleaner on the engine. The involvement of Metro-Cammell in this programme is perhaps part of the story to be included in any future history of that Company, but because it involved personalities from Weymann's it is worthy of inclusion here for completeness.

AEC had traditionally been the supplier of London's buses. Indeed, until 1933, they had been part of the same organisation that had operated the majority of buses in the capital, and there was an agreement that at least 75% of London Transport's requirements would be supplied by AEC. However, it was apparent that during the post-war recovery period AEC would not be able to meet all of London's requirements, and thus Leyland were approached and it was confirmed in late 1946 that they would be able to provide 1,500 chassis, 500 of which were to be bodied by Leyland themselves. These, in fact, materialised as the RTW class and were the first 8ft wide buses for London delivered under peace time conditions. It will be remembered that when the original RT contract was agreed with MCW, it was determined that Metro-Cammell could be involved if Addlestone was overloaded. However, in October 1946, 18 months after the original agreement, Homfray Davies was again involved in discussions which led to Metro-Cammell agreeing to body the balance of the Leyland order. By this time speed of delivery was more important than standardisation, and so Metro-Cammell developed its own body to fit to what became the London Transport RTL class. One outcome of this was that since Metro-Cammell were now building an RT-type body the chassis for Coventry Corporation, which had been delivered in March 1946, eventually received in 1951 a body to RT design built at the end of the London Transport order. But this whole project was not without its difficulties, and in the event only 450 RTL bodies were ever built in Birmingham – interestingly in another 'new' factory at Marston Green (yet another former aircraft hangar) whilst the financial balance was achieved by awarding them a contract for 700 bodies on the AEC Regal IV, the RF class, But the detail of this entire story really is for another book.

Transport of components between the two factories, or elsewhere as required, was handled by the signwritten works lorries, a Bedford (above) and an AEC (opposite). (BB; PG)

By a happy coincidence, in June 1950, during the Silver Jubilee year of the Company, Weymann's completed their 1,000th RT body. Arthur Froggatt arranged for Bowers to send a photographer along to record the various events as the partially completed vehicle made its way from J-Building through to the Station Road finishing and paint shops, and then it was polished and driven round to the front offices to be presented to London Transport and the trade press.

In this picture the J-Building team, a self-contained workforce, pose with the bus which became RT3201. Note that someone with a sense of occasion, and awareness of the past, has arranged for the inclusion of Charles Weymann's patent logo to be put in the number blind area of the destination display.

The vehicle will then be driven 'down the road' to the main Addlestone factory.

Meanwhile, on 28th April 1947, the first complete post war RT was delivered to Chiswick works, RT 402, and it proudly entered service on the 10th of the following month, some two days before the first Park Royal example was delivered. It must have quietly pleased Jack Guarnori that his team delivered the first post-war RT to London, comfortably ahead of his old foreman Ted Needs' team's example from Park Royal. The last RT3 body to be delivered to the London Passenger Transport Board was RT466 in December that year, as from 1st January 1948 the Board was replaced by the London Transport Executive after an eventful 14 years.

It had been intended that all the first 500 bodies would be for the Central Area and painted red, but in the event the last 55 of the Weymann production were painted green and allocated to Country Area services. No green RT bodies were, in fact, ever built new by Park Royal, The final bus of the initial order was delivered in September 1948, but by this time a further order for 50 RT3 bodies had been placed, this time all were green and these were completed within the next two months, and brought to an end, as far as Weymann's were concerned, a distinctive feature of the bodywork not generally repeated outside of London, namely the roof mounted box for the display of the route number. This decision to change had, in fact, been made by LT in October 1946, but such was the nature of the order, supply and use of materials that it took until this time for the decision to become effective. Thus the 301st body built was redesignated RT3/1 and was the first of a further order for 100 units, the majority of which entered service in the Country area.

Following this, the next batch of bodies were again redesignated, this time to RT8, an alteration which made them suitable for placing on the short lived LTE SRT class. A total of 640 bodies were supplied from March 1949 through to September 1950, amongst them being the 1,000th RT body supplied to London Transport by Weymann's since work on this important contract commenced, and a suitable public relations exercise was carried out to celebrate its delivery. RT 3201 was much photographed by the trade press at the time, partly because the Directors at Weymann's used the opportunity to link this milestone with celebrations to commemorate the 25th Anniversary of the formation of the company (see Volume 1). September 1950 marked the end of the original contract with both Park Royal and Weymann's which had in fact been a continuing one and did not link production to a specific number of vehicles. This was, perhaps, just as well for whilst the total

Next came the photo-call for the Station Road finishers and painters who were transforming the shiny empty shells into complete buses ready to be delivered to Chiswick. Arthur Froggatt, Harold Cook and Jack Davies are in the centre of the group to the left in this view, whilst upstairs the ladies of the offices put the new upholstery to the test.

Number 1,000, or RT3201 as we should really call it, now looks the part and would have that indefinable smell of new paint, upholstery, lino, varnish and all the other items which made travelling on a brand new bus such a delight.

83

number of bodies constructed was impressive, only once did it meet the original intention of supplying 450 per annum. Weymann's figures for the first four years of production (1947-50) were respectively 62, 297, 420 and 481.

The new contract which came into effect on 1st October abandoned the target cost system in favour of a conventional fixed price contract. Rather than the open-ended nature of the previous one, this contract was subject to two years notice of termination. The new arrangement was of great importance to Weymann's, as the post-war demand for new buses had abated a little, and the possibility already existed of staff reductions occurring. A continuing shortage of raw materials did not help either, and as late as 1952 certain steel sections were difficult to obtain. The post-war boom seemed to be over, and London Transport was already beginning to find that new buses were not wanted in the same quantity as previously anticipated. Indeed, in that year 50 RT bodies were deducted from Weymann's quota and transferred to an order of equivalent value for 56 low-height double-deck buses on AEC Regent chassis. An order for 20 similar vehicles had in fact been diverted to London Transport from Midland General two years earlier. This was the famous RLH class whose vehicles, at least among enthusiasts, were to be almost as synonymous with Addlestone as the Weymann factory itself. The final substantial design modification was made in April 1952 when the RT8/2 body first appeared. RT 3528 was the first Weymann body to this classification, but as with the change from RT3/1 to RT8 the difference could not be detected by the passenger; this reclassification involving the strengthening of the front bulkhead which was of a redesigned riveted construction. Confirmation that the market was declining finally occurred later that year when, in line with the two year clause in the manufacturing agreements, London Transport indicated that its requirements for further new RT buses would cease in 1954.

One of the difficulties facing the post-war austerity years in Britain was that of deficits on the balance of payments. To help ease this situation the Government was keen to encourage people from other countries to come to Britain, and what could exemplify a visit more than the sight of a red London double-decker bus. Thus, over a number of years in the 1950's London Transport was asked to provide vehicles and crews for overseas visits. The first such trip involved four RTs (two of which carried Weymann bodies) which traversed eight European countries in 1950 to promote the 1951 Festival of Britain. Buses with Weymann bodywork were also to be used on the final European tours in 1957. But perhaps the most significant visit was that to the USA and Canada in 1952, when three London buses covered 12,000 miles from March to August. One was used exclusively to give rides during the official city visits whilst the second acted as a combined crew/stores unit. The third bus, whose history is most relevant to this narrative, was built by Weymann's and fitted out by them as a mobile exhibition and information unit. It was the first Leyland chassis to be fitted with a Weymann's body and became RTL 1307. At this point in time there had been no plans for new RTL chassis to go anywhere near Addlestone, although towards the end of the programme in 1954 a further 31 bodies were fitted to Leyland chassis in order to provide Weymann's with sufficient work during the run down of RT production. Interestingly these latter buses were then placed in store until 1958 due to falling demand, a similar fate befalling 59 RTs built in the same year, although in their case they were destined for the country area and their into service dates were spread over 1958 and 1959.

But we are running ahead of ourselves a little; back in 1952 the RT production lines at Addlestone were still busy and more than 500 RT bodies remained to be built. Actual figures for the final four years of production of RT bodies (1951-54) were 337, 220, 208 and 145 respectively. It should be recalled that by this time, in line with the original capital investment and share allocation, Weymann's were building two RT type bodies to Park Royal's three: the 1949 MCW agreement required that the new 55:45 ratio should be met between the Surrey and Birmingham factories. Such production juggling could not have been easy, and some observers doubt whether such mathematical targets were actually kept. It is appropriate here to refer to the United Molasses Board minutes of November 1954, when it was recorded that Metropolitan-Cammell were seeking recompense of £20,000 in respect of an imbalance in the division of the accumulated build proportions

This advert from Passenger Transport magazine in September 1948, the Motor Show issue, confirms Weymann's weekly output of RT bodies by that time. United Molasses would have been delighted at the profit potential if 15 new buses a day were being wired; did the electricians only work one day per week or did the copy writer slip up? The combined LT and non-LT output was only 15 per week at this time and would never approach 15 per day.

If driver's ergonomics and convenience were a strong point of the RT design, conductor comforts were perhaps less so. The batteries were neatly housed in such a way as to make the under-stair storage area virtually useless where luggage and push chairs, the two items most likely to be placed there, were concerned. Access to the batteries was via a removeable external panel.

— instead of the revised 1949 figure of 55:45 (from 60:40) in MCCW's favour the actual split was 54:46 *in Weymann's favour.* Twenty thousand pounds does not sound a great deal of money today, the price of a decent family car perhaps, but at that time it was sufficient to have put even a company of Weymann's size into liquidation. The matter would only be resolved by an adjustment to the ratio until the necessary sum had been recouped by Birmingham. There was some hard bargaining involved, with a suggestion of an adjustment to a 50:50 ratio, and also a revision in the percentage paid by the two companies to maintain the Sales Organisation. All was not sweetness and light at this time!

That Weymann's had exceeded their quota so handsomely gives a clue that they were also busy in the main factory, where business was still good and spread widely across their customer base as we shall see in the next chapter. Alan Townsin in his history of Park Royal (TPC 1980) records that in the years 1952, 1953 and 1954 PRV were building buses respectively for 8, 8 and 10 customers only. Weymann's comparative figures were 16, 15 and 18 customers.

This difference was to mean that whereas Park Royal were becoming more dependent (for bus work) on the RT contract, Weymann's were not. In 1952 almost the whole of Park Royal's double-deck output – 320 from 347 – was of RT's. In 1953 the comparative figures were 358 RTs from 470. In 1954 210 from 270 were RT's. This sort of dependence meant that when the RT orders finished there would be difficulty in finding work for that factory. It was significant that only then, between 1952 and the conclusion of the RT contract in 1954, did PRV follow the MCW philosophy of seeking orders from the larger operators where, hopefully, the orders would be both substantial and regular.

To conclude this chapter it should perhaps be recorded that the last RT body built by Weymann's was fitted to RT 4794 in November 1954, a total of 2,170 bodies having been constructed over the eight years of production. All construction henceforward would be at Station Road and the lease on the building in Weybridge was relinquished. But this was not quite the end of the story. Even by the time the last RT was leaving the factory, London Transport was planning for its next generation bus, and the prototype RM, which was to be the forerunner of a type initially intended to replace London's trolleybus fleet, had been taken into stock. No doubt conscious of the contribution made to London Transport's post-war recovery, the directors undoubtedly hoped that they would be sharing in the capital's business once again.

It was perhaps not surprising, therefore, that when RML 3 was eventually built at Addlestone in mid 1957, the body was given number W2201 in the RT series. But no further orders for bodies on this model were forthcoming; in view of the comments above about Park Royal's situation it is perhaps also not surprising that the entire post-prototype build went to that organisation. Whilst all of this had been going on, it is now time to see what had been taking place in the main factory at Station Road.

Once the exterior and interior panels have been removed there is surprisingly little left of the body apart from the RT's framing. In the background the successor RM can just be seen. (JAS)

Originally fitted with a Park Royal body, RT91, below, now carries a Weymann roof-box body in preservation. (DC)

86

The RT contract was for the supply of buses designed by London Transport to be used by that organisation in the capital. Only one other operator purchased new RTs, though many, of course, bought them second-hand in later life.

St Helens was the sole exception, though their 40 examples were bodied by Park Royal. Edgley Cox, the Lancashire operator's then Manager, placed the vehicles in service because they were, with their low-profile tyres giving an overall height of 14ft 3ins, low enough to pass below the restricted headroom Peasley Cross railway bridge without the need for lowbridge buses with their inconvenient side gangways and bench seats upstairs.

Although the RTs were more expensive than a normal 56-seat double-decker, the St Helens Transport Committee were convinced of the logic of their Manager's advice, and two batches, of 15 and then 25 vehicles, were purchased.

Surprisingly, perhaps, they gave only ten to twelve years service with St Helens before finding second homes elsewhere. BDJ 67, seen here, was later preserved and is now back in full working order.

Unlike the inter-changeability of Park Royal and Weymann's bodies, the Metro-Cammell ones fitted to RTL 551-1,000, although outwardly indistinguishable were not inter-changeable. The narrower cream band on the front of the RTL serves as a point of identification to the builder. (JAS)

87

The lower deck view clearly reveals the classic design of the RT: neat, uncluttered and showing that passenger ambience had not been forgotten when the concept was put together by LPTB staff at Chiswick works. Note that the MCW lettering, normally cast into the flywheel housing, is conspicuous by its absence.

The upper deck interior of a typical RT shows the neat and stylish effect of London's seats and moquette, and attention to detail.

In 1953 it was time to record the 2,000th vehicle, RT3824, but time was running out and there would be less than two hundred more before the contract ran out, and J-Building became redundant again, along with its workforce.

The adjacent view shows the familiar rear aspect, upright and uncompromising, yet at the same time dignified and functional, almost as though the designer had been thinking of the stiff-backed mounted cavalrymen the buses would pass as they wended their way down Whitehall. These RT buses would be a familiar part of the London traffic scene for fifty years, though which parts of which vehicle were anywhere near that old became a matter of conjecture in later years thanks to the overhaul methods employed at the Aldenham works, now also only a memory.

The higher bonnet level of the Regent III chassis is immediately apparent in this view of the London RLH class lowbridge buses, seen here before delivery. These vehicles, 20 in 1950 and a further 56 in 1952, were taken by London Transport to make up the value of RTs not built, as explained in the text.

89

CHAPTER 11 – THE EARLY NINETEEN-FIFTIES

A decade of constant changes begins

After the various ups-and-downs during 1949, the Directors must have been very pleased when they reviewed what had been achieved. The combined output from the two Surrey factories was 972 vehicles, 421 of them RTs for London Transport assembled in J-Building. This represented a total of 19.44 vehicles per working week, putting Weymann's well into the 'first division' of British bodybuilders. BET contracts had resulted in vehicles being supplied to seven of that organisation's fleets, in addition to six municipalities, and the completion of Weymann's part of the large South African contract plus London Transport vehicles, quite apart from the RTs already mentioned. It must be noted, however, that Liverpool's large order for framed but unfinished bodies artificially boosted this total.

As the buses left the factory gates at the start of the new decade there was an air of stability around the town of Addlestone and its principal employer. The elegant designs long associated with the name Weymann, the traditional colourful yet dignified liveries of the long-standing customers – in many cases unchanged for years – all supported the feeling that things were getting back to normal and 'everything would be all right'. Yet within only a few months major changes would begin to make their presence felt and the size, shape and specification of the buses built at Station Road would change beyond all recognition.

There was no way of knowing then that 1949 would be the peak year, and that output would never reach this level again. Although materials would gradually become more readily available, demand would now start to decrease and the trend for bodybuilders to give up the struggle and cease trading, sell out, or divert their workforce to other products would increase. Yet looking at what was in progress in 1950 in the two factories, all must have seemed very promising.

Upstairs the pressure was telling, however, and 1950 was to be a year of many changes. Arthur Froggatt was now 69 years old and started to ease back on

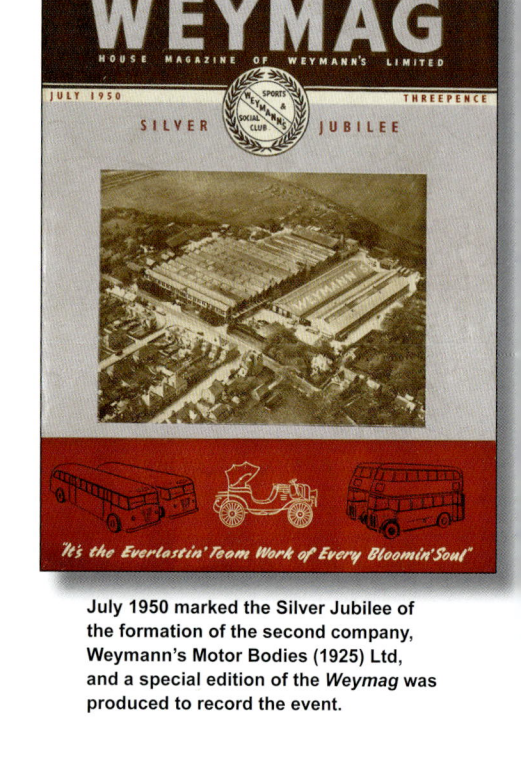

July 1950 marked the Silver Jubilee of the formation of the second company, Weymann's Motor Bodies (1925) Ltd, and a special edition of the *Weymag* was produced to record the event.

Bournemouth's three-axle trolleybuses with their twin entrance/exits and twin staircases followed from a batch of full fronted PD2 motorbuses, M4264-93, with the BUTs having body numbers M4294-4317. KLJ 357 is seen here in 1960, by which time it had been renumbered to 257, having originally been numbered 223. This was the last of the batch, the first having been shown at the Commercial Motor Show in 1950, as seen on page 92 on the stand. (JAS)

Aldershot & District, and then Maidstone & District, were the first to start rebodying through Weymann's, at the end of 1950 and the start of 1951, replacing utility bodies on wartime chassis. Here, A&D's EHO 173, a 1942 Guy Arab, is seen with its new body, M4532. (PG)

Car parks would eventually replace the traditional cycle racks – though not in Weymann's time – here we see the view from the drawing office window one lunch time. (BB)

some of his commitments, allowing him to concentrate on his principal interest, Weymann's Ltd. He stood down as President of the Institute of British Carriage and Automobile Manufacturers after four years in that position, though remaining a Council member, and later in the year would retire from the Board of MCW. He maintained his involvement with many other organisations, however, and the list of his interests and commitments was an impressive one.

Pressures were also mounting elsewhere, and in January 1950 it was announced that a General Election would be held in February; it was, and Labour were returned to power but with a majority of only six. Their position was now almost untenable and all thoughts of further Nationalisation were shelved 'until 1951'. As one of a series of measures to try to ease the country's finances, fuel tax was now doubled, a move which sharpened the appreciation of the need for weight saving in buses, an aspect forming an important part of the story for the remainder of Addlestone's life as a bus building town. It is a sobering thought that even after this hike, petrol, which came off ration that year, was still only 3/- per gallon (15p) and that this was the most expensive it had been since 1920. In today's parlance that's about 8p per litre.

Another sobering thought was that although new cars were almost non-existent because of the export drive, an Austin A40 four-door family saloon – if you could get one – would cost just £654. It was in this year that Austin and Morris announced that they had agreed terms for a merger; the result would be that as mass production progressed, more cars became available on the home market, and prices came down such that by 1953 a Ford Popular would cost only £320 including tax. This was the time when the working man could afford to buy his own car and patronage of the buses began to fall off markedly. It was also the time when, slowly at first, company car parks began to replace the traditional bike racks! The other weapon which bus companies were facing – the increase in television ownership – was also about to be given a boost; the manufacturing industry announced that it planned to make and sell 225,000 sets in 1952. Soon the evening trips to the cinema by bus would become a thing of the past.

In September 1950 final work was completed on the three exhibits for the Commercial Motor Show. In an interesting sign of where MCW presumably considered its future might lie at that time, two of these were trolleybuses and the third was an integral home-market single-decker. How wrong could you be? The integral single-decker (L30, overleaf) was, of course, the HR40 Olympic and was for the BET flagship fleet Ribble Motor Services of Preston, Lancashire, and a near neighbour of Leyland Motors. Ribble was a new customer for Weymann's, having previously taken a high proportion of its body requirements from Brush, Burlingham, English Electric and Leyland; the latter three were situated in the area Ribble served. At this time Ribble were also taking 14 examples of the Sentinel STC6 underfloor-engined buses, to add to the six of the earlier STC4 model of 1949, all with bodies and chassis built in the factory in Shrewsbury, though there were those who said that this was just a ploy to irritate and then awaken the

The two company stands, adjacent as always, at the 1950 Motor Show. Prominent is the Leyland Olympic for Ribble, Weymann's number L30, seen also below passing its tilt test with ease at London's Chiswick works facility. Also clearly visible on the stand is a Bournemouth three-axle BUT trolleybus, M4294, and just discernible through the Olympic's windows is the Glasgow standee single-deck trolleybus M4705 seen on the opposite page. Metro-Cammell were showing an Olympic overseas demonstrator, and this is seen alongside, by the Pyramids, whilst in Egypt as a joint Leyland-MCW exhibit for the December 1950 International Motor Show in Cairo. It later travelled quite widely.

Buses have to be tested for stability, to demonstrate that they will not easily overturn in the event of an accident or other mishap. Weymann's used the London Transport facility at Chiswick works where a commercial facility was available to bodybuilders lacking their own tilting table or preferring to have the work done under contract. A vehicle from a batch would be 'type tested' and if it was satisfactory then the others would be deemed to also be so. The left hand scale indicates that 34° of tilt has been achieved – the requirement being 32° for a single-decker. The right hand scale indicates that the body is leaning over further on its springs, giving an angle of 38°.

The Glasgow single-deck BUT model RETB1 was originally numbered TB35, following on from 34 MCCW-bodied three-axle BUT 9641T vehicles in that Scottish fleet, but was later renumbered TBS1 in 1953. *Modern Transport* considered the vehicle, with its seated conductor and cash desk to be 'most interesting' but passengers and crews were less impressed with its low seating provision (26) and space for 40 standees. Accordingly, this vehicle, together with a further ten similar examples supplied with bodywork by East Lancashire Coachbuilders of Blackburn, Lancashire, was rebuilt between 1959 and 1961, closing off the rear entrance and increasing the seating capacity to 36. Passengers in Britain still expected to have a seat for their journey and similar experiments with single-deck standee buses and trams in other towns and cities received equally short shrift.

Bournemouth continued its policy of taking full-fronted motor buses to give a semblance of commonality with its trolleybuses, both types of vehicle having dual entrance/exit and twin staircases. In consequence, this batch of Leyland PD2 Titans, including body M4289 seen below left, seated only 48 passengers. In the right hand view Jack Davies, left, and Harold Cook pose with their charge, Chief Inspector Page being out of the picture on this occasion but seen in the inside view. The RTs in the background were perhaps also from Weymann's.

Mansfield District's AEC Regal III single-deckers were finished in this attractive blue livery, reflecting the company's origins with the Balfour Beatty group and Midland General. This 1949 example, M4122, is now preserved as seen here. (JAS)

Splendidly preserved and in full working order are two Leyland PS1 Tigers which had also been ordered for the Mansfield fleet but diverted to Crosville by the Transport Holding Company as mentioned in the text. The vehicles were almost complete when the new instructions were received at Station Road and they went to Crosville complete with the extra brightwork seen in this view at Victoria Coach Station, London, celebrating that organisation's 70th Anniversary. LFM 302, body number M4143, was new in 1950. (DC)

Another Weymann product from the ranks of preserved buses is this former Morecambe & Heysham Corporation Regent which had a long life operating in the Lancashire seaside resort. M4684, MTE 639, was a standard highbridge model as seen throughout the country in both municipal and BET fleets, being delivered to its owners in February 1951, one of a batch of six. (DC)

94

Bradford's FKY 28, M3406, was delivered in January 1950. Basically similar to the Morecambe vehicle opposite, it differed in having top sliding windows and scoop ventilators. (IGMS)

By contrast the BUT trolleybus seen here, and delivered in November of that same year, had a five-bay body but with the same ventilation arrangements. FKU 753, M4513, was photographed in 1956 and withdrawn for scrapping in 1970. Bradford's blue was particularly prone to fading and when a change of Manager to CT Humpidge resulted in extended time between repaints the problem became even worse. The solution adopted was to gradually darken the colour year by year, resulting in a variety of hues in the fleet! (JAS)

There was no such problem at Rochdale where the Corporation's smart blue and cream livery enhanced the lines of the Weymann body, in this case M3265, GDK 144 of 1948. It was one of a batch of 13, with seating for 57 passengers, one more than the norm for this product. Later deliveries, in 1949 and 1950, would increase this to 59 seats. (STA)

sleeping giant down the road from Ribble's headquarters. The other two show exhibits on Weymann's stand were the single-deck Glasgow standee trolleybus and a Bournemouth three-axle double-decker trolleybus as seen earlier.

The reduction in evening leisure travel was a portent for the future, however, although on the shop floor business and bonuses were good. BET orders were in evidence, as always, whilst an order for Liverpool Corporation for 140 double-deckers, started in 1949 at body number M3833, seemed never-ending; indeed it would not be completed until 1951 with many framed chassis then making the long journey northwards. AECs still dominated the lines, and an order for Midland General made the news when some of the vehicles were 'diverted' to London Transport to form the famous RLH class of lowbridge buses (*ie* with a side gangway in the upper saloon). Earlier that year another diversion from Midland General had seen a batch of Leyland Tiger PS1 models diverted to Crosville, of course, as already mentioned. Orders passing down the line included some Guy Arab double-deckers for Chesterfield, and Leyland Titans for Bury and Stockton, both now taking the updated PD2 variants, and PS2 Tigers for Birmingham. These would be the last front-engined single-deckers Weymann's built, for a new era was about to begin with underfloor-engined chassis sweeping the board. Birmingham, therefore, took the last half-cab front-engined single-deckers whilst simultaneously taking the new Olympic integral underfloor-engined machines – the effects of manufacturer delays. Bury had been taking 5-bay bodies on its PD1 Titans, but now decided to switch to the 4-bay being offered on AEC Regent III models. This resulted in a delay until 1953 when M4413-21 were delivered, along with AECs BEN 176/7, M4429/30, whose chassis had been held back by AEC. The latter of the two Regents survives in preservation in the Manchester Museum of Transport.

A big order for 30 motor buses and 24 trolleybuses for Bournemouth added both colour and originality to the vehicles in build, for both types featured full fronts, twin entrance/exit layouts with two sets of staircases. Seating capacity was, naturally, somewhat reduced. More colour was added when a third order from Rochdale appeared, but here the emphasis was on more seats, not less, with 59 seated passengers being accommodated in batches M3712-26 and M4254-63.

During June the Construction and Use Regulations were amended to allow an increase from 27ft 6ins to 30ft in the length of two-axle single-decker buses, and

People often ask the photographer to 'take their best side'. The offside of Bury's M4429, BEN 176, a Regent III shows the excellent symmetry achieved on the four bay body. The nearside was not quite so neat, for the extra length when regulations changed to allow double-deckers to be 27ft long, indicated by the just-visible beading behind the rear wheel arch, is matched by a shallow panel as can be seen on the view of matching bus BEN 177 on the title page. This, therefore, can be taken to be 'the best side' of an undoubtedly handsome vehicle.

By 1950 many of the wartime utility bodies were in need of major reconstruction, though others soldiered on for some years – it depended how good, or bad, the timber that had been used for framing had been. Maidstone & District and Aldershot & District undertook a major rebodying exercise involving wartime Guy and Daimler chassis and one of the latter, GKP 262, from a batch now carrying body numbers M4554-82 of 1951 is seen here. It is fitted with the new glazing, using aluminium window pans, as fitted to Show exhibit M3595. Shortage of aluminium meant that export orders had priority for this scarce commodity. (AEJ)

When Glasgow started reducing its vast tram fleet, alongside the replacement of life-expired buses, it needed large numbers of replacement vehicles. It had standardised on the MCCW-outline design as built in Birmingham, and the first post-war deliveries were indeed 20 examples from Metro-Cammell. Later, and more substantial, orders were handled at Addlestone but still to the MCCW outline, as seen here with body M4907, above left. Just to make sure that no-one was fooled the usual MCW bodymaker's window poster has been replaced by a bespoke version from the Station Road drawing office, boldly stating BODYWORK BY WEYMANN'S. Later deliveries, including that above right on an Albion CX37SW 8ft wide chassis, were Weymann-bodied although those had been intended to be supped as frames to be completed by the Corporation. M4974 of 1953, FYS 500, is seen above in St George's Square. This batch, M4963-87, included the last Albion double-decker to be built. (RM)

London's RLH class of lowbridge vehicles, below, were popular with enthusiasts, being unusual in the capital and far outnumbered by RT and RTL classes. KYY 508 was one of the first batch of 20 provincial style Regent IIIs new in 1950 and had originally been ordered by Midland General but diverted after that company became part of the THC empire.

97

South Wales took regular batches of lowbridge and highbridge Regents with Weymann's bodywork. Left is M5687, delivered in March 1953, and the first of a batch of 15 lowbridge examples. Below are four official views of GCY 522, M4431, from an earlier delivery of 46 in April 1950 where M4431-53 were lowbridge and M4454-76 highbridge. The interior views show the bench seats and side gangway, together with the platform and under staircase area which allowed the conductor some (rather sparse) room to retreat from the madding crowds. (Top: AEJ)

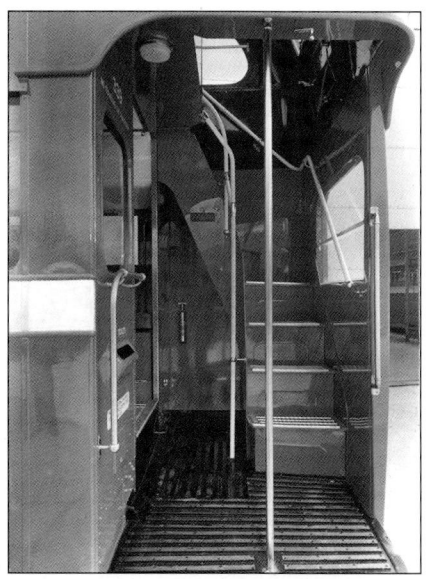

Glasgow's standee single-decker in service in its original form, before the rear door was closed off and the seating capacity marginally increased. It had been an exhibit at the 1950 Commercial Motor Show as mentioned on pages 92/3, registered FYS 765 with body number M4705. It was later renumbered TBS1 as shown here.

Freddy Rayer now moved from Brush Coachwork Ltd to Tube Investments Ltd.

26ft to 27ft in the case of two-axled double-deckers. Two weeks later (!) the general use of 8ft wide vehicles was authorised – the bureaucrats were still clearly on top of things. It was actually not until December that the universal use of 8ft wide coaches on extended tours was authorised, reflecting how many of our modern 'A' roads were still quite narrow highways in those days.

At the end of June, following his 69th birthday in January, Arthur Froggatt retired from the Board of MCW, reluctantly but under pressure because of the age limits set by law on the company and its Directors. WH Gray also retired from MCW that year, and the two events triggered a series of new appointments. PD Brunton (of Metro-Cammell) and Jack Davies were appointed to the MCW Board in ATF's stead whilst Bon Cole, who had earlier resigned from the role of Managing Director on health grounds, took Gray's place. Godfrey Chesson, previously with Eastbourne Corporation Transport, was appointed as technical sales representative, assisting Bon Cole. Although he had long been away from MCW, Freddy Rayer, who had worked with Philip Brunton to design the original Metro-Cammell metal-framed body pre-1930 (see Volume One), made the news when he left Brush Coachwork Ltd and moved to Tube Investments Ltd as a consultant on metal framing for bus construction.

Whilst metal-framing had undoubtedly come to stay, it was during 1950 that fibreglass – introduced in clothing during the war and later to be widely known as glass reinforced plastic (grp) – made its appearance at Addlestone. Many manufacturers experienced labour problems with this development, which was usually seen as an area where women could be employed. Although the pattern making was an extremely skilled job the later processes were semi or unskilled, and the whole routine replaced the unquestionably highly-skilled panel beaters who could turn a flat sheet of metal into a three-dimensional dome or mudguard. How this innovation was received at Addlestone appears not to have been recorded but it seems unlikely to have been accepted without some serious bargaining.

The new process was (and still is) ideal for producing low cost 'copies' from a master pattern, and lends itself to complicated shapes such as domes, and, later, complete front and rear full-bay assemblies from the top deck floor up to and including the roof. Important as grp was, however, opening up a new way of manufacture of awkward components, the real step change would be in the chassis, where the engine was moved from its long-established position and put under the floor in single-deckers.

Meanwhile, Back in the Boardroom

Nineteen-fifty drew to a close with mixed signals being discussed by the Directors at their Board Meetings. Bank rate had been raised from 2 to 2.5%, we had been thrown out of Persia and the British financed giant Abadan oil refinery in that country (now Iran), and those oilfields had been nationalised, so that there was real unease about what would happen to oil supplies and prices. On the positive side, orders were being completed for Stockton and Aldershot & District and expectations were high on the news that Leyland's Henry Spurrier was off to Africa for another three-month business trip.

The combined workforce from the two factories, Station Road and J-Building, with the associated office staff, was now 1,500, a figure which would never be exceeded. The total output for 1950 was slightly down on 1949 at 909 vehicles, just below 16 per week, but again the Liverpool order was boosting the figures. It was becoming obvious now that in output terms the magic 'one thousand' number was unlikely to be reached.

The devaluation of the pound in September 1949 had paved the way for some spectacular export business for which Leyland had laid the ground work between 1948 and 1951. The company was competing with American and other manufacturers in South America and the Caribbean, but a 30% devaluation against the dollar gave Sterling an edge they could not match. The MCW organisation was now in line for many of the body contracts, though Saunders Roe located on Anglesey also shared in some of the biggest export orders ever recorded up to that time.

Devaluation meant imports, including oil of course, were made even more expensive, and in January 1951 it was announced that because negotiations with Argentina over meat had deadlocked, the British domestic meat allowance would be further reduced. At the crucial moment, this was the time when passenger vehicle exports finally came good and Leyland's buses soon began to be exported to meat- and sugar-rich countries across the globe with enormous benefit to the balance of payments and weekly food allowances.

Despite all these difficulties 1951 was earmarked as the year for the Festival of Britain, one hundred years after the Great Exhibition, and a chance to show the world what we could do. It opened in May in a scenario reminiscent of the 2000 Millennium shindigs, and London's South Bank hosted a variety of events and buildings, including the Skylon and the Dome of Discovery, which will long remain in the memories of those old enough to have seen them. Transport items on display included one of MCW's Birmingham-built South African Olympics.

As already mentioned, the beginning of 1951 had seen Arthur Froggatt's 70th birthday, and again he made it plain that it was the requirements of the 1948 Companies Act relating to large organisations which saw him forced to step down as a Director and Chairman. James Don, the United Molasses Director who had joined Weymann's board in 1942, now succeeded ATF as Chairman. Mr Froggatt would have wished to carry on in some other capacity, and in fact did not retire from the company until June, by which time United Molasses were also apparently pressing him to reduce his continuing and fairly regular presence. With a very sad heart, he finally retired, and was given a heart-warming and rousing sendoff in the works canteen on Wednesday June 18th. Less than 24 hours later he was dead, having collapsed whilst walking to the Green Line coach to take him home from a function at the Grosvenor House, Park Lane, to honour Henry Ford. Such had been the speed of events that there were still many gatherings booked where it had been intended to allow other groups of friends and fellow workers to express their own thanks. A truly remarkable man had passed away.

There was a brief period of anticipation until, in August, United Molasses announced that Jack Davies had been appointed Managing Director of Weymann's Ltd, with Harold Cook as General Manager and Walter Dodsworth as Works Director. In the middle of all these changes Peggy Newton joined the office staff, to work for Cyril Ward, and found amongst her new colleagues Edna Bubb, Maurice Bullivant, Ron Barratt, Walter and Marcelle Healy and Keith Barkham, all regulars at the reunions throughout the 'nineties when the Author was interviewing former employees, and all contributors to the story. Peggy recalled that even at such a time of upheaval the firm was a happy one to work for – "the offices were like a holiday camp at times" she recalls!

When the year's production figures were checked they confirmed that 796 buses had been built during 1951, down from 909 in 1950. Included in this figure were the first rebodies of wartime utilities for BET fleets Aldershot & District and Maidstone & District, as mentioned earlier.

> Arthur Froggatt was born in 1881 and worked his way up the ladder in the coachbuilding industry to reach the top. He was elected a fellow of the British Carriage & Automobile Engineers in recognition of his work in the industry. He was awarded the MBE in 1945 for his work during World War 2.
>
> Arthur Froggatt's standing with his workforce was recognised when they turned out to a man to see his cortege pass, the church was filled, and men stood outside to hear the service. Amongst the charities he supported was the Gordon Boys School at Woking and many of its lads were given employment at Weymann's.
>
> After his death the family donated a five-bedded ward in the Epiphany Convalescent and Rest Home in Truro, where his daughter Sister Anne, a Nun, was in charge.

Arthur Froggatt relaxing at one of the sports days – his daughter-in-law recalled that his pockets were always bulging with sweets for the many children, and here we see the evidence!

The underfloor-engined revolution arrives

At the 1948 Motor Show it was clear that a new generation of single-deck buses would not be long in making their appearance. Heavy goods vehicle chassis manufacturer Atkinson, based at Walton le Dale, Lancashire, not too far from Leyland's base, had shown an underfloor-engined chassis for a passenger body. This had been developed with the active encouragement of North Western, seeking a Gardner-engined chassis now that it could no longer buy Bristol products. HS Driver, North Western's Chief Engineer, and HR Lambert, the General Manager, were quoted in the Trade Press as recording the excellent working relationship with Atkinsons which was to manifest itself in two Weymann-bodied single-deckers, bodies M5050/1.

Also at the 1948 Show Leyland had announced a horizontal version of its O.600 engine, fuelling speculation that an underfloor-engined chassis from that manufacturer could not be far away. When the announcement came at the end of 1949 that it had collaborated with MCW and would be producing an integral transit type bus, using that new O.600 engine, there was some surprise in the industry since chassisless buses were known to be unpopular with British operators.

Four home-market prototypes were built at Birmingham in Metro-Cammell's works, all to the then maximum UK dimensions of 27ft 6ins x 7ft 6ins, coded HR40, and seating 40. Perhaps reflecting their builder's railway parentage, and with little experience to draw on, they were more solidly built than was necessary; true heavyweights, they weighed some 7½ tons, around the same as a contemporary 56-seat double-decker. Nonetheless they attracted much interest, particularly in the aspect of easier and safer loading with the doorway directly alongside the driver.

Although it clearly indicated the future direction Leyland and MCW would take, the underfloor-engined concept was not new, of course. The forward-thinking Midland Red company had been using such a layout since 1946 when they unveiled their S6 design, but their buses were no longer produced for the open market and the rest of the industry had to await the arrival of Leyland's Royal Tiger in 1950/1, and then AEC's Regal IV, Guy's Arab UF and the Atkinson Alpha, the four main initial heavyweights, before they too could enjoy the benefits.

Carrying the evocative name Olympic, in honour of the 1948 games, this new single-decker came on-stream at Weymann's during 1950. There were 19 of the original HR40 models, and the first three Addlestone examples, numerically, were for Red & White and United Welsh, with the next five for Birmingham Corporation. There were then eight for Isle of Man Road Services, two for James of Ammanford and one for King Alfred Motor Services of Winchester (now under restoration), a rather strange selection of customers for such a vehicle, perhaps. Also in build for Birmingham at this time were the last front-engined single-decker metal-framed bodies Weymann's would produce, a batch of 30 Leyland PS2 Tigers. The contrast between the two contracts could not have been greater and with the exception of wartime utility double-deckers this is believed to be the only occasion when Addlestone built for the Birmingham operator.

KOC 233, seen here, was the first of the initial four home-market prototype Olympics, built in Birmingham by Metro-Cammell. It was used as a demonstrator before being sold to Jennings in 1951. There would also be some overseas demonstrators. Note the original air intakes either side of the indicator and over the entrance. Below is one of the Weymann's batch of five for Birmingham, body numbers L4-8, working the city's airport service. The MCCW vehicles, as explained previously, did not carry body numbers, whilst those built at Addlestone were in an L or LW series. (MAT both)

101

The external body design of the production models differed slightly from the four prototypes in the elimination of rounded corners to the windows as the illustrations clearly show, perhaps influenced by BET and giving an indication where the manufacturers saw market potential. Indeed, although the Olympic sold to British operators only in small numbers, the same basic body design was used in lighter form for the hugely successful Hermes model which appeared on conventional chassis with the new underfloor-engine configuration from Leyland, AEC, Atkinson, Guy and Albion, many in BET fleets and, to a lesser extent, municipal ones, throughout the British Isles.

The new design allowed the whole of the floor area apart from the driver's 'cab' to be used for carrying passengers and at a stroke the 32-35 seat capacity was increased to 40. All the first 19 – body numbers L1-19 – had front entrances only, but whilst the potential as a bus was obvious the model was far too spartan to be considered as a coach. That market would be wide open for all bodybuilders once the separate chassis models became available.

A problem with the O.600 engine was its size; when turned on its side, and with the statutory 10ins ground clearance below, it produced a floor height of some 36ins; the photographs in this chapter showing passengers boarding the early models will testify to the high floor line. After some early examples were built with rear entrances, the industry quickly adopted the front entrance with all its obvious safety advantages and implications for possible future one-man-operation, and the front entrance single-decker became a mainstay of Weymann's and most other bodybuilders. Some operators took examples with front and centre doorways but the single entrance/exit at the front was by far the most common.

After the amendment of the C&U Regulations in June 1950 a 30ft long version of the Olympic was produced, the HR44 which seated 44, and replaced the earlier

Delays in delivery of single-deck chassis whilst the post-war emphasis was on exports often caused reallocation of body contracts. Birmingham had ordered 35 front-engined Tigers from Leyland but before they were eventually delivered MCW had transferred the body order from MCCW to Weymann's and Birmingham Corporation then changed the final five to Olympics. As mentioned in the text, with the exception of some wartime utility allocations this batch of metal-framed single-deckers M4609-38 and the five Olympics (page 101) were the only Addlestone-built buses supplied to Birmingham by MCW.

JOJ 247, M4626 from 1950, is seen at Weymann's before delivery whilst below a clutch of the 30 vehicles are seen on works service duties where a low bridge under a canal alongside the factory at Bourneville precluded the use of double-deckers. These would be Addlestone's last traditional single-deckers and four of the 34-seat Leyland Tiger PS2 models survive in preservation.

102

The Ribble 1950 Commercial Show exhibit, L30, DRN 112, was the first of the larger HR44 models and the extra length was achieved by increasing the front and rear overhangs. Although only four extra seats were gained in this new model, the unladen weight increased by just over one ton to around 7tons 4cwts. Ribble took 30 of these integrals.

Isle of Man Road Services MMN 300, L16, was one of the original HR40 models. Note the shorter overhang beyond the front and rear axles.

Red and White took just two Olympics and both are seen here. Nearest the camera is HWO 379, L1. Contrary to what may be thought from these views not all Olympics were red! (AEJ)

103

model. The extra length was achieved by extending the front and rear overhangs. By dint of leaving the main body structure unaltered, as also was the wheelbase which remained at 15ft 7ins, it was possible for Weymann's engineers to have the first example at the new length ready for September, and thus L30 was the Show model. Body numbers 20-29 had been left blank (wishful thinking perhaps?) and the HR44 series ran from L30-L120.

The first three to take to the road were delivered to local independent operator Fishwick, based a stone's throw from Leyland's Lancashire works, and an ideal location for keeping an eye on these new machines. Ribble were taking 30, body numbers L30-59, and the Fishwick examples, L80-3, numerically followed a selection of other BET company vehicles. There were then four more, L87-90.

In the event, neither model was popular on the home market – in comparison to large numbers of the Hermes type body fitted initially to the heavyweights and subsequently to the lightweight (*ie* all separate chassis models) from 1951 onwards, only 200 Olympics were built at Station Road, 86 for the home market, and two odd export examples, one for Trinidad and the other to New Zealand, and then 90 for Cuba, numbers L151-240. The balance are accounted for by vehicles completed by Bus Bodies in South Africa. The rugged nature of the successor Series 2 Olympic would lead to more and bigger export orders. Some of the Cuban and South American Olympics were still in service as late as 2012.

One reason the full sized Olympic was never very popular on the home market was that many operators in those days still expected to be able to take a body off its chassis at overhaul time if they felt it necessary or desirable. As an export model, however, it met the needs of many operators who would later also take other Leyland models with MCW bodies, many of which would be built at Addlestone to the end of the company's existence.

Although much emphasis has been placed on exports in this story, home market production was, of course, proceeding apace. In the main factory BET and municipal contracts included repeat orders and some significant first time deliveries including to Bury, Southport and Wallasey Corporations. Down the road in the Weybridge J-Building satellite factory, Jack Guarnori and his team were turning out RTs at the rate of around nine per week and the 1,000th had been given a special send off in July 1950, with London Transport officials being invited down to a handover ceremony with a special photo-call outside the offices as mentioned in Chapter 10. By a happy coincidence it also marked the twenty-fifth anniversary of the Company's formation as Weymann's Motor Bodies (1925) Ltd, and, accordingly, a double celebration took place with the transport press invited *en masse*. A special issue of the *Weymag* was also part of the celebration as seen on page 90.

The badge carried by Olympic buses. A later version, clearly continuing the theme, was produced for the lightweight Olympian model.

Only two Weymann-bodied HR44 Olympic models were exported, one to Australia and New Zealand as a demonstrator, L107, and the other, L102, sold to Trinidad and seen here alongside a Tiger Cub (nearest the camera). Twenty-one sets of running units exported to South Africa were bodied in that country by Bus Bodies (SA) Ltd and appear in Weymann's body lists as L91-101, L111-120 but bodied as stated. (STA)

Fishwicks, the long established independent operator in the town of Leyland, had long enjoyed a close working relationship with the local manufacturer and the co-builder would have been glad of the opportunity to keep an eye on this revolutionary new model. MTD 514 is seen here in the operator's garage and it would be no coincidence that three from the batch L80-3 were the first ones to take to the road. The longer front overhang shows up well in this view. (STA)

Donald Stokes commented on the number of permutations his customers managed to create from what was intended to be any standard design. Two of the most obvious Olympic deviants are shown here, Stockton with its dual-door layout on L109, NPT 858, and Edinburgh JFS 525 with its Scottish cutaway rear entrance. The nearside view of the Stockton bus shows an easy way to different iate between the new HR44 and existing HR40 models – the front wheelarch met the door framing on the latter. Stokes' boss, Henry Spurrier, would have been pleased that putting a body onto these running units was not in his province. Let someone else sort that one out!

Some years later Sheffield took two bodies to the same configuration, with the rear cutaway doorway, and had them mounted on Royal Tiger chassis with crush loading standee bodies. They were not a success.

105

Separate chassis versions arrive

Although the Olympic was prominent on Weymann's stand at the 1950 Show, elsewhere at Earls Court Leyland were showing something far more interesting, the separate chassis model Royal Tiger, also using the O.600 engine and intended to fill the gap for the coach market which the Olympic left, and a model which it had already announced in April. Two chassis were shown, together with a coach-bodied version from Leyland's own South Works bodyshops, representing its return to single-decker and coach construction since 1939. There was an instant and very favourable response to both the chassis and Leyland's coach body. Also at the Show was a Brush-bodied demonstrator bus to BEF specification and registered by Leyland as MTC 757; whether Brush, and later Atkinson, decided to pull out of bus building in the light of MCW's and Saunders Roe's success with Leyland, and their own subsequent shortage of orders, is uncertain, but what is clear is that Brush ceased bodybuilding very shortly after that demonstrator made its appearance. Had Freddy Rayer known of this when he moved to TI as a consultant?

The Royal Tiger chassis had the same 15ft 7ins wheelbase as the Olympic and, therefore, was perfectly matched to Weymann's Olympic body. Although Leyland introduced its own 44-seat bus body for that chassis in 1951, Addlestone's engineers had already been bodying the chassis for some of the BET customers including Western Welsh, Rhondda and North Western Road Car. The result was a handsome bus with a high turn of speed, ideal for express work. Unfortunately, it was extremely heavy, at around 8tons, and fuel consumption and a sometimes inadequate braking system relative to the speed attainable were two concerns.

The first generation of underfloor-engined chassis from manufacturers Leyland, AEC, Guy and Atkinson could all rightly be described as being over-engineered. The

When the 44-seat Western Welsh Royal Tigers were weighed they registered around 7tons 2cwts, the same as the Regal IVs for the same operator, and the same as the chassisless HR44 Olympics. The body design clearly owed much to the Olympic although the external mouldings had been dropped. Wheel nut rings, axle stubs and the sound of the engine now became the manner of identification between the rival manufacturers for the cognisant.

Above left is Leyland Royal Tiger 439, one of 25 carrying body numbers M4823-47 delivered in 1951, whilst above right is one of the 20 AEC Regal IV models, 559 in the Western Welsh fleet from the batch carrying body numbers M5589-5608 delivered the following year.

Hebble, another of the Yorkshire BET subsidiaries, with its head office in Halifax, took eight of these Leyland Royal Tigers, body numbers M5580-7 in 1950.

106

Royal Tiger, Regal IV, Arab UF, Dennis Dominant and the Alpha PM746H range were heavyweights, and much more substantial than was subsequently proved necessary. Fuel economy suffered just at the time when the increased duty already mentioned was making operators more conscious of the need to reduce weight. One additional ton in weight was quoted as being equivalent to an extra mile per gallon of diesel fuel consumed, and accordingly a lighter range was designed of which the Leyland Tiger Cub and AEC Reliance would be the front runners. This was also the time when side and rear destination indicators were dispensed with in many fleets, internal trim panels were no longer fitted, single-skin roofs reappeared, badges and some external trim disappeared, and other small measures were introduced, all to save weight.

The AEC Regal IV, basis of the famous London Transport RF class, had also been announced at the end of 1949, with production beginning shortly afterwards. This model was quite rare at Addlestone, only 24 being bodied including, almost inevitably, 20 for Western Welsh who, at that time, were taking every home model which Weymann's were bodying, and four for Dundee. The huge order for RFs, some 700 being built, was handled by MCCW in Birmingham between 1951 and 1953 in a deal recompensing them for missing out on the RT contract which Weymann's shared with Park Royal. Joining the other manufacturers at the 1950 Show, AEC had a demonstrator of its new chassis, with a Willowbrook body and painted in City of Oxford's colours although the vehicle actually entered service with Douglas Corporation.

Working with North Western Road Car of Stockport, Atkinson had had high hopes for its Gardner-engined Alpha chassis, and potential BET contracts. At the handover of the first vehicle, in an informal celebration at the Walton-le-Dale, Lancashire factory, Atkinson's Chairman, WG Allen, paid tribute to North Western for the advice and co-operation given to his company on their entry into passenger vehicle construction after many years building goods vehicles; HG Lambert, the NWRC Manager, replied by saying his company was looking forward to successful usage of the Atkinson vehicles. Others attending this event included representatives from Kirkstall axles, Gardner engines, Weymann's and MCW. There were to be 14 Weymann-bodied Atkinson Alphas, and a further two from Willowbrook, all in the North Western fleet.

One of the main reasons that North Western was keen to encourage Atkinson was that, as mentioned earlier, it had been cut off from its preferred choice of Gardner-engined chassis manufacturer, Bristol, by the fact that whilst North Western was in the BET camp, Bristol was part of the state-owned Tilling combine and, as such, precluded from supplying outside the group. North Western would otherwise have been ordering the LS and M range, but then Weymann's would have the lost the body business to Eastern Coach Works. Atkinson then produced a lighter weight chassis, which was coded PLH, and several examples bodied by Northern Counties went to the SHMD fleet based in Stalybridge and an operator which had joint workings with North Western. Without the volume orders, however, it was not possible to compete viably. In a final twist, North Western now found it was excluded from buying these since it was required to partake in the large BET Tiger Cub contract. Deja vu!

As consolation prizes go the contract for Metro-Cammell to build 700 RF single-deckers for London was not to be sneezed at. Based on the AEC Regal IV chassis there were four body types as shown in the diagrams on page 129.

One of Dundee's four only other Weymann AEC Regal IV models seen at Station Road on a miserable day in early 1953 before delivery to the Scottish operator. This one, number 20, was later rebuilt by the operator to a dual-door layout, putting the doorway in front of the rear axle and reducing the seating capacity to 40. The vehicle lasted in service until 1971.

It was a brave attempt by a small manufacturer to gain entry into a huge potential market, both at home and overseas, but the chassis was too heavy and too high, when compared to the forthcoming second generation of lighter models from Leyland and AEC. The placing of the large BET requirement elsewhere – 500 of the Leyland Tiger Cub (see below) as an opening order – was a huge blow and Atkinson withdrew from the market. HS Driver, the NWRC engineer, was bitterly disillusioned, although the Tiger Cub was in many ways undoubtedly superior, and BET were talking to Leyland about extensive orders, making pricing more attractive to both parties. Driver left the north west, headed for the far south east, and joined Gardners as a technical representative in Australia. This salutary reminder of the clout which BET's buying power could exercise would not have gone unnoticed at MCW's offices.

107

Another manufacturer showing an underfloor-engined chassis at the 1950 Show was Guy Motors, whose earlier work in converting the Gardner engine to horizontal layout was subsequently marketed by the engine manufacturer as its HLW range (as used by Atkinson in its new chassis). Guy's prototype, designated Arab UF, went into production shortly afterwards but was very much in the minority at Addlestone. Only six were bodied for the home market, with dual-purpose bodies for express work, fitted with coach seats, for Lancashire United. Body numbers M6589-94 were delivered in 1954 and worked the gruelling pre-motorway era trans-Pennine routes. LUT had become a strong Guy supporter after experience with the rugged wartime Arabs, and their standardisation on the Gardner engine was confirmed by these chassis being equipped with the 6HLW unit. In 1956 a further five UF chassis, M7214-7218, would be fitted with 53-seat dual-entrance bodies and exported to Dar-es-Salaam in Tanganyika. This operator also took some UFs with Guy bodies to the same configuration which were built on Park Royal frames.

North Western had taken rear-entranced single-decker buses since the 1920s and the continued use of conductors meant that, initially, the front entrance offered little advantage. Bus stop positioning could make for problems when all other vehicles, single and double-deck, had rear entrances. Thus the arrival of Atkinsons 394/5 in 1951, 395 being seen below, carrying body numbers M5060/1 with the traditional porch arrangement at the rear was not as strange as it might now seem. Their two HR44 Olympics, however, were of what Leyland and MCW had intended to be the standard for that model, with a front entrance as shown alongside on Yorkshire Woollen District's number 736, L76, one of ten delivered to that company. Note the radiussed windows and top sliders are incorporated in the body styling of the Atkinsons but not continued in the Hermes body. (MAT)

108

Although independent operator Lancashire United purchased many BET-style MCW bodies, the tide was turning away from Addlestone by the time these six heavyweight Guy UF coach-seated express vehicles were delivered for the Liverpool-Manchester-Leeds service. Here M6594, the last of the batch and seen in Oldham, gives a reminder of the traffic conditions such services met before the advent of the cross Pennine M62 motorway. Weymann's last contract for this operator was a solitary pair of Hermes-bodied Tiger Cubs M7167/8 delivered in 1956 though there were further vehicles from Birmingham. (MAT)

Guy subsequently produced a lighter version – the Arab LUF in 1952 – of which Weymann's bodied 32 for Northern General between August 1955 and January 1956, with body numbers M7044-65 and M7129-38, and five-cylinder engines. A further 14, M7139/40 and 7726-37, went to BET subsidiaries in Africa. Again, the fitment of 55 seats in vehicles which would be operating on poor roads confirmed that these must have been quite substantial vehicles. Both UF and LUF models lasted in production until 1959, just before Guy Motors went bankrupt and were bought by Daimler.

Meanwhile, Weymann's went on to body 377 Royal Tigers between 1951 and 1955 before the model was replaced for the home market by the Tiger Cub, and for export by the Worldmaster. Of the 377, Station Road would body 200 for Argentina; 55 for Western Welsh; 36 for North Western; 16 for East Yorkshire, 12 for Rhondda; 8 for Hebble; 2 for Sheffield and 2 for Pakistan. There were also 44 intended for Chile, of which the majority were diverted elsewhere when financial arrangements with that country could not be completed satisfactorily.

North Western's 36 Royal Tigers were soon at work on express services. Here M6096, still new with gleaming paint, sets off for Llandudno in the summer of 1953. (JAS)

The bus body Leyland produced for its Royal Tiger was functional rather than elegant, as seen here. Ribble took 110 of this model with examples also going to Trent, East Midlands and Isle of Man Road Services fleets, amongst others. (STA)

109

Jamaica Omnibus Services was formed in 1953, a BET outpost as mentioned, and soon took Royal Tigers and Series 2 Olympics in quantity. By 1954 vehicles from Addlestone and Elmdon were in service and one of each are shown here and at the foot of the facing page. A19, M6368, from a Weymann's batch M6350-6370, shown with the traffic policeman in Kingston shows its Royal Tiger badge whilst the large Olympic badge is visible on the other vehicle on the opposite page. (STA)

The impressive Royal Tiger badge. (JAS)

The order for 44 Royal Tigers to be supplied to Chile as part of the Leyland tour of South America ran into trouble when satisfactory finance could not be arranged. The order was reduced to 20, and Number 160 is seen in Chile, left, with the balance being sold elsewhere.

Seen below in Madrid are two from the rest, some of which went there, with the magnificent Post Office in the background. Others ended up as far away as Kuwait and Damascus. (STA all)

Close scrutiny will reveal that all is not quite as it seems here. M5588 was a partially knocked-down (pkd) Leyland Tiger Cub with a Hermes type body, designed to be exported as a flat pack but seen here reassembled in such a way as to show how the various sections were put back together, though for demonstration purposes a space was left between them. It was exhibited in this form at the 1952 Commercial Motor Show. Named Jason, the model apparently found little or no appeal and this was the only example produced. It was later sold to Trinidad.

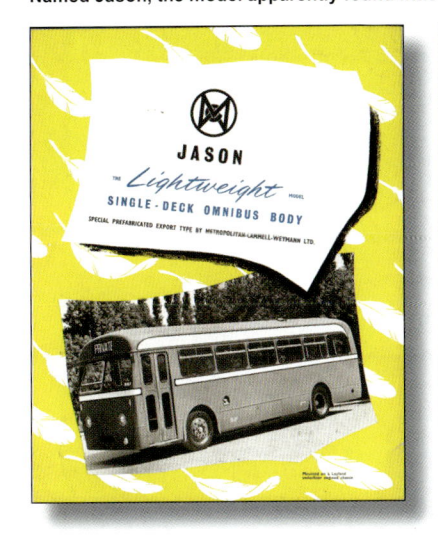

Some time after the Motor Show Jason was quietly taken apart, reassembled complete, painted and shipped out to Trinidad. MCW then marketed the Apollo as its completely knocked-down (ckd) export single-decker.

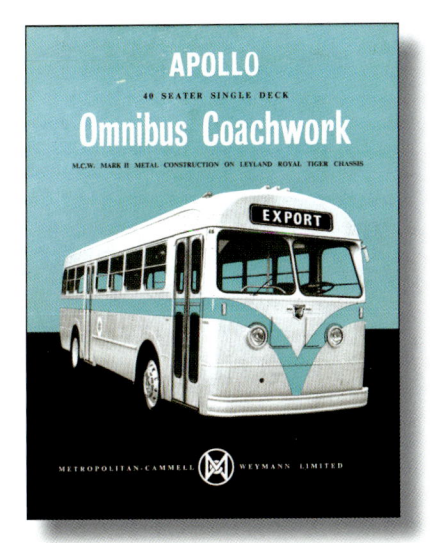

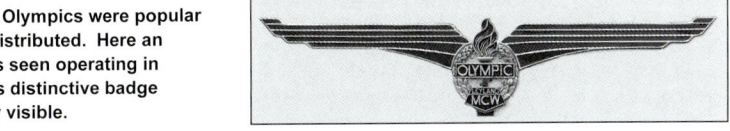

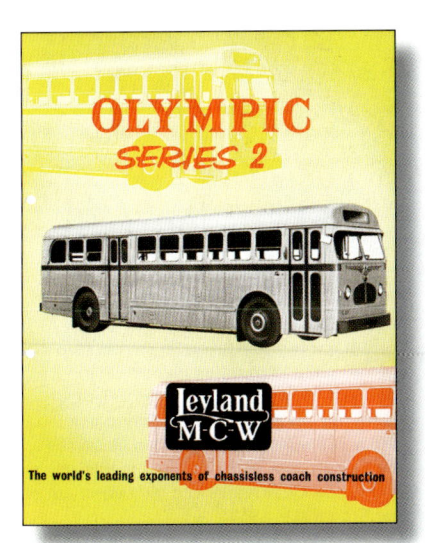

The Series 2 Olympics were popular and widely distributed. Here an ER2 model is seen operating in Barbados, its distinctive badge being clearly visible.

111

Hard Times in Downing Street – Good Times in Station Road

Although Labour had been returned to power in 1950, the slender majority and continual internal differences made Prime Minister Attlee's life a misery, and some time after his government was defeated in a vote over shortages of raw materials, following the coal and coke crisis of February 1951, he announced that he had had enough and was going to go to the country on October 25th of that year. That time he was not alone in having had enough: sufficient disillusioned voters fed up with his hair-shirted iron chancellor Stafford Cripps and his draconian measures made their point to ensure that the Conservatives were returned, though with a majority of only 17 it would remain to be seen whether they could make any real improvements in the country's affairs. Contemporary problems in Greece in 2012, also through strong austerity measures, mirror many British people's concerns in the 1950s.

Meanwhile, work in the factory continued amidst the problems of shortages, but, where materials were available for overseas orders, further export business in 1950/1 included vehicles for Uruguay and Portugal, whilst in December 1951 the trade press were carrying adverts for the manufacturers of components included in Ceylon's first trolleybuses – double-deck Weymann-bodied models which looked very similar to those supplied to Brighton or Notts & Derby. It was in that same month that BET finally moved out of their old-established Headquarters at 88, Kingsway, and moved to their new home in Stratton House, Piccadilly.

January 1952 was marked by the visit of a delegation from Argentina to inspect the first batch of their 200 new Royal Tiger buses. The Argentinian Ministry of Transport would be operating the vehicles in Buenos Aries and elsewhere, and, understandably, was taking a keen interest in this huge contract, now worth over £4million. At an informal gathering in the factory James Don, Weymann's new Chairman, referred to the reciprocal trading arrangements between the two countries, to which the bus order contributed; on behalf of the Argentinians Dr Dirisi congratulated the manufacturers on what he had seen; Bon Cole on behalf of MCW noted that these buses formed part of the largest road transport order ever received by Britain from overseas; on a more down-to-earth note, Donald Stokes, Leyland's then export manager, commented that the order represented many week's meat ration. The party then went to what *Bus and Coach* described as 'a very fine lunch' at a Hampton Court hotel where Stokes reminded the press that Leyland and MCW had also supplied Olympics to Canada, even though it was the big South American

This " Bus & Coach " photograph was taken on the occasion of the inspection by Dr. Domingo Dirisi, commercial attaché at the Argentine Embassy in London, and Senor Juan Gatto, chief of the Argentine Ministry of Transport's purchasing commission, of the first batch of 200 Leyland Royal Tigers with M.C.W. metal bodies ordered by the Argentine Ministry of Transport. Left to right: W. E. Dodsworth (Weymann's), A. Binns (Leyland), D. J. A. Davies (Weymann's), D. G. Stokes (Leyland), R. M. Cole (M.C.W.), Senor Juan Gatto, L. B. Alexander (Metropolitan-Cammell Carriage and Wagon), Dr. Domingo Dirisi, H. A. Cook (Weymann's) Commander Gaud (Metropolitan-Cammell Carriage & Wagon), and James Don (Weymann's).

Above: Bon Cole of MCW with Donald Stokes of Leyland, whilst at the left is a group photograph taken on the occasion of the official Argentine inspection in January 1952 when the first 25 vehicles were completed. More relevant to our story is the inclusion of United Molasses' Mr James Don, at the far right in this other view, now Chairman since the retirement of Mr Froggatt in 1951.

MODERN TRANSPORT

ARGENTINE BUS ORDER

First Ten with M.C.W. Bodies Delivered

THE first batch of ten Leyland Royal Tiger buses with M.C.W. bodywork forming part of an order for 200 ordered by the Argentine Ministry of Transport, were inspected last week at Weymann's, Limited, Addlestone, by Dr. Domingo Dirisi, commercial attaché at the Argentine Embassy in London and Senor Juan Gatto, head of the Argentine Ministry of Transport's purchasing commission. These new vehicles, which were referred to in this journal on November 17, have a seating capacity for 40, with standing room for 22, and are 32 ft. long and 8 ft. wide.

Of M.C.W. patented metal construction, the body is built integrally with the chassis, it being connected directly to the outrigger brackets affixed to the chassis main frame. The outer side and roof panels are riveted to the T-section steel pillars. The floor comprises softwood boards covered with brown linoleum, the traps for access to the engine being edged with non-slip steel tread plate.

The front entrance and rear exit are equipped with C.A.V. electrically operated glider-type doors and there is an emergency exit opposite the rear door. Ventilation is by means of two Airvac extractor ventilators in the roof, two large hinged intake ventilators in the front panelling, and one above the windscreen.

Seat frames are of the service type, stove-enamelled green and having an open-type grab-handle. They are upholstered in green Dulon leathercloth on Dunlopillo rubber cushions, with seat backs covered in green leathercloth. The driving position is accessible through the front entrance and separated from the saloon by an aluminium vertical stanchion and horizontal rail with fitted curtain. The two safety glass windscreens are raked back to eliminate glare and reflection, while a de-mister is incorporated. The driver's seat is of the semi-bucket adjustable type, upholstered to match the saloon seats.

Interior views to the rear and front of the M.C.W. bodies for the Argentine

The Leyland Royal Tiger with M.C.W. bodywork

Senor Gatto and Dr. Derisi at the front entrance to one of the Weymann-bodied Royal Tiger buses for Buenos Aires.

Senor Gatto and Dr Derisi *(sic)* pose with one of their vehicles for this view also taken on the occasion of the official government inspection in January 1952. The Argentine Royal Tigers were left-hand drive models with dual-door 32ft long Hermes bodywork.

113

orders which made the news that day. He might have quietly mentioned that there would have been many more Royal Tigers for the home market if the 'exports first' situation hadn't applied. In the event it was a good thing, for the more-economical lighter-weight chassis were developed during the period that the big export order was being handled.

The following month the Port Elizabeth assembly plant was opened in South Africa, reflecting the increasing degree of skill and independence being achieved there and elsewhere throughout the world. RM Morter took charge, having previously been Assistant Works Manager at Addlestone, but earlier with Hall, Lewis (later Park Royal), and the company would grow in importance as the volume of British-built vehicles operating in South Africa diminished. East Africa was in the news next, in February, when Princess Elizabeth, on holiday in Kenya with husband Prince Philip, learned of the death of her father, King George VI.

A Changing World

We have seen in the previous chapters that the post-war years had been no bed of roses so far. Shortages of men and materials, a labour government hell-bent on nationalising almost everything in sight, despite there being no money in the kitty to implement these policies, unions fighting for better living standards

1952 saw the ratification of the European Iron and Steel Schuman Plan. Here at home, continuing shortage of steel was confirmed by this Government-sponsored advertisement.

Export business was brisk and included Africa, Canada, South America, India and Ceylon, Spain and Portugal amongst other countries. Lahore took a batch of ten Guy Arab double-deckers at this time, body numbers M4848-57, and this cutting is believed to show one posed near to the Guy factory in Wolverhampton.

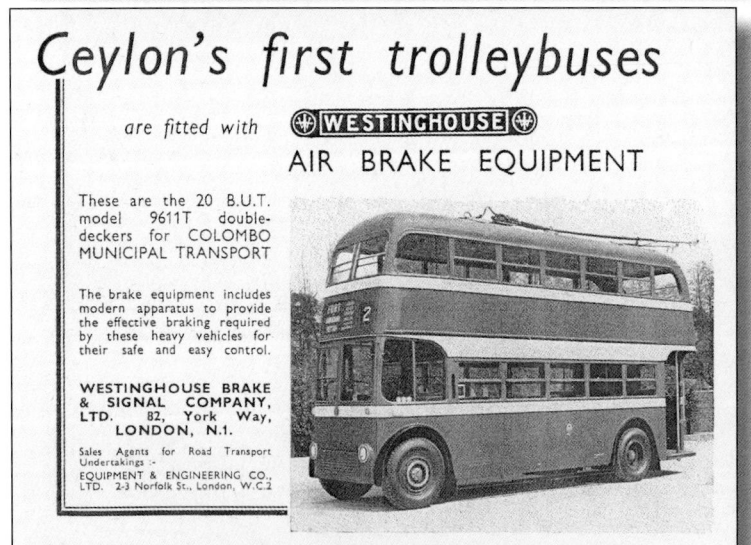

The twenty BUT trolleybuses supplied in 1952 to Colombo in what was then Ceylon were overshadowed by the huge Argentinian orders, but were nevertheless significant in being the only post-war double-deck trolleybuses Weymann's produced for export. They carried body numbers M4712-31.

Marcelle Penton, one of three sisters working at Weymann's, seen at the switchboard console where she worked as receptionist for ten years. Marcelle married Walter Healy, from the buying department, in 1958 and both worked at Station Road until made redundant in 1965.

Double-decker buses hadn't changed much in appearance; this smart City of Oxford Regent with its splendid livery meticulously applied was, at first glance, not so very different from buses being supplied to the same operator five years later though in fact they were by then a little wider and longer. To the casual observer the same paint scheme, rear open platform, destination layout and other details conveyed an air of continuity. Here MWL 978 from a batch of 20 AEC Regent IIIs delivered in 1948 has centre stage in a typically quiet street of that time. (KWS)

for their members but not always willing to concede better working practices in return, bosses still maintaining their living standards and attitudes from the best of the pre-war years and equally unwilling to face up to a changing world could only collectively add up to trouble in the making. And so it was to be.

Looking from outside in 1952 it might have been thought that, in fact, things were starting to improve. Actually, much of the improvement in the transport industry was being driven by Leyland Motors, still very much a *tour-de-force* worldwide, and a major contributor to the nation's wealth through its success in bringing home the bacon (and beef and sugar) with vast export orders for its buses and trucks. The world was moving on, and developing countries were looking to update their transport infrastructure, whilst commonwealth countries were replacing ageing buses and trolleybuses though often still looking to the mother country for those replacements.

Leyland's new underfloor-engined chassis were about to give Britain its biggest ever export orders, and although it did not yet know it, Addlestone was to benefit to some tune. Although single-deck bus (and coach) design had taken a quantum leap forward, the traditional double-decker was still some way away from making a similar step-change. Thus, much of the output from Station Road looked broadly similar to the vehicles delivered in the past 15-20 years, with the exception of those built during the war.

Methods of production, and materials, had changed little, and customers' buses still carried broadly the same fleet names and liveries, and were delivered to the same towns and cities.

In the offices, secretaries still used shorthand notebooks, whilst the girls in the typing pools (many firms still did not employ married women) used manual typewriters and produced multiple carbon copies on thin paper – flimsies – which became less and less legible towards the bottom of the pile. The age of the Xerox, later 'the photocopier' had not yet arrived. The lady on the switchboard ruled the roost; only she could connect you to the outside world through her polished mahogany console with its mass of wires, buzzing buttons and headphones. Subscriber trunk dialling (STD) was also some years away yet and buttons A and B still reigned supreme in the red telephone kiosks.

There was an orderly routine, based generally on hard work and respect, and whilst money was hard-earned and not over abundant, expectations were less and consumer demand much less than today. National Service kept the youth of the day out of mischief and the age of the laddette was, thankfully, light years away.

However, this age of graft and, some would say, subservience, was about to come to an end. In some ways this was due to the use of materials and routines developed during the recent war when the costs could be ignored with so much at stake. Now the new technology, particularly in plastics and electronics, would change the way things were made and the way we lived. Formica became a buzz word and transistors began to find their way into every aspect of life.

Whilst the actual sequence of events may not reflect their individual importance – 'all the right ingredients but not necessarily in the right order', as it might be put – without a doubt the first and most important event at Station Road had been the death of Arthur Froggatt. He had been in charge at Weymann's since 1934, and it is said that he knew everyone in the factory by name – all 1,500 at this time. Saddened by the continuing militant attitude of some of the workforce, and by the fact that he was about to stand down before his 70th birthday, he had through his kind and perceptive nature kept the Station Road plant going through thick and thin. And there was to be more thin than thick in the coming years. There were still many on the shop floor who had been at Addlestone even longer than ATF; some remembered the more abrasive days of Izod and Black before ATF came from Park Royal. Others saw an opportunity for making some changes . . .

Changes in the offices were mentioned earlier. United Molasses appointed James Don, their nominee director who had been overlooking matters for some years now, to be Chairman. Jack Davies became the new Managing Director, a popular and wise choice. The two remaining key posts went to Harold Cook, as General Manager, and Walter Dodsworth as Works Director. Here there were to be tensions which resulted in an unfortunate outcome, of which more later.

Whilst all this was being chewed over in the works canteen during the lunchtime, perhaps over the rice pudding, the topic probably then turned to the Suez Canal and the many other trouble spots in the world, places where men had served during the recent war, or where they had spent their National Service, and often where the buses they were building were to be sent.

Whilst the so-called Super Powers were busy developing and testing nuclear bombs capable of destroying the whole planet, and mankind with them, tensions in Asia and Africa, including India, Egypt, Persia, Israel, Kenya, Rhodesia, Cyprus

London Transport's second batch of lowbridge Regents, RLH 21-76, were delivered in the autumn of 1952. Unlike the earlier members of the class they had been ordered for London Transport as part of the rebalancing of the giant RT contract when it became apparent that LT was considerably over-blessed with RT buses. Previously, of course, vehicles had been diverted from the Balfour Beatty contract. Despite their awkward side gangway layout they were popular with enthusiasts, though perhaps less so with passengers, and several survived into preservation, including RLH 32 seen above. Their lower overall height also made them popular on the second-hand market and several were exported to Canada and into Europe. In 2012 three Canadian ones were repatriated for preservation or for spare parts for others in museums. (PG)

Facing page: The South American Olympic receives a final check over before leaving Elmdon for the Festival of Britain in 1951.

The West Bromwich fleet was well kept, but in later WMPTE days as here, standards declined and its smart livery, with discrete gold lining, enhancing the lines of the Weymann's body looks as though this vehicle was taken out before the cleaner came back from his tea break. Usually the fleet took its MCW vehicles from MCCW but here is one from Station Road, M5081 of 1952. It was one from a batch of 20 Daimlers. (AEJ)

Norman and Beryl Froggatt seen here at the front in this group at a function of the Worshipful Company of Coachmakers and Coach Harness Makers of London.

Norman, son of ATF, joined Weymann's in 1936 after his father had moved across from Park Royal, becoming an estimator. By 1946 he was Chief Estimator, moving up the ladder to become the last Works Manager. He was at Station Road until the end, moving then to Duple at Hendon as a Director, and going north to Blackpool when Duple took over the Burlingham company and its factories.

He and his wife retired into the rural midlands where Norman died.

and elsewhere were often more relevant if potentially less devastating. Oil or independence was usually the catalyst, and the former was a constant worry for the west, particularly so here in Britain with the growth of the motor car linked to the reduction in numbers of electric trams and trolleybuses, and the gradual switch away from coal following the Clean Air Act and the use of liquid fuel in the power stations. But it was the threat from nuclear fission – which had spawned many of the commonplace items which we now use and take for granted in our everyday lives – that was in most people's minds.

In an age where suddenly nuclear-tipped Inter-Continental Ballistic Missiles (ICBMs) could take over where Germany's Doodlebugs, and later V2 rockets, left off, and reach anywhere in the world without warning in a matter of minutes, many people felt their lives seemed to be constantly under threat. Norman Froggatt and his wife would have remembered when a nearby V1 severely damaged their house during the war, forcing them to evacuate their family into temporary accommodation.

Moving ahead only slightly, and giving an indication of how communications were changing and needed to do so, the Duke of Edinburgh is on record as saying that when he first entered Buckingham Palace he found internal communications were based on the use of uniformed flunkies who took handwritten notes from room to room – often remotely placed in relation to each other – when he was used to instant contact on board ship in the navy. His introduction of Walkie Talkies was to seem like science fiction in the hallowed portals, but even 'sci-fi' was now being recognised as becoming reality as Russia and America were getting ready to launch satellites and were talking about putting a man on the moon. Technology, and expectations, were changing the way we saw the world and land transport would be affected one way or another.

Earlier in 1951 the Festival of Britain had been an opportunity for everyone to see just what British workers could do and make, and as mentioned earlier, MCW had taken the opportunity to show a South American Olympic, see adjacent illustration. At the end of the year output was recorded as 796 vehicles.

The announcement that Austin and Morris – motor car manufacturers – had merged in November 1951 may have seemed pretty irrelevant to Weymann's employees, many of whom still used their bikes to get to work, and few of whom would have had a car. But it set in motion a long-lasting series of crippling strikes which made Weymann's agitators seem like amateurs – until 1964. Peter Sellers outdid Tony Hancock when his film *I'm All Right Jack* was screened, lampooning both unions and bosses and causing audiences to laugh or cry depending on which side of the accurately portrayed fence they found themselves.

Leyland were still working hard to obtain business throughout the world and one of its service engineers returned to Lancashire in 1952 after a year-long stint in North and South America backing up the Sales teams' efforts. This was part of the strategy which saw Olympics being exported to both countries. The later shotgun marriage of Leyland Motors with what had become BMC meant that when serious management deficiencies needed to be addressed the solutions were thought to be found by moving some top-management from Lancashire to Birmingham. Sadly, this left a vacuum in Lancashire and marked the start of the decline in Leyland's fortunes, and with MCW and Leyland working hand-in-glove, Addlestone was going to suffer through no fault of its own. The growth of car ownership was now spreading, however, and coupled with the increase in television sets predicted earlier and the greater amount of air time given to this growing medium, evening travel to the cinemas dropped off catastrophically, meaning that there were now many less people using the buses.

Television output and capability had grown steadily since 1950 when, in August, the BBC had achieved a milestone with its first overseas broadcast to France. By 1952 four out of five people in the country were said to be in range of the signal, and in 1953 the go-ahead was given for a second (commercial) channel which began broadcasting in 1955. These straws in the wind were gathering momentum.

In January 1952 Weymann's vehicles were in the news when Ceylon's first trolleybuses entered service, with chassis built at Kingston, Surrey by British United Traction, the joint Leyland-AEC Company set up to manufacture trolley vehicles. BUT's home market aspirations had been dealt a body blow, however, with the change of policy by London Transport whereby its trams were to be replaced by *motor* buses as they were taken out of service until final withdrawal in July 1952. At a stroke the relevant market potential was put in jeopardy, and indeed sacrificed, since the whole electrical manufacturing industry had lost much of its market potential in the UK and BUT now turned its attention to the growing railcar industry.

Britain's economic ills continued and bank rate was raised to 4% in the March 1952 budget, whilst restrictions on hire purchase would slow down spending, particularly on motor cars. But the tide could not be turned and the figures at the end of that year would speak for themselves. In early July London's last tram ran,

Cutting edge TV technology in the mid-1960s. Three black and white channels, 19in screen, only 42½p per week – oh, but an extra two guineas for the legs!

Leeds were still taking 7ft 6in wide double-deckers in 1952 and the official view of PUA 563, M5380, illustrates the difference the later paint scheme (below) made, brightening up the appearance. This body incorporates equal depth windows, as does the Wallasey body on page 122, but the four-bay design looks much neater with the deep glass. In the lower view, another from the batch of six passes the infamous Quarry Hill council flats, now just a memory. Leeds would still remain a Roe customer, but taking MCW metal-framed products from both Birmingham and Addlestone in preference to the teak composite construction from the Cross Gates manufacturer. (AEJ)

118

reminding those in J-Building that had things gone as planned, the replacements would have been trolleybuses and not RT3s. Weymann's management had a real reason for worry where J-Building was concerned, for London Transport had just given the statutory two years notice to terminate the RT contract. Just exactly when this body blow percolated down to the shop stewards is not clear.

All was not gloom and doom, however. A second week's paid holiday was granted in 1952. Other good news was that the first scheduled flights to South Africa, using Comet jet airliners, had just started. This was unlikely to have affected Weymann's employees except perhaps for those who would later travel there on business, whilst those who did travel abroad would have been pleased to hear that the overseas travel allowance was to be increased – from £40 to £50! This would presumably be academic to Park Royal's Chairman who was in India inspecting the new PRV subsidiary Hydrabad Allwynn Metal Works plant!

Travel much nearer home would see Weymann's men going to the 1952 Commercial Motor Show to assess trends and make comparisons with their own products. There would be much to consider, as we shall see shortly.

When the year's performance was reviewed, James Don reported to the United Molasses board that "Weymann's have operated satisfactorily, and have orders on hand for full employment". They had built 784 buses, a slight drop on 1951, but there had also been 41 vehicles for the Ministry of Supply. Between 1952 and 1956 Weymann's would built 535 vehicles for the MoS, including many of the famous Green Goddess fire tenders. The spread of customers was in marked contrast to Park Royal where strikes had meant that almost the whole of that company's output had been meeting the contractual obligation to deliver RTs for London Transport – very much a case of all their eggs in one basket.

Movements of men at this time included Lloyd Thompson joining MCW from Hairlok, and the appointment of Bill Shirley, Weymann's one-time joker in the fitters' shop, as Director and General Manager at Park Royal as Bill Black moved to higher things within the ACV group. Addlestone's Messrs Cook and Davies were in the news in November when their car was in a crash one night, and United Molasses became involved in claims for compensation for injuries incurred. Better news for UM was that James Don was able to report that the results for 1953 were satisfactory, that 800 Olympics had now been built, and that full production had been maintained despite intense competition at home and abroad.

Despite Mr Don's assurances the figures were actually dropping steadily now; 649 buses built in 1953 represented only 13.25 per week against almost 20 only four years earlier. The workforce headcount was dropping accordingly, of course.

Weymann's were only one of several bodybuilders producing examples of the famous Green Goddess fire tenders. One is seen at a steam rally at York though perhaps unnoticed by some of the enthusiasts in the crowd. The Goddesses had their lives extended by periodic instances of industrial unrest by the fire brigade's union, and at such times they were manned by the army. (JAS)

Ten of these smart Guy Arab III vehicles in their distinctive and attractive, if rather dated, gold-lined livery were supplied in spring 1952 to Tynemouth, a subsidiary of the major BET Northern General concern. M5425 is shown.

119

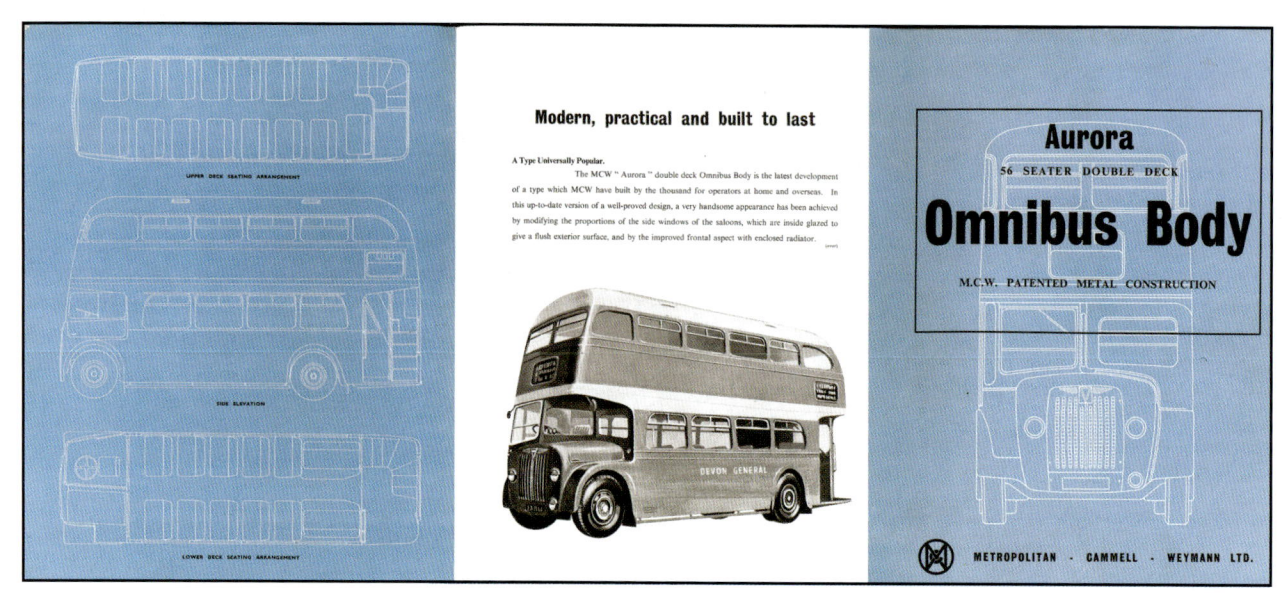

As mentioned in the text, this vehicle seemed a strange choice for the 1952 Show. The Aurora was listed in the MCW internal description papers as *'Old established MCW structure. Upper and Lower deck saloons separately constructed. Has also been used for single-deck construction'* – it clearly represented the end of an era. Weymann's double-deck bodies were indeed still built in two sections, upper and lower decks, and then put together. The new Orion was built with framing reaching from the foot of the lower deck skirting to the upper deck window level, with the top 'lid' incorporating the complete roof and window pillars as can be seen in the view of upper-deck manufacture on page 126.

Devon General had not yet adopted the 'tin-front' concept and so this rather handsome 56-seat 8ft wide bus was ahead of its time in the fleet until 1954. The assembly is believed to be based on a Crossley unit, logically used from within the ACV group. The bus has been preserved and is maintained in full running order as an example of what might have been. Weighing in at 7tons 18cwts, some 34cwts heavier than the competing 58-seat Orion (6tons 4cwts), when weight saving was the issue it was outclassed from the very beginning.

120

The eye-catching MCCW entry on its 1952 Show stand was this lightweight double-decker. The body weight for this 7ft 6in wide bus quoted in the adjacent advert was 36cwts 1qtr – only 1 qtr heavier than a Hermes single-decker 44-seat body, but with two decks, a staircase and 14 extra seats. The completed vehicle weighed 6tons 4cwts whereas the Weymann Aurora weighed 7tons 18cwt as recorded and painted on the vehicle in the official picture opposite. Below we see the Orion in action with purchaser PMT, a BET fleet located not too far from MCCW Birmingham, enabling it to be easily monitored if necessary. There was also a London Transport Regal IV RF from the contract for 700 vehicles on MCCW's stand.

Reproduction of an extract from MCW's internal papers showing that the Orion range included the following options:

MARK IV.	"ORION" LIGHTWEIGHT DOUBLE DECK. NORMAL AND LOW HEIGHT.	Tubular steel pillars and light alloy lining panels. Combined structure for upper and lower saloon. Emphasis in this design is on Lightweight whereas in Mk.V, emphasis is on lower cost.
MARK V	DOUBLE DECK NORMAL AND LOW HEIGHT	As Mark IV, but all steel structure and lining panels. Emphasis in this design is on low cost whereas in Mk.IV, emphasis is on Lightweight.

121

Wallasey had taken Metro-Cammell bodies for many years, Weymann's first deliveries being made in 1951. Their rather dull livery – the infamous sea green and cream – does little to improve the lines of this November 1952 PD2, body number M5452, with its unusual choice of equal depth windows. It was one a batch of 12. Leeds also took a batch of vehicles with equal depth deep windows on both decks as seen on page 118.

Southport, a genteel seaside Lancashire town, was a staunch Leyland supporter, taking both chassis and bodies from its nearby manufacturer. In 1952 Weymann's secured their first order, for double-deck bodies, and maintained the business without difficulty when Leyland withdrew from bodybuilding shortly afterwards. Its vehicles were always extremely well turned out in their bright red and off white livery, supporting the high class image of the town. This Leyland PD2, M5104, was from the first order.

North Western took six of these handsome lowbridge PD2 Titans in 1953 and M6079 is seen here. These were the second batch of double-deckers Weymann's had supplied to this all-lowbridge fleet, one of the bigger ones in the BET empire, the first being ten – M4017-26 – being delivered in 1949. Already operating 25 Hermes-bodied Royal Tigers, it would shortly be taking further large numbers of that body on a selection of chassis makes and models. This popular version of BET livery was always well maintained by North Western and its vehicles lost some of their attraction when more red and less ivory became the order of the day.

Sales promotional material still had some way to go when this rather basic specimen was produced for the Commercial Motor Show in 1952. It was actually in colour, as shown on the page 121, but the drawing of the bus is hardly flattering.

It seems that this was the time when model names came to the fore and fancy brochures were produced. Drawing Office feeling was that this stemmed from MCW acquiring a honcho from the motor car industry who was still thinking in terms of hundreds of thousands, or millions, of each model. The presentation of these varied hugely, and some can only be described as amateurish with drawings bearing only a passing resemblance to the finished product. Those produced for the Orion and the first Aurora are perhaps a good example of this latter point.

In November 1953 the MCW organisation celebrated its 21st Anniversary, with suitable advertising in the trade press, and a special commemorative booklet, whilst also creating a small private London Motor Show – mid-way between the 1952 and forthcoming 1954 Commercial Motor Shows. Here it mounted an exhibition of current vehicles from long-standing major customers including six double-deckers and four single-deckers displayed in an LTE bus depot. The object of the exercise was to remind its guests, on the morning of the Public Transport Association's Annual Dinner, that MCW had been around since 1932, and that during that time it had supplied large numbers of vehicles to some of its customers – since numbers were the name of the game it was proud to point out that of the ten vehicles on display, an RF and an RT3 were the 4,899th and 4,990th built by MCW for LTE; Birmingham's 1,877th was alongside Manchester's 1,213th, Sheffield's 230th, Midland Red's 496th, Maidstone & District's 420th and Western Welsh's 227th. The single-deckers included an Elmdon-built Olympic for Jamaica Omnibus Services and one of the new lighter-weight Olympians.

The inevitable lunch followed and Sir Archibald Boyd, MCW's Chairman, acted as host and mentioned some of the highlights of the 21 years, and paid tribute to the then Managing Director, Homfray Davies; the latter acknowledged the tribute but took the opportunity to remind the guests that more buses could be built if there were not so many special requirements. His light-hearted jibe that ten customers would produce twelve designs seemed apposite when looking at the photographs in this book of the so-called standard Olympic body with three different doorway arrangements! Had Henry Spurrier been there he would most certainly have endorsed these comments, for, although there were as yet no indications, Spurrier would close Leyland's famous South Works bus bodybuilding plant only a few months later. Whilst poor labour relations played their part, he always maintained that building buses was as bad as building fire engines – which he had also stopped at Leyland – since every customer wanted a different specification. Whether the ever-growing relationship with MCW was now a consideration must be a factor to be questioned. Not for the first time, and certainly not for the last, there was a feeling in some quarters that the Leyland's management might have cleverly marched the stroppy shop floor into a *cul-de-sac*. Other wags said Leyland's management definitely weren't that clever.

A single-door Olympic – L117 – operating in Southern Rhodesia with Salisbury United, part of the United Transport empire with its Red & White and James origins, now with BET associations. The shells for this batch of three – L116-8, built in 1951 – were finished by Bus Bodies (South Africa) Ltd as were others including eight for Cape Town and an immediate difference will be noted in the deeper sliding windows for extra ventilation.

The Tiger Cub and rivals make their mark

The heavyweight chassis were now to be succeeded by a range of lighter and more economical models. Forerunner here, and reflecting Leyland's prowess in those good old days, was the PSUC Tiger Cub, though only by a short head. This new chassis featured the smaller – and lighter – O.350 engine which ran at higher speeds than the O.600 and was, as a consequence, much noisier making for a less comfortable passenger environment. On the plus side the chassis was lighter than the Royal Tiger, through a combination of weight saving measures, and a typical 44-seat bus body showed a saving of some two tons against its predecessor.

One of two prototype Leyland demonstrators was bodied by Weymann with a Hermes body, M5450, in June 1952, registered OTD 301 and demonstrated quite extensively. The body weighed 36cwts and the completed vehicle 5tons 10cwts, giving a much better unladen weight-to-passenger ratio. It was shown at the 1952 Commercial Motor Show where it attracted considerable interest. The body was then refurbished and placed onto a later production chassis registered RTB 49, and the complete ensemble was eventually sold to Rossendale Transport in 1955 after further demonstration work.

Weymann's drawing office staff would see the benefits of the development work done on the Olympic by Philip Brunton from MCW and Stanley Markland from Leyland which had produced the Hermes body, and the knock-on effects where the same basic body would be capable of meeting the requirements of a wide variety of customers for some years ahead. Whilst there had clearly been great progress in single-deck design and weight reduction it should not be thought that double-deckers had been forgotten. Now it was time to prepare the other vehicles for the 1952 autumn Motor Show where Weymann's would be exhibiting a somewhat special Devon General AEC double-decker, M5523, a Regent III with a Crossley style 'tin front' and rather stylish four-bay body with shaped end windows to the lower saloon in its new Aurora body, and then a very novel item, a partly-knocked-down single-decker for Trinidad, but very cleverly re-assembled, thereby showing how it was sent overseas.

Sadly, neither exhibit seems to have been a success. Although the model name Aurora was later used for two further designs this Devon General Aurora, the last of a batch of conventional Regent IIIs for the operator, became a one-off while the flat-pack Jason also failed to make any sales impact. The choice of two competing double-deckers on the two MCW group stands seems a little strange but clearly it was soon decided that the MCCW Daimler for Potteries would be the frontrunner. Even more strange was the production of two very down-market brochures for the Orion and Aurora, both using a rather poor artist's impression, one lettered PMT and the other Devon General in the separate brochures. When weight saving was the object of the exercise then there was simply no contest. The lightweight MCCW vehicle, already being branded Orion, a 7ft 6in wide 58-seat body on a Daimler chassis and weighing 6tons 4cwts, was 34cwts lighter than Weymann's 8ft wide 56-seat Regent III at 7tons 18cwts. Why should Weymann's have been showing a face-lifted double-decker where even its own sales brochure seemed to list no real new selling points when on the next door stand MCCW was in the run-up to the now famous Orion range. Was the right hand not talking to the left at this time? After a spell of extensive demonstration, and a change from the original Daimler engine to a smaller Gardner 5LW, the new lightweight double-decker, registered REH 500, would end up with Potteries Motor Traction in Stoke on Trent. The Aurora remained in service with Devon General and is now preserved in full working order. Also displayed on the adjacent MCCW stand was one of the 700 strong RF class single-deckers for London.

After the 1952 Show MCW were able to assess the response to this new somewhat austere looking rather gaunt double-decker. It clearly demonstrated what *could* be achieved in weight saving, and work now began in the drawing offices to take the concept further. Weymann's drawing office staff must have been particularly busy at this time since they had developed the very handsome designs which Wallasey, Birkenhead, West Bromwich, Southport and Leeds, amongst others, were taking, whilst still keeping up with orders for the existing designs for Devon General and other BET fleets, and at the same time becoming involved in the Birmingham-led new Orion designs which would eventually cover light-, mid- and heavyweight variants. Fibreglass was now making its presence felt, especially for front and rear domes, and so there

This was Weymann's Hermes body M5450 seen in June 1952 on Leyland's prototype unbadged, and hence anonymous, Tiger Cub chassis demonstrator, OTD 301. The body, which weighed just 36cwts, was later transferred to a newer, production chassis registered RTB 49 and the vehicle continued working as a demonstrator. It was later sold to Rossendale Transport as seen below. (STA; MAT)

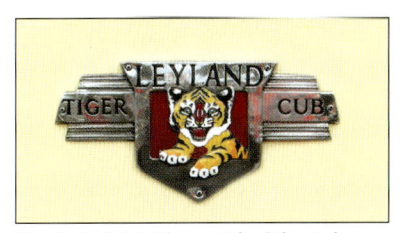

The Tiger Cub badge matched the style of the earlier Royal Tiger and would be followed by the Leopard and other members of the cat family. (JAS)

The Hermes body soon became recognisable throughout the country, the basic outline derived from the Olympic being unmistakable. BET fleets took many hundreds but there were examples in municipal and independent fleets as well. This official drawing shows variations for Leyland and AEC chassis.

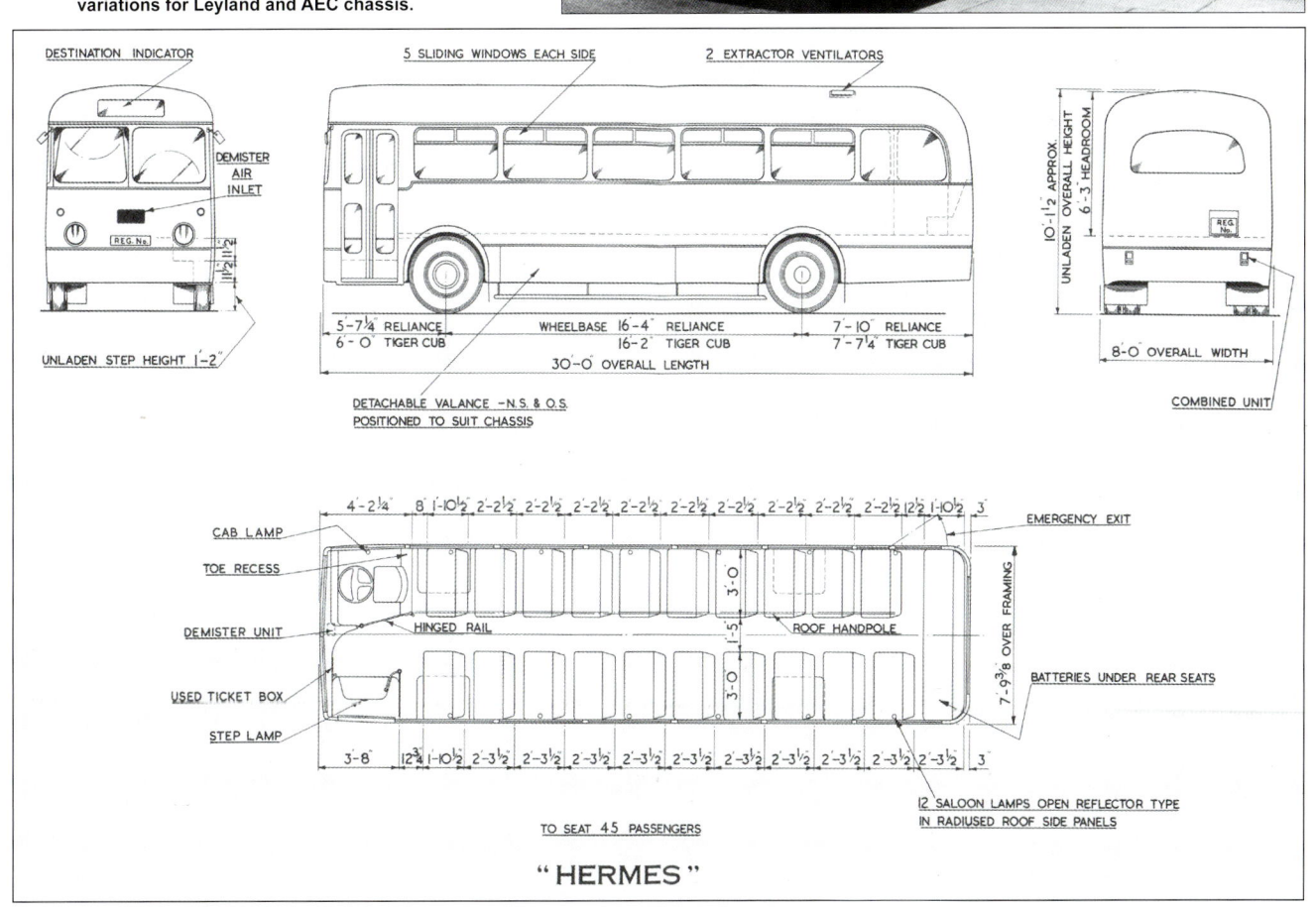

"HERMES"

125

Northern General, Exeter and PMT all took examples of the highbridge Orion on Guy chassis. Northern's batch of 20 were numbered M6202-21 and the first of them, delivered in October 1953, is shown above.

The Orion body was designed to be built from the outriggers to the upper deck waistrail in one unbroken section, with the roof being added as a lid with windows as can clearly be seen in this official photograph. Before long the method of construction would change again as fibreglass replaced the front and rear domes. Looking at the lightweight construction it is easy to understand how a bus can lose the complete roof section in accidents involving low bridges. There were two versions of the Orion, using aluminium (which was more expensive) for lightness or steel where cost saving was considered more important than weight reduction.

As new materials came on stream methods of production were adapted to make use of them. One such example, fibreglass, or grp, used semi-skilled labour to brush pungent smelling chemicals into the white fibre mat which had been laid in the master mould. After curing it produced a perfect copy and the process could be repeated over and over again. It replaced some of the most highly skilled panel beaters for producing items such as domes as seen on the left. No wonder that labour relations became ever more strained. (STA)

Orion bodies are usually remembered for their sparseness, and the need to have external fixing points on the domes to hold the internal strengthening and safety rails across the front windows. They are also remembered for the rough finish on the inside of those same domes before the art of making smooth double-sided fibreglass was perfected. This official factory photograph taken in the autumn of 1953, above, shows a highbridge vehicle for Rhondda. Below is a lowbridge example for South Wales with the bulbous Crossley bonnet assembly before the Regent V front from AEC had been introduced. A similar tin front was fitted to a batch of Dennis Lances for Aldershot & District.

would have been changes on the production lines to meet these requirements (see page 126). To add to the variety some operators were still taking 7ft 6in wide bodies, not yet being ready to change over to the new width dimension of 8ft which was now generally available for operators to use from July 1950.

A run of body numbers from M6138 to 6235 was allocated to Orions ordered for BET fleets and amongst the first true Orion bodies from Station Road were, in late 1953, examples for Maidstone & District on wartime chassis sent for rebodying, followed by bodies on new or existing chassis for Devon General, Rhondda, Northern General, Potteries and Tynemouth. This was also the time when traditional radiators were being replaced by 'tin fronts' and Devon General were the first to take Orions so fitted, using a rather bulbous Crossley version. They also produced some interesting rebuilds from older chassis using Weymann components for the new bodies.

Whilst all this was going on the steady flow of export single-deckers to Argentina continued unabated whilst smaller orders saw vehicles being exported to Jamaica and Portugal. Lisbon was rebodying some of its AEC Regal III single-deckers using sets of Weymann's components assembled in Portugal.

On the single-deck front, the Hermes was now carrying all before it. Western Welsh, Rhondda, Mexborough & Swinton, North Western, Northern General, King Alfred and PMT were now keeping the production lines flowing. One order was for 100 Tiger Cubs for Western Welsh and they would amass over 180 of this single-deck model from Station Road. Next down the line came AEC's new chassis, the

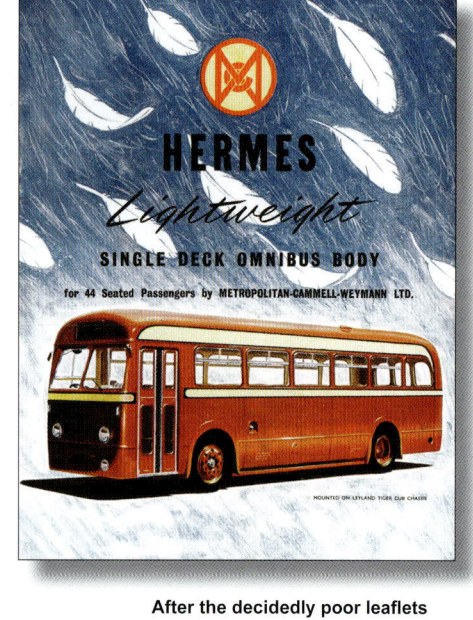

After the decidedly poor leaflets for the 1952 Show MCW moved up a gear with its publicity and the new colour brochure for the Hermes, above, was typical of the new order. It was certainly more in keeping with both the organisation and the models to be promoted.

The two paintings prepared for the 1952 Celebrations were remarkably detailed and some people portrayed here were able to identify themselves to the author many years later. The single-deckers are thought to be an export order, with their rear destination boxes, but the double-deckers in the distance seem to be more elusive. Imagine working in an office above this area.

The MCW organisation came of age in 1953, produced a suitable commemorative brochure, and placed eye-catching advertising matter in the trade press. It also commissioned two splendid paintings showing the assembly lines at Addlestone and Elmdon, reproduced here. The Addlestone line shows Hermes bodies in build whilst the Elmdon one has the first of the London Transport RF sightseeing buses, together with export Olympic models amongst the vehicles in build.

Devon General's M5504 was a traditional-bodied Regent III from the same batch of 20 as the 1952 Show prototype Aurora model. It would be some while before enclosed 'tin-fronts' sported by the Aurora replaced the radiators in this fleet, but that body was destined to be unique. (KWS)

Reliance. This weighed 5¾tons as against 7¾ for the Regal IV of which Station Road had bodied just 24. The Reliance would prove equally attractive to operators as the Tiger Cub and Weymann's first examples were for BET companies, with body numbers M6599-6602 for North Western being followed by M6782-91 for Potteries Motor Traction, all with Hermes lightweight bodies. Brewers of Caerau, treading cautiously, took one Tiger Cub and one Reliance for comparison in 1954.

In amongst the home orders, and the big headline-grabbing exports, there were smaller contracts which took Weymann's vehicles to various far flung countries. In 1954 an order for 44 Royal Tigers for Chile caused some problems when satisfactory finance for the deal could not be arranged and Leyland was obliged to divert 24 of the order elsewhere. These vehicles went to Madrid, Damascus, Kuwait, Uruguay, Venezuela and Yugoslavia but little, if any, futher business came to Station Road from this exotic arrangement. There must have been some serious rearranging to do between left and right hand deliveries now.

More conventional orders saw Liverpool and Sheffield taking approaching 150 Leyland Titan PD2s with traditional Weymann bodywork in contrast to the Orions which were now becoming more common. Sheffield then took another 36 handsome vehicles on AEC chassis, thus keeping the body design alive.

Events outside MCW which caught the world's attention included the launch of the new Boeing jet liner, the 707. Air travel was really going to change now, for soon it would be possible to cross the Atlantic by scheduled passenger jet propelled planes. Another dock strike neatly brought that point home to some people!

By the time the 1954 Motor Show came round Leyland had produced a lightweight integral which reflected the Lancashire company's unwillingness to write off the home-market Olympic; they decided instead to produce a lightweight version – the Olympian – using the smaller engine and other components from the lighter Tiger Cub model which had been introduced in 1952. Once again, the Olympic type of structure was utilised, though weight reduction was now a major consideration and this time the integral model would show a saving of some 2cwts against the comparable bodied Tiger Cub.

The prototype duly appeared at the 1954 Motor Show, with body number LW1, and LW2, part of Western Welsh's order, was also shown there. A further 59 – LW2-60 – were built between then and 1957 when Leyland finally got the message, gave up, and the model was dropped. Six were exported, the rest being supplied to home market customers of whom Western Welsh took the lion's share with 47 vehicles. Lancashire independent operator Fishwick, already operating eight Olympics took six Olympians and some of these were later the subject of an interesting makeover when they were sent to Duple Northern for conversion to be suitable for express work to London, with coach seating and additional smart, but discrete, trim.

Moss Nelson is believed to have joined Weymann's around the same time as Bill Black, circa 1927. He remained at the factory until closure by which time he was Design Engineer, having previously been Chief Draughtsman. He then went to Frimley and when that facility closed he retired. (BB)

FANFARE
SINGLE DECK COACH BODY
To Seat 37 Passengers

North Western's eye-catching Fanfare coach of 1954 represented Weymann's first foray into the luxury coach market when it appeared at the Motor Show. Initially, it was fitted to Reliance chassis, but Northern had some on Guys and later examples for Sheffield and Southdown were on Leylands.

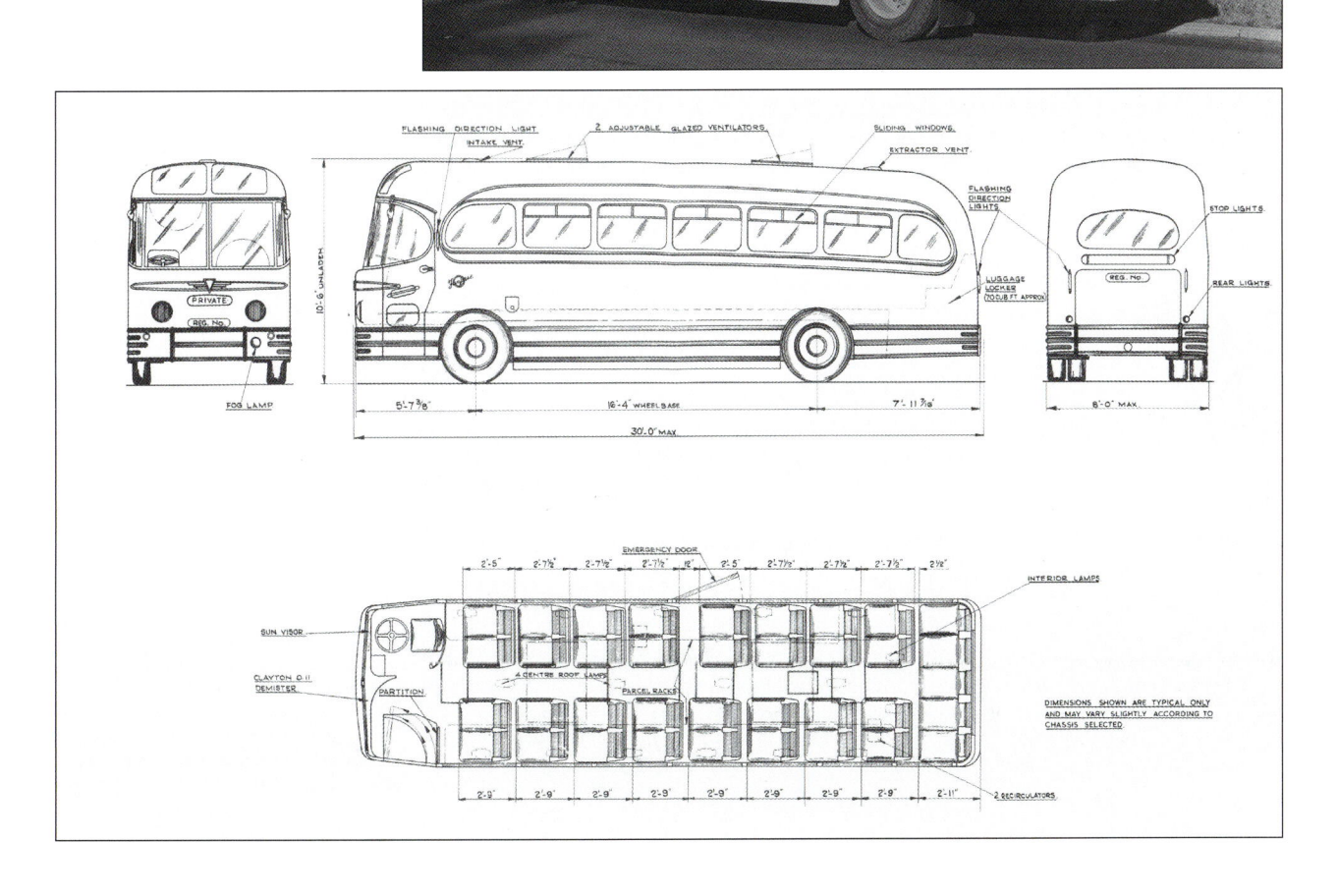

131

The adaptability and popularity of this body, now marketed as the Hermes as mentioned earlier in its lightweight form for separate chassis, was such that it could be found in use with nine or ten different chassis or sets of running units. Moss Nelson and the drawing office staff must have been very satisfied when they saw the variety of orders for this single-decker going down the lines below their offices.

Also at the 1954 Show, however, was a far more interesting body on a Reliance chassis when North Western's M6628 displayed the first Fanfare coach body. This had been designed in conjunction with Frank A Mason, Chief Engineer of BET's Welsh subsidiary South Wales Transport and it came as little surprise that the majority of these stylish vehicles would be found in BET fleets. BET took 24 further Fanfares on Reliance chassis in 1955.

The Fanfare was, of course, Weymann's first true coach and immediately following numerically was M6629, a left hand drive Worldmaster model with air conditioning and other special features, intended to be used for work on the continent. The finished vehicle, the Arcadian, made its debut at the 1956 Motor Show and then joined the ranks of the one-offs before quietly disappearing to Madrid.

Leyland now joined the tin front revolution with its PD2/20 series Titans, with Southport being amongst the first to have Weymann's bodies fitted, whilst South Wales took some lowbridge Orions which looked completely overwhelmed when fitted with the bulbous Crossley front. AEC must have thought so too, and before long they would introduce their own tin front for the Regent V which must rank amongst the neatest of all the new style fronts.

It was at this time East Kent took 40 dual-purpose bodies where the Hermes shell had a new front end grafted on. The same body was also soon taken by North Western and Aldershot & District, thus extending the life of this popular design whilst giving it a neat facelift. Also around now a new youngster began work in the bodyshop, and formed a lifelong friendship with the previously mentioned Vic Smith. Dave Humphrey, who acted as coordinator for the Author in tracking down former employees, joined the ten-bar-two darts team and still attends the firm's annual reunions. He was teamed up with Vic for one particular routine whereby the metal-framed bodies were squared-up by adjustment with a sledge hammer, it being Dave's job to hold the wooden block. Since the friendship lasted we have to assume Vic's aim was always good. To then see these two men delicately and accurately throwing darts was an eye opener!

It must have seemed that things were going reasonably well for Weymann's at this time, but a succession of bombshells was waiting just around the corner. It appears that despite a difficult market the company had managed to produce a reasonable profit though this was earmarked for distribution to shareholders. Jack Davies wanted some of this reinvested into the Company at Station Road. UM were not for giving ground and also raised the matter of the sales budget having been exceeded. The matter became contentious and Jack Davies was forced to stand down. This was a

The East Kent Reliances delivered in spring 1955, M6933-72, featured a revised version of the Hermes body for dual-purpose or express work. These bodies had high-backed seats incorporating headrests as can just be seen. Later versions for A&D and North Western were just fitted with slightly deeper than normal seats.

Two men who shaped Weymann's for many years and who left, separately, in 1956. DJA Davies, left, and Homfray Davies, right.

Harold Cook is believed to have worked at the Cunard Motor Company, joining Weymann's at the time they took Cunard over. By 1934 he was Chief Engineer and in 1946 became a Director, whilst still holding the position of Chief Engineer. He was appointed Deputy General Manager of Weymann's in 1947 and in that same year acting, and then substantive Managing Director of MCW. By 1950 he was Director and General Manager of Weymann's, and by 1956 Managing Director. He remained at Station Road to the end, and thus appears to have been one of, if not the, longest serving employee. A proud record and a distinguished career.

very sensitive issue for United Molasses since James Don knew only too well how popular and well respected he was. Davies was persuaded to resign, and to go quietly, for the good of the company, since the unions would have backed him with industrial action if they felt he had been badly treated. Accordingly, in March 1955, DJ Davies left Addlestone and shortly afterwards sought refuge at Beadles, (John C Beadle [Coachbuilders] Ltd), a Rootes Group member, in much the same way Bill Black had done in 1932. We shall see a result of that move shortly, but he later, and more importantly, moved to Marshalls of Cambridge where his BET connections, forged over many years at Weymann's, would have been invaluable. He had been at Weymann's for 25 years, latterly as Managing Director, and joined the MCW Board in 1950.

Jack Davies was followed by Homfray Davies as Managing Director but hardly had the ink dried on the new letterheads when in 1956 he left, going into the new industry handling waste disposal. This was a body blow of some magnitude for here was another man known and admired throughout the industry and whose pedigree stretched back to the stormy days at Hall, Lewis in the 1920s, before Park Royal was formed.

Another significant loss from Weymann's management soon occurred in 1956 when, according to Maurice Bullivant (Buyer) and Edna Bubb (Senior Secretary), in whom he had confided according to their (separate) interviews for this book, Walter Dodsworth had left through a mis-timed letter to the UM Board, expressing dissatisfaction with the new arrangement whereby he and Harold Cook jointly shared the position of General Manager. It had been intended, with James Don's approval, to revise the arrangement to a single occupancy – Walter Dodsworth. Unfortunately, and unbeknown to the unfortunate Mr Dodsworth, James Don had been called away to America on shipping business and at the crucial Board Meeting was unable to explain the reasons behind the letter. The Board, thus unenlightened, felt they were being asked to accept a resignation – and did so! Walter Dodsworth was soon snapped up by Park Royal. The loss of three key players in such a relatively short space of time cannot have been good for morale or for Weymann's reputation in the industry.

Sales were becoming harder to obtain throughout the industry now and although matters had been helped by the abrupt closure of Leyland's famous South Works in 1954, there was still over capacity in the industry. Weymann's share of the important BET cake was now being reduced partly by the Loughborough-based Willowbrook company, some of whose products were almost indistinguishable from Weymann's. This, coupled with the more vigorous approach from the revitalised Scottish Alexander Coachbuilders concern, would become a serious problem and the departure of Homfray Davies would have almost certainly been crucial now.

Nevertheless, life had to go on, and even losing three star players would not have to stand in the way of holding the ship steady. Harold Cook now became sole incumbent as Managing Director.

There was unrest outside the factory again at this time, and Fleet Street flexed its muscles and called a newspaper strike. In the pre-television days this was a great inconvenience, of course. This may well have helped the Tories to increase their majority to 58 when they were re-elected. Better news was the announcement that Britain was to have a national motorway network, and the announcement that Saunders Roe, who had shared in the enormous export orders to South America, were pulling out of bus building. But there was still overcapacity . . .

More and more of the business going down the lines now featured the uninspiring Orion designs, and the number of the former and more elegant double-deckers continued to decrease. Brian Burton looked out of the Drawing Office window and saw buses leaving for what until 1950 had been his uncle's fleet in Chesterfield and was pleased that the connection remained. But although life went on, it seemed that an era where elegance counted had truly come to an end.

Metro-Cammell perhaps also thought some things had come to an end, for they attempted, unsuccessfully, to have the General Working Agreement amended, though to exactly what effect is not recorded. The year end figures for 1954 were 615 buses and 65 Ministry of Supply vehicles; for 1955 they were 472 and 138 including command centres and Green Goddesses. UM Minutes record the situation as conditions being difficult and profits substantially down but down to what level they do not reveal. The question now was what would 1956 bring?

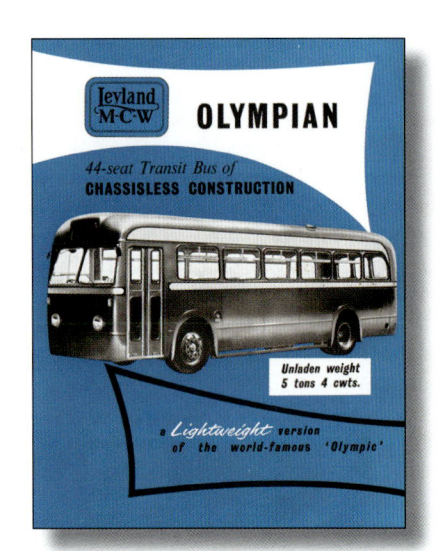

Leyland were still convinced that there was a place for their home market integral, and in a final fling for the model put two into the 1954 Motor Show, one destined for Western Welsh and the other one from their own demonstration fleet. As the leaflet states, it was seen as a lightweight Olympic using Tiger Cub components, and weighed 5tons 4cwts with a 44-seat Hermes body.

Western Welsh took 47 of these Olympians with Hermes bodywork, in addition to coach seated versions from Willowbrook. In 1958 they took six examples of a Weymann dual-purpose version, seen on page 150. Western Welsh were major Weymann users, as we have seen, and built up a huge fleet of Hermes bodies, on Leyland Royal Tiger, Tiger Cub, and here Olympian chassis. This is the Leyland demonstrator and first of the model, LW1, registered TPH 996, at Weymann's. It confirms the on-going collaboration between Leyland and MCW's engineers.

Experiments with standee vehicles continued in various undertakings – we have seen the Glasgow trolleybus on pages 93/9 – but there was no national legislation covering such operation. Sheffield took two Leyland Royal Tigers, M5850/1, in 1953 and had them fitted with these Scottish rear entrance type bodies with provision for 30 seated and 30 standing passengers. The local licensing authority was having none of it until an additional emergency exit had been provided by modifying the *rear* panel (!) as shown here. The capacity was then 31 seated and 26 standing, with 2+1 seats and a roving conductor. They were confined to just one route whose passengers' opinions seem not to have survived. (KWS)

134

Glasgow took 20 Sunbeam F4A trolleybuses in 1953, five with Alexander bodywork and the remaining 15 bodied at Station Road. They were all delivered in July and M5647, FYS 785, from the batch FYS 781-95, is seen here in later life. They were all in service until 1965/6. (IGMS)

This batch of 1950-built Albion chassis became embroiled in local politics in Glasgow. The 8ft wide chassis had been used for export until 1950 when UK regulations were changed to allow the wider vehicles to be operated here. Glasgow accordingly ordered 25, which were delivered that year, and intended to build the bodies in its Coplawhill workshops. There were delays due to the pressure of work at Coplawhill and it was eventually decided, after much wrangling, that the bodies would instead be built complete by Weymann's. The chassis were stored in one of Glasgow's bus depots until 1953 when they finally made their way to Addlestone. M4968, FYS 501, was completed in August of that year. Once again it is seen in later life when economies had brought about this much less attractive, but cheaper to apply, livery. (IGMS)

Bury Corporation was taking Leyland and AEC chassis in the post-war years and ordered two AEC Regent 9631 chassis in 1950, but then decided to have them modified to take advantage of the new synchromesh gearbox option on offer, model 9631S. This caused a delay until October 1952 and the two AECs were finally delivered from Weymann's in 1953, along with nine Leyland PD2s, all with 4-bay bodywork. The bodies on the Leylands had to be modified to suit the different front bulkhead position. One of the AECs, M4430, survives in the Manchester Museum of Transport and is seen here soon after withdrawal from passenger service. (JAS)

135

Southport was a municipality whose name stood for pride and excellence in turnout, in this case using a well kept red and cream livery. With its Victorian shopping parades on Lord Street it held out for the elegance of the traditional body. The first sign of dilution would be the arrival of the tin-front on its classic Leyland PD2s but here we see the last of the old order, number 24, M5104, delivered in July 1952 and ready to make the long trek to its new seaside home where Brian Burton's cousin was the General Manager – as Brian no doubt reminded his colleagues in the drawing office from time to time.

The arrival of the lightweight Orion, and also its heavier but cheaper version, meant that quite clearly the days of the elegant double-deckers being built at Station Road, Addlestone had to be numbered. Some customers held off the evil day as long as possible and one example is shown here. Birkenhead had been a shining example of civic pride for many years, and its vehicles were always extremely well turned out in their blue and ivory livery. They took ten of these fine Aurora-bodied vehicles in the year that Manager George Cherry was President of the MPTA. Here CBG 563, M6435, delivered in May 1954 cuts a dash a couple of years later. Mr Cherry's son David was also no stranger to Weymann's bodywork, having been through the engineering departments at North Western, Western Welsh and Rhondda before becoming Chief Engineer at Western Welsh in 1966. He moved north in 1972 to Northern Counties of Wigan, taking charge of the coachbuilding firm the following year. (KWS)

It was no surprise that the Orion gained few friends in the styling departments but the weight saving it offered could not be ignored. Once fibreglass technology improved, and customers realised that the body trim did not have to be so austere, some quite reasonable vehicles began to appear, though this was perhaps not one of them. Leyland were well represented with MCW double-deckers at the 1954 Motor Show, including examples for Edinburgh, Newcastle and Walsall, the latter TDH 770, fleet number 823, being shown. In addition to the MCW lettering painted on the windows the paper posters confirm that this Orion is indeed an example from the MCCW factory. There was a suggestion that Weymann's drawing office staff put them there – as if to say 'not invented in Addlestone'! (MAT)

136

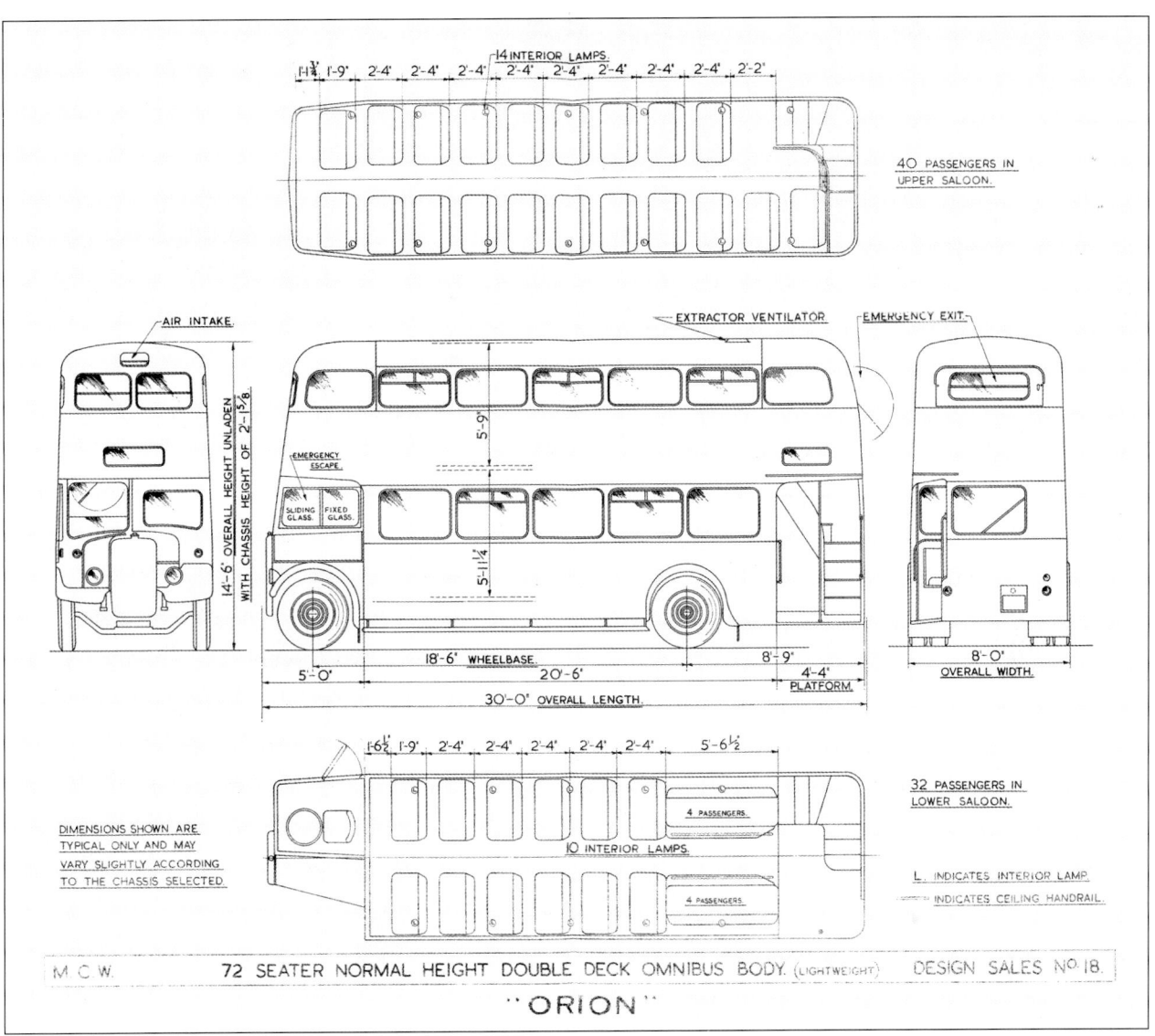

By the time of the 1956 Motor Show, two years after the Walsall vehicle shown opposite had been on view, the maximum length for two-axle double-deckers had been increased to 30ft and this 72-seat Orion for PMT and registered 700 AEH was on display. Built in Birmingham it showed once again what could be achieved in a lightweight body. It was a Titan PD3/2 but the chassis had been rebuilt from an OPD2/2. After demonstration work it entered service with PMT. The official general arrangement drawing for the production version is shown above. Liaison between MCCW and Weymann's became ever-closer now, with staff from Addlestone being regularly seconded to Birmingham.

137

CHAPTER 12 – 1956-60

Engines to the rear

Nineteen-fifty-six began at Weymann's with the completion of a batch of lowbridge Daimlers for Chesterfield. These six vehicles, YRB 193-8, completed a contract where the first six vehicles were delivered in November 1955. However, the year will forever be remembered by many as the one in which Colonel Nasser nationalised the Suez Canal and Britain went to war to reopen it. Some may prefer to remember that this was the year ERNIE came to our attention, but he brought sunshine to only a very few, for he was the machine selecting the new Premium Bond numbers. More significant to the transport industry were the numbers 27 and 30, for the former had given way to the latter in June as the maximum legal length for home market double-deckers. The outcome would be seen at the autumn Motor Show of which more shortly.

Northern General were in the news when they took ten Fanfare coaches, but on the comparatively rare Guy LUF chassis when all others at this time were on AEC Reliances. Guy Arab IV double-deckers were also going down the line at this time, but they would travel much further afield, being for Kenya, Tanganyika and Uganda, part of a United Transport contract, all with Orion bodywork.

At the 1956 Motor Show Weymann's exhibits included the Arcadian coach, number M6629 and a handsome (though tin-fronted) double-decker for Southport, body number M7322. As always, some vehicles were on the MCW stands, some were on chassis manufacturer's stands, and some were in the demonstration park outside the main exhibition hall.

One of the highlights at the Show had not yet come Weymann's way, though that would very soon change. Leyland was showing its Leyland-MCW Atlantean, a revolutionary new type of double-deck bus with the engine mounted at the rear and entrance at the extreme front. Potential customer reactions varied, but a capacity of up to 78 seats was not going to be ignored. After the Show it was put out for demonstration and operator reaction was assessed, and engineering matters were addressed. Three main conclusions were apparently reached: the concept was very good, the price was likely to be a discouragement, and the integral construction was even more likely to be a deterrent. Leyland went back to the drawing board.

As autumn 1956 gave way to winter a series of events took place which brought good news to some and bad news to others. In November United Molasses purchased Homfray Davies's 2,474 shares which at that time were valued at 25 shillings each, (£1.25p). Sadly, however, with the end of the RT contract some time earlier, J-Building was closed with many redundancies. Walter Dodsworth would have seen first hand how Park Royal coped with the end of the same contract; not having had a separate workforce must have made matters even more difficult. The year end results showed 528 buses plus 105 MoS vehicles. Again, the report concluded that conditions were difficult but that there was a satisfactory profit.

During 1956 and the early part of 1957 there was a fascinating variety of export business from Station Road, with single-deck Worldmasters and Tiger Cubs being sent to Africa, Persia (Iran), South America, the Caribbean, Portugal, Ireland and the Isle of Man. More unusually for Africa, 15 Leyland OPD2 Titans with Orion bodies were completed for Kampala in Uganda, following the earlier order for Guys mentioned above. Unfortunately, before very long the rough roads in Uganda combined with regular overloading caused problems with the main bearers and a remedial team led by Jack Guarnori was sent out to rectify the problem but the facilities were rather basic and the work was carried out *al fresco*.

In the political field, world events again hit the headlines in 1957 as Harold MacMillan took over as Prime Minister from the ailing Anthony Eden. Changes nearer home in the Weymann's boardroom in the City saw CG Allott, who had earlier been UM's Secretary, appointed as Weymann's Chairman in February, whilst GW Scott jnr was appointed a Director as a UM nominee. Two further major

Atlas shouldered the weight of the world – some operators of early Atlanteans knew just how he must have felt. (JAS)

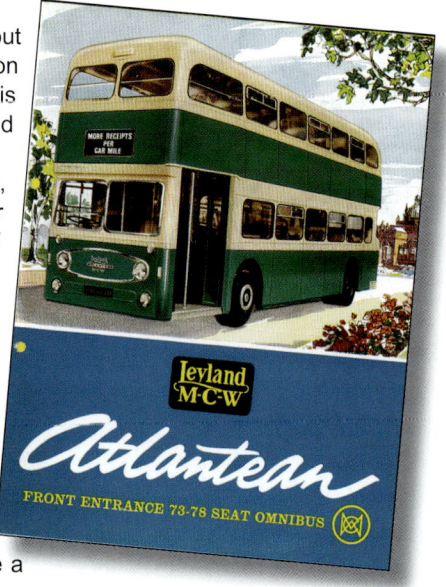

138

The huge output of RTs and RTLs from the separate factory 'down the road' at Weybridge had carried their own series of body numbers, using the prefix W, by then superfluous since the Flexible Patent bodies had been discontinued from 1940. That series finished at W2170 and a new series was started at W2201 for the prototype Weymann's Routemaster, RML3. Sadly, it was destined to be a series containing just the one number. (PG)

Opinions as to the merits of tin fronts varied; Sheffield took Regent IIIs and improved the otherwise unattractive Orion by having the Regent V front end fitted, as seen here on M7067, WWB 754, from a batch M7066-7101 for the Corporation and M7102-10 for the joint railway fleet. The vehicles were delivered between April and July 1956.

Facing: Chief Inspector George Page with one of the Kampala Orions, complete with its bi-lingual wording on the bulkhead and international advertising. George came to Weymann's with Arthur Froggatt in 1934, and remained there until final closure. His wife worked in the buying department with Maurice Bullivant, whilst his daughter Shirley and son Bob were also part of the huge Weymann's 'family'.

events occurred away from the factory in March when the Treaty of Rome was signed, forming the Common Market, and Commercial television broadcasting began. Which was to be the lesser of the two evils depends on your point of view.

In the Station Road works a small team were working on what they saw as the bright hope for the future – a new integral double-decker bus for London based on AEC running units and with a body designed by London Transport. This was to be the next generation's means of transport but with a large surplus of brand new RT buses (many sitting without wheels and supported by oil drums in London country depots) no more production orders were expected until 1958. The Weymann Routemaster, RM3, the third prototype, used Leyland running units and was delivered to its new owners in July 1957 but when those orders were announced they went to Park Royal. This naturally meant that in Addlestone there was little acceptance of Harold MacMillan's provocative declaration that collectively "You've never had it so good". At the year end the output was recorded as 508 buses,

139

Where elegance and presentation were concerned some of the municipalities were still in the premier league in the late 1950s, though spray painting and minimal relief colour were already the order of the day with BET and Tilling fleets. Rochdale took 40 of these handsome Regent Vs, which had Gardner engines, in 1956, M7174-7213, spread from May to November. The four-bay body and AEC front sit happily together. M7182 was photographed by AEC at Windmill Lane works in May, showing off its dark blue and cream livery before heading north.

Southport also maintained high standards and M7322, MWM 38 from a batch of six buses delivered in 1956, is seen in the famous Lord Street. The four-bay body is an Aurora, the third batch of almost identical vehicles. The Leyland front is perhaps not as neat as the AEC one above, but even so this must be classed as a very handsome design. MWM 42 from this batch had been shown at the 1956 Motor Show. Manager Jackson Hoggard was the son of the late Richard Hoggard who had been Manager at Chesterfield for 20 years until 1950 when he retired through ill health. Richard's brother worked for Crossley Motors and his cousin Brian Jackson Burton (above) was employed in Weymann's drawing office until closure. (KWS)

140

North Western Road Car Co, based in Stockport, took substantial numbers of Weymann's bodies in the 1950s, including lowbridge double-deckers on Leyland PD2 chassis, as seen here with M7346, KDB 669, in Manchester's Piccadilly bus station. The newly delivered vehicle looks pristine in its red and ivory livery, but the batch of ten lost their smart appearance quite quickly and never had the panache of the previous delivery with 'proper' Addlestone bodies. When they acquired the later mainly red livery their appearance soon became very mundane indeed. (MAT)

The single-deck fleet included Hermes single-deck buses on Leyland Royal Tiger, Tiger Cub, AEC Reliance and Albion Aberdonian chassis, in addition to the small number of Olympic and Atkinson models seen on page 108. The neat and businesslike interior reminds us of the days when seats were intended to be comfortable and inviting. The line-up in Buxton would be typical of North Western's fleet as seen in many locations, working local or express duties. The later BET livery, adopted as cost cutting measures were implemented throughout the group, is now evident. Comparison between the three Tiger Cubs – FDB 562/3, and the later KDB 638 – shows that the latter's body has deeper windcreen glasses, perhaps to improve driver visibility. (MAT top; KWS foot)

141

The Fanfare, the name coming from the fan-like cross section of the framing, made clever use of flat glass around the front whilst giving the impression of streamlining. The 37-seat body, on a Reliance chassis, weighed in at 6tons 4cwt 2qtrs. This Grey Cars example was registered ROD 750 with body number M7017 from May 1955. Below is the Fanfare interior from the North Western Show model, and below right the 'continental step' which allowed passengers to alight safely when the coach was being used in left hand drive situations 'on the other side of the road' overseas.

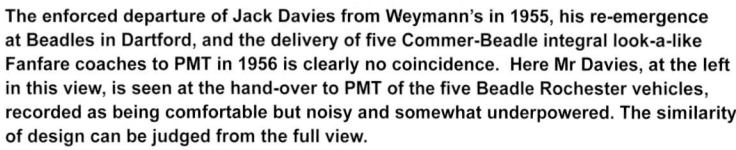

The enforced departure of Jack Davies from Weymann's in 1955, his re-emergence at Beadles in Dartford, and the delivery of five Commer-Beadle integral look-a-like Fanfare coaches to PMT in 1956 is clearly no coincidence. Here Mr Davies, at the left in this view, is seen at the hand-over to PMT of the five Beadle Rochester vehicles, recorded as being comfortable but noisy and somewhat underpowered. The similarity of design can be judged from the full view.

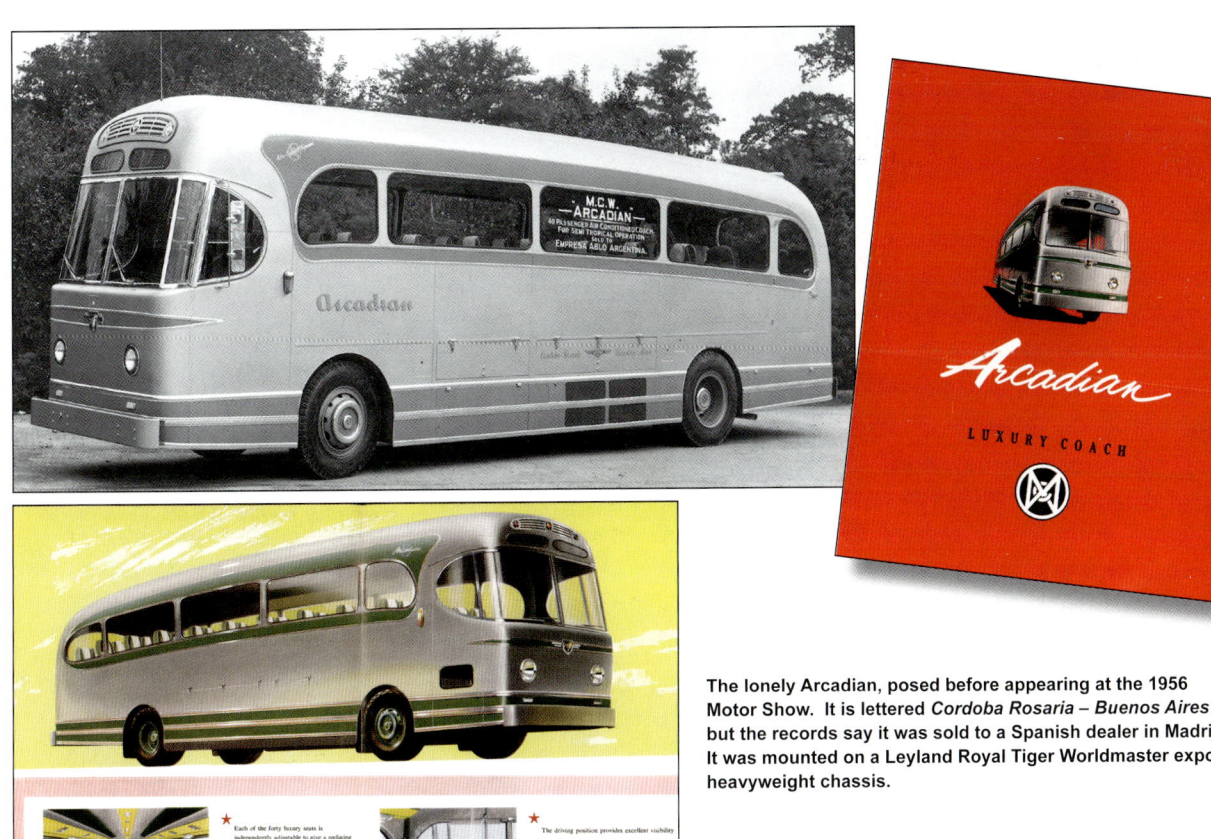

The lonely Arcadian, posed before appearing at the 1956 Motor Show. It is lettered *Cordoba Rosaria – Buenos Aires* but the records say it was sold to a Spanish dealer in Madrid. It was mounted on a Leyland Royal Tiger Worldmaster export heavyweight chassis.

with apparently no MoS deliveries that year. UM's comments merely repeated the previous two year's remarks. There was, however, one milestone. It was noted that 1,000 Olympics had now been built.

The following year (1958) was once again Motor Show year and yet again Leyland would be calling the shots, now with production versions of its new type of double-decker with the engine situated at the rear. The Atlantean would be a mainstay of MCW's double-deck output from now on, although there were still many operators who heeded their engineer's advice to leave well alone until others had sorted out the problems. And there was to be no shortage of those for some time to come.

Nineteen-fifty-eight saw a series of landmarks, some directly affecting Weymann's, others signifying the ongoing march of technology. Motoring buffs will remember the year for the introduction of Alex Issigonis's BMC mini car and Beardmore taxi production at Station Road; aircraft and travel enthusiasts will recall that regular jet passenger service to America began now. This new form of propulsion reduced travelling time such that the round trip sales visits to North America, South America and Africa, for instance, could now be accomplished in days rather than months as previously. On a different level, but much more important to most ordinary people, the arrival of Subscriber Trunk Dialling (STD), inaugurated by Her Majesty Queen Elizabeth, meant that it was now possible to reach more and more places by dialling direct instead of having to ask the operator to make the connection. The days of the in-house telephonist having sole contact with the outside world were coming to an end, though international dialling was some way off yet.

Another form of communication which would soon directly affect Weymann's finishing shop personnel probably meant nothing to most of them when it was announced that the first motorway in Britain – the Preston by-pass – would shortly be constructed. Some 250 miles from Addlestone its significance would become clearer when a Metro-Cammell shell on Atlantean chassis for Ribble Motor Services (of Preston) arrived for completion as a motorway coach to be fitted with galleys and toilet, reclining seats and provision for a hostess to look after passengers.

143

When Glasgow decided to take some single-deck buses for a standee experiment in 1956 they took 30 of the Royal Tiger Worldmaster export chassis, doubtless thinking of the heavy loads these buses were likely to be carrying. The frames were supplied by Weymann's, M7383-7412 and they were then fitted out and completed in the Corporation's famous Coplawhill works, where so many trams had been built. The single-deckers were finished with two doors and 42 seats, as seen here. When the experiment was over, like the trolleybus from 1950 (page 99) they were converted to single door configuration as seen in the centre view. Glaswegians were not for standing, no matter how hard the management tried to convince them of the merits and the fact that their continental cousins always expected to have to stand. Four of the converted batch saw further service with Southend after a busy life in Glasgow. (MAT; STA)

North Western took a leaf from Midland Red's books when their dual-purpose versions of the new Hermes body arrived in 1957 and used a striking red with black top livery. Aldershot & District's two shades of green was equally striking but perhaps slightly more refined. Here a 1957 Reliance, M8198, stands alongside a Trent Weymann-bodied Tiger Cub. (JAS)

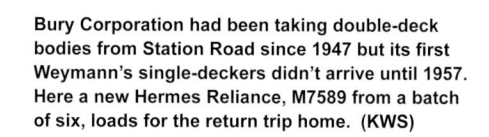

Bury Corporation had been taking double-deck bodies from Station Road since 1947 but its first Weymann's single-deckers didn't arrive until 1957. Here a new Hermes Reliance, M7589 from a batch of six, loads for the return trip home. (KWS)

Stockton Corporation took eight of these Titan PD2 models, M9157-64, and M9163, 276 DUP is seen here in October 1959. Note the opening windows at the front of the upper deck and the somewhat unusual hoppers in the side windows. Since Stockton is not known to be blessed with above-average hot sunshine perhaps it had a high proportion of tobacco smokers using its upper saloon seats.

Conversely, Newcastle Corporation decided to do without any side window ventilation in its 30ft PD3 Titans as shown on M7657, 182 AVK, from a batch of ten M7651-60 delivered in September 1959. This would be part of the weight-reduction drive which gave many early Orions such a bad name. (AEJ)

The stylish Regent V front as seen here was rather spoiled by Rhondda's all-over red livery which looked good only if seen in the sunshine, and otherwise had little to commend it. M7508, VTX 426 from a batch of 20, is seen when new and clearly shows the forward entrance, then making a come back, doubtless partially influenced by the new Leyland Atlantean with its entrance at the very front. The angled bulkhead window to allow the driver to turn round and collect fares was some years ahead of its time. (STA)

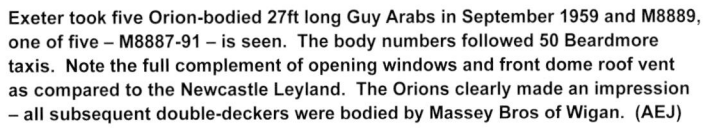

Exeter took five Orion-bodied 27ft long Guy Arabs in September 1959 and M8889, one of five – M8887-91 – is seen. The body numbers followed 50 Beardmore taxis. Note the full complement of opening windows and front dome roof vent as compared to the Newcastle Leyland. The Orions clearly made an impression – all subsequent double-deckers were bodied by Massey Bros of Wigan. (AEJ)

145

Bournemouth took three batches of these splendid Sunbeam MF2B trolleybuses with dual-door bodywork and body number M8235 was the 1958 Show Exhibit. Here M8241, WRU 266, from that first batch of 20, M8233-52, delivered from October 1958 to spring 1959, negotiates Richmond Hill, one of the town's steep roads out of the famous Square. Further batches followed later, in 1959 and then in 1962. The bodies seated 62, a low capacity due to the two entrances and two sets of staircases. Bournemouth's trolleybus system was closed in 1969, making a depressingly short life for such fine vehicles. (JAS)

In direct contrast to the Rhondda vehicle on the previous page, here we have a City of Oxford Regent V with the exposed radiator Regent III front end. Gleaming even on a dull day and having been preserved, M7531, built in 1956, was photographed at an enthusiasts' day at the Gateshead MetroCentre. (JAS)

Facing page centre: Fishwick's Orion M7831 was one of six delivered in February 1958, and is seen here after withdrawal for preservation. The company was Leyland's nearest customer, being only minutes away from the various factories belonging to the chassis manufacturer (and earlier body maker) in the town from which it took its name. It was posed where generations of works buses had stood, waiting to take employees home at the end of their shifts before the age of mass car ownership speeded on the demise of bus manufacturing. (JAS)

Addlestone-built Orions can be identified by the right-angled junction of cantrail and windscreen, above, whereas Birmingham examples feature the corner moulding, below. (JAS courtesy Chris Lonnergan)

Brighton Corporation took 20 of these 27ft long Leyland Titan PD2s in 1959, body numbers M8355-74, and more would follow later. The later Brighton buses were amongst the last to be built at Weymann's factory. (STA)

146

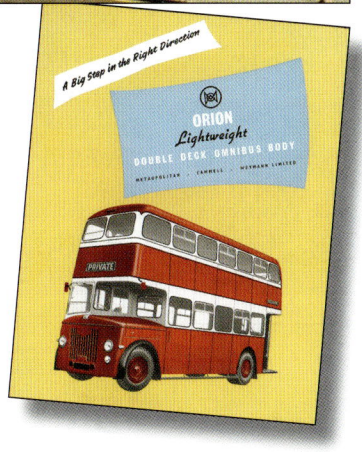

Top of the page: A contrast in body types as two Chesterfield vehicles approach the camera. On our left highbridge M9181 of January 1960, 233 LRB, comes alongside M46 (post fire numbering) of July 1961 with a lowbridge body. Both vehicles have the slight V-fronted body design shown more clearly on the illustrations on pages 136/7. The two bonnet front styles will also be noticed. The flat-fronted development of the Orion body seen on the other four vehicles on these two pages always struck the Author as more workman-like and rather more in keeping with the rest of the body design. (STA)

Offering another comparison, this time between the 27ft version opposite and the 30ft Orion bodies here, is Bury Corporation's GEN 201, M7556, once again seen in preservation and with its lady owner at the wheel. Bury took 25 of these 73-seat vehicles in 1958/9. (JAS)

147

The 30 Reliances taken by Aldershot & District in spring 1957 were fitted for one-man-operation and express work. Higher backed seats than normal were fitted and M7672, RCG 624, from the batch M7667-96 is seen above left. The driver's cabin, above, on a later delivery, seems rather elaborate by today's standards.

Mexborough & Swinton took two Hermes standee vehicles, M7528/9, in January 1957. Fitted with a partial 2+1 seating arrangement as seen left, they carried 32 seated and 29 standing passengers. Second of the pair M7529, SWW 51, is posed on the railway crossing at Denaby. (STA)

Relegated to driver training duties, this Southend Leyland PD2, M7708, MHJ 925, was one of six – M7708-13 – delivered in July 1956. Southend were also taking bodies from Massey Bros of Pemberton, Wigan at this time. The town's trolleybuses had been withdrawn in 1954 but Weymann's had never bodied any of them. (RM)

CUTSCA and AMDET were the two principal operators in Uruguay and here we see a Royal Tiger Worldmaster from the batch M7783-92, delivered in 1957/8, in the yard behind the factory. Much larger orders would soon follow.

During September 1957 Hull took ten Hermes two-door bodies, M7928-37, on Reliance chassis and M7937 is seen here operating a driver-only service. (STA)

Exports much nearer to home involved four sets of frames – M7876-9 – in 1957 for Lough Swilly in Ireland. The bodies were completed locally and ZP 4344, M7877, which was finished by Dublin Vehicle Builders, is seen here alongside a wartime Bedford bus. (MAT)

149

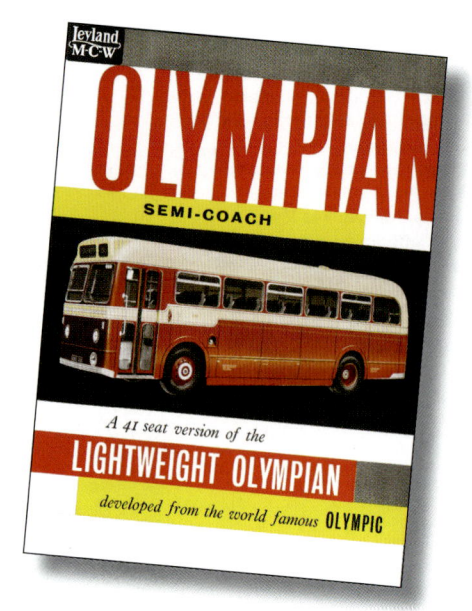

Western Welsh took the only coach-seated Olympians, LW53-8, in November 1958 and OUH 490, L58, last of the batch, is seen here. (GW)

The Weymann Fanfare coach was designed in conjunction with the Chief Engineer of South Wales Transport, Frank Mason. Initially fitted to AEC Reliance chassis but later also to Leyland Leopards, it was Weymann's first true luxury coach though an express version was also later produced. M7646, NCY 626 of June 1956, has been preserved and is seen here in Bristol docks at a vintage vehicle rally. (JAS)

Fanfare coaches were usually found with BET fleets but an unusual exception was this example delivered to Salford City Transport with a high-specification body for use by members of the council's various committees. On the formation of Selnec in 1969 it quickly found itself on more lucrative outings, including an Executive Express service to Manchester Airport. (GMTS)

Aldershot & District and North Western Road Car shared a common Chairman at the time these one-man equipped Reliances, the last single-deck bodies from Station Road, were delivered, both fleets taking the new style body with almost identical mouldings and paint style. Perhaps it was no coincidence. M9485, delivered in February 1961, is seen here on a local service rather beneath its standing, although they could be used for express work when required. (RR)

150

Hermes bodies were less common outside the BET fleets but Leicester was one of the municipalities to take the model. Here M7706, OJF 193, one of four on Tiger Cub chassis delivered in October 1956, unloads at the terminus of the outer circle route as the driver watches progress. In 1958 a further, single, example was delivered, body number M8460, registered SJF 212. (STA)

Not quite what it seems – URR 353 delivered to East Midland Motor Services in December 1956 was an example built in the MCCW Elmdon factory. MCCW also supplied batches of double-deckers to EMMS in between Weymann's deliveries. The next Hermes bodies from Station Road for East Midland would be body numbers M8051-60 in June 1957. (AEJ)

Maidstone & District took 12 Reliances with 42 seats and equipped for one-man-operation in late 1956 and early 1957. The provision of the roof side panel for advertising, here shown in relief colour, markedly changes the appearance of the Hermes body. M7723, XKT 993, is seen on a quiet afternoon with just one solitary passenger. (AEJ)

151

The Atlantean Era Arrives at Station Road

We saw that in 1956 Leyland had displayed its new and advanced rear-engined double-decker at that year's Motor Show. Now, two years later, the fruits of its reassessment would become clear, and MCW's involvement would mean both factories would soon be busy building bodies on the separate chassis replacement. The 1956 prototype, registered 281 ATC, had been designated as model PDR1 and incorporated an underframe with a flat floor onto which the body had been constructed. Now the new successor, designated PDR1/1, was a more conventional chassis, except for its engine position.

When the Commercial Motor Show came round again in September 1958 Leyland were showing three Atlanteans with bodywork from the MCW organisation and one with Alexander bodywork for Glasgow (their LA1). MCCW had bodied RTH 637 for James of Ammanford, a BET Company, and FHF 451 for Wallasey, being of lowheight and normal configuration respectively. The Weymann-bodied vehicle, M8776, another lowheight vehicle, was the first of a batch of 14 for Maidstone & District, and registered 43 DKT. It was to feature extensively in advertising and publicity material, some linked to the changeover of the Hastings trolleybuses to motor bus operation in June 1959.

The PDR1/1 model differed in several major respects but crucially it did not allow the incorporation of a low gangway in the lower deck and thus to produce a lowheight version it was now necessary to go back to the unpopular but effective side gangway layout, this time at the rear of the upper deck and affecting the rearmost three rows of seats. The overall unladen height of the two models was 14ft 6in and 13ft 4in respectively. Clearly, the full height model with level floor in the upper saloon was more attractive but the solution did not appear until Leyland announced the PDR1/2 model with the Albion drop-centre rear axle, and it became possible to have all seats accommodated in a normal saloon layout without losing the ability to maintain height under 13ft 5in unladen.

Orders were placed for over 200 Atlanteans at the 1958 Show, the majority for BET fleets, and during 1959 Station Road bodied lowheight PDR1/1 examples for Maidstone (14) and PMT (35), with smaller orders being completed for Yorkshire Traction (12), Trent (11) and East Midland (10). Deliveries began in 1959 and ran through until the year end. Because MCW had been involved in the concept from the start, working with Leyland, they had valuable experience of potential problem areas, especially concerning the cantilevering of the hefty power pack at the rear of the body. Additional strengthening was built into the body structure to compensate, but experience in service would later prove that more was necessary. Quite separately it became necessay to fit stronger road springs and a modified model became available, being designated the PDR1/1 Mark 2.

Well-known operator, Silver Star of Porton Down, became the first independent to take an Atlantean, M9014, TMW 853, yet another lowheight vehicle, for use on

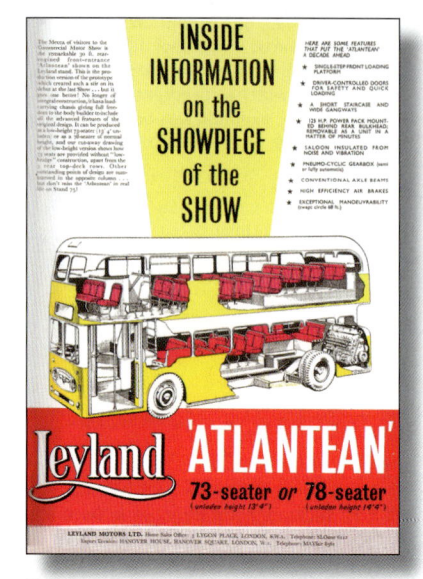

Brochure for the PDR1/1 Atlantean with its partial side gangway layout for the low height – 13ft 4in – version.

The interior of Silver Star's semi-low height coach-seated Atlantean, M9730, is believed to be unique with this type of seating. Seen right is the preserved bus-seated version, M358, showing the splendid livery of this one-time favourite. (JAS).

152

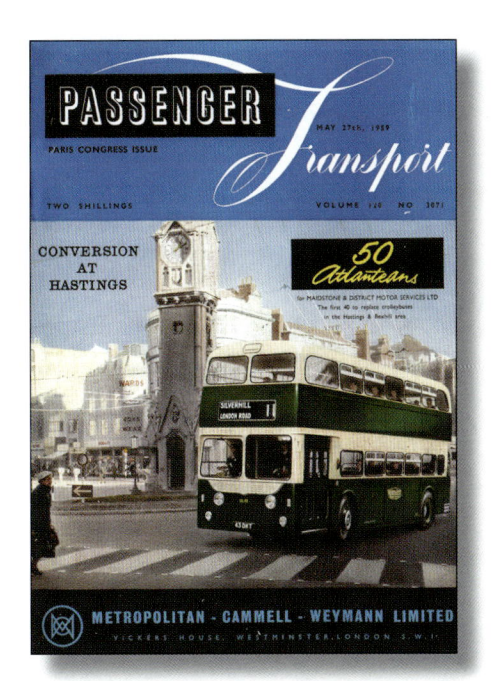

The M&D contract made good publicity material as seen here on a trade magazine cover advertisement.

its troop contracts. Silver Star would take three more Atlanteans, including one – M9730 – with coach seating within its lowheight structure as shown opposite. Another, M358, 1234 MW survives in preservation as a reminder of that organisation's splendid livery and turn out.

Maidstone's DK 43, mentioned earlier and displayed at the 1958 Motor Show, was the first Atlantean from Weymann's and was fitted with the lowheight body. It featured in publicity material as seen opposite. Arrangements between the two factories were such that for some time most lowheight models were produced at Addlestone. Potteries Motor Traction were amongst the next customers for this combination, and although the model quickly gained a reputation for being unreliable and problematical, PMT went on to take 105 examples – claimed to be the largest fleet of lowheight PDR1s in the world – and operated them successfully right up to 1980. Where there's a will . . . ? Clearly, the BET engineers were in a position to pool their knowledge and experience but the successful day-to-day operation had to be down to careful monitoring and good engineering practices. One obvious problem was the location of the driver, some 30ft away from the engine, and thus out of earshot of any warning noises. When these came they were advance notice of expensive problems.

Alongside these Atlanteans there was still a steady flow of front-engined Leyland Titan PD2 and PD3 models, together with AEC Regent Vs. There was a reluctance to adopt the so-called 'tin-front' in some fleets, and South Wales took a batch of Regent Vs with traditional radiators. Conversely, there were those who adopted it with some relish. This variety would keep the drawing office staff busy for there was quite a selection of tin-fronts available, including at least two from Leyland, in addition to those from AEC, Crossley and Guy.

In a different league, two of the big export contracts, single-deck Albions for Ceylon, were completed at the end of 1959 with the last of 160 vehicles being despatched from Station Road.

While all eyes were focussed on the Atlanteans the Fanfare coach quietly joined the Leyland camp, having until then been on Reliance chassis only, when Sheffield took six 41-seat express examples in August 1959 on Leopard L1 chassis, M9016-21 as seen here with M9019, 1504 WJ. Southdown took Fanfares on Tiger Cubs soon afterwards as shown on page 166. After the Construction & Use Regulations were amended in 1962 the Fanfare body was lengthened to 36ft and became the Castilian, see page 173. (JAS)

153

Following the 20 Sunbeam model MF2B trolleybuses delivered in 1958 and seen on page 146, Bournemouth took a further ten of the 63-seat dual-entrance vehicles, M8574-83, in late 1959 and M8581, YLJ 284, is seen here in its operator's fine and much loved livery. (JAS)

This Tiger Cub, M8461, 964 DTJ bodied in February 1958, had been a Leyland demonstrator. It was sold to Merthyr Tydfil. (STA)

Jones Bros of Aberbeeg took this Reliance, M9496, XAX 448, seen leaving the factory in 1960. It has the later BET standard body, but three earlier Hermes examples would join the fleet in 1961 as seen on page 168. (BB)

This page, right, top to bottom:

Weymann's first Atlanteans were 14 semi-lowheight for Maidstone & District. At first the full-height vehicles were built at Metro-Cammell's works but soon both factories built both types, though the lower PDR1/1 were usually associated with Station Road. (DT)

A Weymann-built full-height example in the Yorkshire Woollen fleet of Dewsbury, M43, 665 BWB, originally with Sheffield as seen below, illustrates the difference in body appearance. (AEJ)

The first production Atlantean was delivered to Wallasey Corporation in December 1958, and was built in Birmingham. A full-height example, it survives in preservation and is seen here in nearby Birkenhead docks. (DT)

Below: Completed vehicles were subjected to a water spray test to ensure there were no leaks, and here Sheffield's 1165 awaits its soaking. Peter Gascoine recalled that his aunt's bungalow was situated immediately over the fence here, and if the wind was in the wrong direction when spraying took place on Mondays she had to dash out and take her washing in! (PG)

155

Ribble and PMT were two operators in the BET empire who took quantities of the semi-lowheight Atlantean for bus work, in addition to the former's famous motorway coaches. Such was the demand for this PDR1/1 model, despite the awkward rear seating arrangement which can be clearly seen in the three photographs on the opposite page that production had to be shared between Birmingham and Addlestone, rather than concentrated on the latter as was originally intended. Ribble's RRN 405, left, one of 14 and a 1962 Elmdon product, can be compared with Weymann's M9046, 766 EVT, for PMT, one of 35 delivered in 1959. Both the examples seen here survive in preservation.

Ribble, staunch Leyland supporters, but adopting a cautious attitude, continued to take conventional Titan PD2 and PD3 models, though some had full-fronted forward entrance bodywork. (JAS both)

Ribble's motorway coaches – the Gay Hostesses – were actually distributed between the main fleet and subsidiaries Standerwick and Scout, all being regular attendees at Victoria Coach Station, London. The interior included very comfortable seats, galley and toilet, and a hostess was on board to dispense snacks and ensure passengers were comfortable. The opaque windows at the rear confirm the location of these facilities. The marginal view shows the access to the power unit, looking like the mouth of some basking shark in the original one-piece version. Ease of access and the need to eliminate a sometimes badly fitting engine shroud led to a three-piece alternative later being introduced.

Top: The rear aspect of the Atlantean bustle soon became familiar throughout the land as the model joined more and more operators. PMT's fleet of the semi-lowheight Atlantean PDR1/1 bus was reputed to be the largest in the world.

Above: Ribble allocated these full-height coaches into its three fleets, instantly recognisable with their distinctive livery and opaque rear glasses. The open hatch for topping up the cooling water may not be a very good sign so early in the journey. (JAS: STA)

This page top to bottom:

The lower deck interior sported a five-seat bench which neatly fitted over the power pack.

The rear three rows of seats on the semi-lowheight PDR1/1 incorporated a side gangway layout reminiscent of the original awkward 'true lowbridge' models which Bristol had superseded when its Lodekka was launched some years earlier, and Dennis was now also offering in its Loline, built under licence from Bristol. Note that the rearmost seats in this example are divided into two, with one seat slightly forward of the other, a trick first employed by West Yorkshire Road Car nearly twenty years earlier in an attempt to prevent well nourished passengers exceeding their legitimate space! After clambering up to the seats the elevation did give passengers slightly better vision.

157

CHAPTER 13 – 1960-62

Fire; Motor Show; Exports save the day

After the relative success of the early to mid-'fifties, the end of the RT3 contract, and the associated redundancies, marked a watershed and five years later it appeared that the company was still facing the future with some concerns. Certainly the United Molasses Board saw it that way, recording that "production was still unsatisfactory due to lack of orders".

From a high of 972 buses built in 1949, a figure never to be achieved again, the output as recorded by Norman Froggatt in his summary of the annual output between 1929 and closure in 1966 shows a downward spiral. Norman, the last Works Manager of the Company, prepared these figures as the records and documentation were being packed away to be sent to Birmingham in the final clear out in January 1966. I am grateful to Keith Barkham for having the foresight to keep Norman's original list which has been most useful.

Norman's figures are particularly interesting since they are taken from the official contemporary records by the man in charge, and also because they record the summaries of non-psv content of Ministry of Supply contracts, and taxis, something which does not feature in the enthusiasts' lists prepared by the PSV Circle. There are apparent discrepancies between the summary which Norman bequeathed us and other published lists and I believe these can be explained by the following factors: the difference between calendar year-ends and financial year-ends and/or the difference between completion, delivery, and into-service dates. All the information published is offered in good faith, however.

The 'sixties were to be a time of great change. The 42-hour week made its appearance in 1960, as did Lady Chatterley when 200,000 copies of the unexpurgated version of that famous book were finally printed after a ruling that it was not obscene. Marking the march of technology the Government agreed to part fund a supersonic airliner – Concorde as it became – whilst the laser and the first vertical-take-off plane (VTOL) made their appearance. National Service was now coming to an end and the last conscripts were called up during this year.

In the factory Godfrey Chesson was now Contracts Manager and was addressing the fact that James Don was still telling him (and UM) that overcapacity and small profits were a serious problem, even though there was steady production. He noted in the *Financial Times* that Jaguar had taken over Daimler and wondered how that would affect matters, especially as there was to be a Weymann's-bodied Daimler exhibit at the Motor Show later in the year.

Godfrey Chesson joined MCW in 1950 as a technical representative, having earlier been part of Eastbourne's maintenance team. He later moved to Weymann's, becoming Contracts Manager by 1960. (BB)

The Trent Motor Traction Company, a BET subsidiary based in Derby, took 16 of these semi-lowheight Atlanteans soon after their introduction in 1959/60. The next ten were supplied after the 1961 fire and carried body numbers from the new series, M246-55, and here the first, 65 ACH, is seen arriving in Derby in July 1962. They joined a fleet which operated many vehicles bodied at Station Road including single-deck and double-deck buses, dual-purpose vehicles and Fanfare coaches. Latterly their buses were finished in the darker BET shade of red as seen here. (STA)

158

Lisbon's transport origins owe their finance to Weymann's original owners, the Bernhard Scholle Bank, owned by Central Mining and Investment Corporation of South Africa, as explained in Volume One. They bought their first buses in 1940 to be used in the celebrations to commemorate Portugal's Centenary. They remained regular customers and between 1958 and 1960 took two batches of AEC Regent Vs totalling 46 vehlcles. One of the 64-seat front-entrance buses is seen here in a vibrant city street scene. (STA)

Edinburgh took a fleet of 50 Tiger Cubs, M9430-79, between July 1960 and January 1961 and M9469, VSC 93, is seen here in busy Princes Street operating a flat fare service which cost 3p. The Hermes bodies carried 47 passengers by having 3+2 seats in most of the saloon. Externally the vehicles were fitted with the heavy duty mouldings from the Olympic style bodies to Edinburgh's own specification. M9444 was displayed at the 1960 Commercial Motor Show. Following the success of the vehicles in service a further order was placed for another 50. (STA)

Contracts going through the works in the early months of the year included four Atlanteans for Chesterfield (following on from a batch of PD2s), and Atlanteans for Trent, Western Welsh, Newcastle and Ribble subsidiary Standerwick, together with a single example for Silver Star. There were large numbers of Reliances to be seen, including batches for South Wales, Maidstone & District, Oxford and PMT.

As the year progressed there were some interesting export orders including Regent Vs for Lisbon, and Albion and Leyland single-deckers for Barbados.

It was once again Motor Show year and a varied selection was prepared for display on the MCW stands and by other manufacturers, notably Leyland. One of Halifax's forward-entrance Titan PD2 models in its distinctive livery was shown, and carrying the name Aurora (again), whilst an Edinburgh Tiger Cub with its mainly 3+2 seating managed to accommodate 47 passengers and was one of only two full-sized single-deckers in the hall. Across the aisle was one of Sheffield's Atlanteans in its attractive cream and blue livery. Most significant, however, was the Weymann's double-decker on the Daimler stand. Looking for all the world like an Atlantean the difference soon became apparent when it revealed that by the use of a drop-centre rear axle it could seat 78 passengers in normal configuration – *ie* without the side gangway on the upper deck – and yet keep within 13ft 4in overall height. MCW had designed a new body to suit both chassis, and the brochure is reproduced here. Leyland would now have to adopt the same driveline for its Atlantean or it would find itself being left behind. The Daimler, christened Fleetline, used a Daimler power pack but this was later exchanged for a Gardner unit. On the Leyland stand was one of the single-deck Worldmasters similar to the Belgrade vehicles from Addlestone from a Birmingham contract for 120 for Madrid.

By the time of the Motor Show there had been a worrying development for MCW when Duple, who had already acquired Willowbrook, announced that they had purchased Blackpool-based builder Burlingham. Although Duple were principally coach builders these acquisitions were builders of both buses and coaches and whilst the Willowbrook factory would later be closed there was considerable capacity in Blackpool with two factories, one being quite modern.

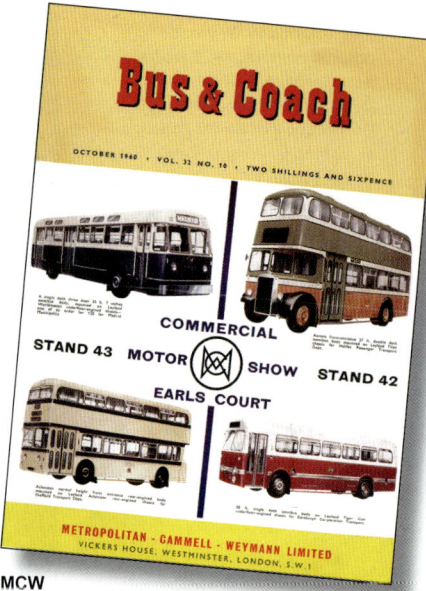

MCW advert on the cover of *Bus and Coach* for October 1960 showing Madrid, Halifax, Sheffield and Edinburgh vehicles displayed at the Motor Show.

MCW's 1960 brochure showing the different possible seating arrangements for Atlantean and Fleetline models, and also the MCCW Liverpool design on the Atlantean chassis.

160

Newcastle took 20 Atlanteans, M1331-50, in late 1963 using Alexander front screens as specified by the operator, thereby making them similar to examples for Bournemouth delivered in 1964. M1333 stands in the yard waiting to be delivered to its customer. Further examples would be built for Newcastle in 1965, as seen on page 181.

Jamaica Omnibus Services was a BET outpost whose General Manager in 1955-7, Ivor Gray, was well-known to Weymann's. He had previously been GM at South Wales Transport and after his two year contract returned to take charge at Rhondda, and then the giant Western Welsh concern. JOS took three Leyland Comets, M9502-4, built at Station Road in 1960 but the main business was with Metro-Cammell for hundreds of Olympics in a contract which was still running after Weymann's had closed. One is shown in the lower view.

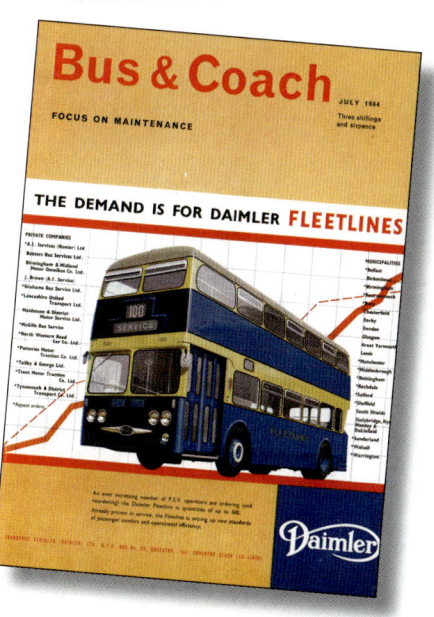

M9617, the Daimler CRD6 Fleetline registered 7000 HP, was shown at the Motor Show in 1960. Finished as a demonstrator in Birmingham's dark blue and pale cream colours it was later sold to Tailby & George as seen in the lower right view. Sadly, it was destroyed by fire in their garage in 1976. Note the very severe upright aspect of the upper deck, much more so than the similar body for the Atlantean, and the projection of the body beyond the engine bustle. Its technical advances obliged Leyland to follow suit. (STA; AEJ)

Autumn 1960 saw this line up being recorded. The Beardmore taxi faces one of the Olympic Series 2 buses built at Addlestone, L151-240, followed by an Atlantean PDR1/1 for Potteries, a Lisbon Regent V and, bringing up the rear, one of Edinburgh's 50 Tiger Cubs.

However, fascinating as the details of the vehicle contracts might be, there can be no doubt that the defining moment in this part of the story occurred during the night of Tuesday 4th July 1961 when fire swept through the factory causing what the *Surrey Herald* on Friday of that fateful week described as 'Addlestone's worst night since the war'. One third of the main factory was gutted and 450 employees were temporarily put out of work. Fortunately, no one was injured but the Chief Fire Officer was quoted as saying that only a drop in the wind had allowed them to save many parts of the works. Even the offices, fronting on to Station Road, were in danger of being totally engulfed.

Below left: Bournemouth's later motor buses could not match the elegance of its modern trolleybuses as this PD3 rear-entrance front exit Orion, M9530, 8151 EL of October 1960, demonstrates. There were ten in the batch, numbers M9526-35. (STA)

Below: After being withdrawn from service 225 LRB was presented to Chesterfield's German twin town of Darmstadt for display. It was later returned to its home town where it passed into the care of one of the employees and can regularly be seen at vintage vehicle rallies. (STA)

162

MOORES of Weybridge — FORD DISTRIBUTORS — CARS · VANS · TRUCKS · SERVICE · PARTS

Surrey Herald

No. 3,590 70th YEAR   FRIDAY, JULY 7, 1961

FIRE GUTS WEYMANNS WORKS

Addlestone's worst night since the war

450 EMPLOYEES ARE PUT OUT OF JOBS

FIRE swept through Weymann's factory at Addlestone on Tuesday night. In a few terrifying hours flames leaping 100 ft. gutted a third of the main factory.

Damage has not yet been assessed, but it is believed to be at least £500,000. Approximately 450 employees are temporarily out of work.

It was the worst night Addlestone has seen since the end of the war, with the streets alive with huge crowds. The roads were jammed with parked cars as police drafted in from all over the area battled to keep the roads clear for the fire engines and ambulances. The blaze lit up the sky and could be seen several miles.

Damage would have been much worse but for a lull in the wind that had whipped the building into a blazing inferno within 20 minutes of the fire starting. At one time it was feared that the whole office block, fronting the main road, would be involved.

Firemen from surrounding sections in the county, using 10 appliances, including several pumps and 15 jets, fought for over an hour to bring the blaze under control.

Headed by the Chief Fire Officer (Mr. Johnstone), they cordoned off the area, but it was only the drop in the wind that saved many parts of the works.

Inside, many thousands of pounds worth of coaches and double-deck buses were ablaze. The "secret" 40 ft. cabin cruiser on which work had been in progress only for three months was severely damaged. No personal injuries were reported.

'VERY SERIOUS'

On Wednesday morning, the General Manager, Mr. W. H. Lawrence, said the situation was "very serious." He could not give an accurate estimate of damage nor could he say how long the men would be laid-off.

It was hoped to re-start production "shortly," and employees would be notified.

The welded hull of the boat which was the cause of the catastrophe stands by fire-damaged buildings in the view alongside, with the extent of the destruction being plain to see above right.

One of Bournemouth's trolleybuses was damaged beyond repair and a one-off replacement was financially out-of-the-question. Accordingly, the contract was completed with only nine vehicles being delivered. Two M&D buses were also destroyed. (PG)

The sorry remains awaiting the insurance assessor's verdict. In the event two single-deckers from a contract for Maidstone & District were condemned but were able to be replaced, the Reliance chassis being readily available from AEC, unlike the bespoke Sunbeam trolleybus chassis.

163

After Effects Of The Fire

On the morning following the fire the General Manager, Bill Lawrence, confirmed that the situation was extremely serious and that only the Works Firemen, Maintenance Men and General Staff would be allowed in. All other employees were to be sent home while the situation was assessed. The London Salvage Squad had been brought in to help clear the terrible mess and make the damaged buildings safe. Amy Partridge and her neighbour Ray Cox still remembered being woken up in the middle of the night as the word went round and that her husband Bill and the works firemen had been called out when I interviewed them in 2001.

The cause of the fire was an overflow of pitch from a barrel which had been left, by design, on a low level of gas heat to prepare it for use the following morning. The heat was slightly too great and the pitch overflowed onto the open flame causing an immediate conflagration. The pitch was being used as caulk to make watertight the hull of a metal boat which was being built as just one means of trying to find alternative sources of work for the factory. Reports vary as to whether there was more than one boat, but the *Surrey Herald* for 8th May 1962 records the handover of the replacement for the fire-damaged hull, and its imminent departure to Southampton for fitting-out. The hull cost its owner, AT Priddle, a local man and a friend of Managing Director Harold Cook, £3,100. The exact cost of the fire is not recorded.

Inside the ruins of the factory in July 1961 many vehicles had been damaged, some only relatively lightly, others more seriously. Some needed replacement

Ministry contracts were always hard-fought for, and usually only marginally profitable. Ten of these 39-seat army buses on Bedford SB3 chassis were completed in March 1961, numbers M9715-24. The chassis alongside has not so far been precisely identified but is believed to be one of the four tractor units for hauling sugar trailers, body numbers M299-302. (PG)

Rochdale Corporation continued taking Weymann's bodies when it ordered five Reliances of which M190, 2120 DK, was one. They were delivered at the end of the eventful 1961. Nearby Salford City Transport ordered ten Reliances for delivery the following year, nine with single-door bus bodywork of this general outline and one equipped with a high specification Fanfare coach body with tables and 28 leather seats, for use by members of the various council committees going about their official visits.

Below is the James Atlantean, YTH 805, M229, by then in the Oxford fleet and parked amongst vehicles showing the original and later City of Oxford liveries. (JAS)

164

The Belgrade contract for 160 Leyland Royal Tiger Worldmasters took the phrase 'standee-buses' into a new league. The buses were designed to seat only 23, but to take a further 100 standing passengers. And that was only the *designed* load. Just how many would actually be carried might well be something else! Extra strengthening, including double bearers, was incorporated and the vehicles were delivered in two batches between October 1961 and February 1962, carrying body numbers M72-161 and M359-428. Doug Jack in his history of Leyland's activities in this field in *The Leyland Bus* recalls further orders being received following their successful operation. Fare collection might just have been somewhat of a challenge, one imagines. A Leyland contract for 120 Worldmasters for Madrid, built at MCCW's Elmdon plant, used this same body shell as did Weymann's for AMDET and Cuban contracts.

Numerically following the Belgrade contract were 75 Worldmasters for Buenos Aires, M429-503, part of another big Leyland contract split between Olympics and Worldmasters, some bodied by MCW, some by Marshalls, and some chassis to be bodied locally. (PG both)

Ivor Gray was now back from Jamaica and in charge at Western Welsh where his Chief Engineer was facing the challenge of internal reflections in night time coach operation. His solution was to have Weymann's equip a batch of Reliances with bodies incorporating this unique windscreen design. M9672, WKG 134 of May 1961, is shown outside the factory ready for delivery. There were 15 in the contract, M9659-73, and they followed a batch of Fanfare coaches for Trent, making a somewhat startling contrast to passers by. Not surprisingly, perhaps, they remained unique. Gray's boss as Managing Director at Western Welsh was WT James, who, as Chairman of Jamaica Omnibus Services, had been his boss in Gray's stint overseas. Mr James had been a BET Director since 1948 and the Atlantean seen opposite had been new to the BET subsidiary James. (PG)

165

Following the revision of the Construction & Use regulations in 1962 to allow single-deck vehicles on two axles to be up to 36ft long the Hermes body was redesigned and Maidstone & District took advantage of the opportunity to use some of this extra length when they purchased M9208, 290 GKK, with 40-seat dual-purpose bodywork as shown on an AEC Reliance chassis. It was one of a batch of 20, M9197-9216. (AEJ)

By 1959 the Fanfare coach was available on Leyland chassis and Southdown was amongst the first to take up the new option. This Tiger Cub, M9024, XUF 132 of January 1960, is one from a batch of fifteen, M9022-36. Later in 1961, after the fire, a further batch, M57-71 with a mix of 37 and 41-seat bodies, would follow. (STA)

Two of Standerwick's motorway coaches await their return to Blackpool, with a third just out of view. Such duplication confirms the attraction of these vehicles with their on-board snacks, toilet and deep comfortable seats. The 24 vehicles in the batch, M9394-9417, were split between Standerwick and Ribble's main fleet, with the first four going to the Blackpool subsidiary. M9395/7 are shown and would return via the M1 motorway and the Preston by-pass, the first such length of motorway in the country. The driver does not look too impressed with the situation – let's hope things improve. (STA)

Trips to the south coast were *par for the course* from Station Road but trolleybus deliveries were always more interesting, the vehicles needing towing of course. In this view one of the 'Bournemouth Nine' makes its way through the New Forest to join its colleagues and the many motor buses also in that fleet. Judging by the foliage this is early in the migration which took place between July and October 1962. In the upset after the fire some chassis were stored in Bournemouth until they were able to be handled at Station Road, thus making this trip an extra time in each direction. (PG)

In the lower partial extract from the local paper the *Surrey Herald* for May 8th 1962 the infamous and doubtless unloved boat makes its way to Southampton to be fitted out. Might there have been some in the factory who harboured uncharitable thoughts as to what might happen when it entered the water?

bodywork, including two Reliances for Maidstone & District, but a poignant loss was one of the last batch of trolleybuses built for Bournemouth, the last such production vehicles ever built in this county. One was so badly damaged that even the chassis was a total write off. It was not viable to build a single replacement chassis and thus Bournemouth's last batch of Sunbeams was one short when delivery was eventually made between July and October 1962.

Work continued on clearing up the aftermath and then resuming production in areas unaffected by the fire and its after effects. The first deliveries after the 4th July catastrophe appear to have been the 28 undamaged Reliances for Maidstone & District and one immediate action taken after the fire had been to start a new sequence for body numbers, beginning at M1 once again. It seems most likely that a combination of forthcoming insurance claims, accounting considerations, inaccessibility of existing records and expediency would have accounted for this move. The M&D vehicles thus carried body numbers M1-30, with numbers 27/8 being the two replacements. Delivery was completed by Christmas, except for those two which were not completed until April 1962.

The next vehicles out of the factory appear to have been ten Leyland PD2s for Chesterfield, then two Leopards for Southend and five Reliances for Rochdale. One Atlantean was also delivered, M229 to James of Ammanford, a BET subsidiary. Thus, although it was to be October before things got back to anything approaching normal, this handful of vehicles had been despatched to their customers in the interim. What happened next, however, was little short of spectacular.

Leyland Motors were, at this time, very active indeed in South America and the Caribbean, and also in what was then Yugoslavia. Donald Stokes, the company's Sales Director, was blazing a trail of some magnitude. This was before the amalgamation of ACV and Leyland Motors, and Leyland, with MCW, was competing head on with the ACV Group which contained, amongst others, AEC, Park Royal and Roe. Stokes was securing the biggest orders ever recorded in Britain for buses, and Weymann's, through MCW, were about to feel the benefit.

From October 1961, when deliveries started, until October 1964, over 560 export single-deck buses on Leyland Royal Tiger or Worldmaster chassis were produced at Addlestone, in addition to a smaller number of Olympics, including some for South Africa. The huge orders were split between Birmingham and Weymann's, and in some cases also with Marshall's of Cambridge.

Returning to the post-1961 orders, there were deliveries for Argentina, Uruguay, Montevideo, Jamaica and a series of small orders for South Africa. Sir Donald rightly became Lord Stokes, and the value of the business was well in excess of £10 million at 1980 values.

Home market business, whilst less spectacular, was fitted in and around the exports at Weymann's and included BET and municipal work as previously. Oddball orders included a Bedford SB3 in a vain attempt to get into the lightweight coach market. Two Albions were bodied around this time, an exception to the norm, and went to Ghana as illustrated on page 169. This was, however, just a drop in the ocean, for the Ghanaian Transport authority had commissioned a report by ERL Fitzpayne, Glasgow's Manager, on its future needs. The upshot was an order for 150 Worldmasters with MCW bodies built at Elmdon.

Bournemouth's trolleybuses had marked the end of that particular market, not just for Weymann's but for the UK. It seemed ironic that these fine vehicles should have such a short life after all the trials and tribulations of getting them built. With the exception of survivors in museums, including some Weymann's examples, and one Dennis prototype bodied for South Yorkshire PTE by Alexanders – also a museum piece – the British trolleybus had evidently become extinct.

Coach-builders cultivate a second string

OUT OF WEYMANN'S ROLLS . . . A BOAT

ON Thursday morning the massive doors of Weymann's Addlestone factory were rolled open. From out of this famous coach-building works was wheeled a brand new 43 ft. long boat.

Mounted on the back of a trailer, the grey and white painted boat was en route for Southampton, where she will be fitted out in three months time.

This is the first boat ever to be built by Weymanns, and wrapped in her sleek all-steel hull is a story of disaster and a legend of a gamble.

The disaster: On the evening of July 4, 1961, fire swept the Weymann's factory. Thousands of pounds worth of damage was caused. Inside, the hull of a new "hush-hush" boat was burned out. Months of work had gone up in flames and the project was temporarily abandoned.

He has kept constant watch on the progress in the factory. He now looks forward to sailing his new cruiser to Spain this summer.

Facts and figures about the boat. She is a five berth cruiser weighing over six tons. Length is 43 ft. 3 in., breadth 12 ft., draught 3 ft. 7½ in. with displacement of 14.5 tons. She will be powered by two Perkins 30 horse power diesel engines.

Among her special features are built-in fuel and water tanks, steel fore-cabin, cross-drained rear cockpit and synthetic resin-rubber non-slip deck covering. Her cruising speed will be 11 knots and her top speed is estimated at 14 knots.

SURREY HERALD 8-MAY-62

167

Portsmouth put its first underfloor-engined single-deckers into service in 1960, and, like the later Leopards seen here, they were equipped for driver-only operation. YBK 139, M9740, delivered in December 1961, was one from a batch of twelve used as replacements for a trolleybus route discontinued from April the previous year. They seated 34 passengers with standing space for a further 16 and were equipped with centre exit doors as seen. A further seven, M672-8, still with centre exits but this time with seating for 41, followed in 1963. (STA)

After the nine Royal Tiger Worldmasters of 1958 Halifax took 15 of these 42-seat Leopards in 1962, with six being allocated to the Joint Omnibus fleet and nine to the Corporation. PJX 35, M330, and now preserved, is one of the latter. It is seen here operating a heritage service in its home town. (JAS)

889 AAX, M8812, was one of three OPSUC1/3 export Tiger Cubs intended for Trinidad but never sent. In 1961 all three were modified to comply with UK regulations and then purchased by Jones of Aberbeeg. Unusually for Tiger Cubs they had four-speed pneumocyclic gearboxes. After withdrawal and passing through various hands this one was acquired by Alan Roberts in 1994 and extensively restored to concours condition. (JAS both)

168

Two Albion vehicles were exported to Ghana in 1962, one to Kwame Nkrumah University, M840, seen right, and M56, believed to be the one below. (PG both)

Building bodies for Midland Red was not normally an Addlestone occupation but a batch of Leyland Leopards, M598-622 with 53-seat bodies, as shown here, were built in 1962 and one, M598, was shown at the 1962 Motor Show. The balance of the order, M623-47 was completed at Elmdon, although Weymann's body numbers had been allocated. Number M611, 5157 HA, delivered in November 1962, is shown post-1968 when its ownership had passed to the National Bus Company. (AEJ)

The reincarnated Aurora, now a front-entrance Orion as seen below, adds a touch of class to the elegant Lord Street, Southport. M9745, UWM 44, was one of four delivered in July 1961, M9743-6, UWM 43- 6, with the balance of the order, M9747-50, WFY 47-50, delivered the following October. (AEJ)

169

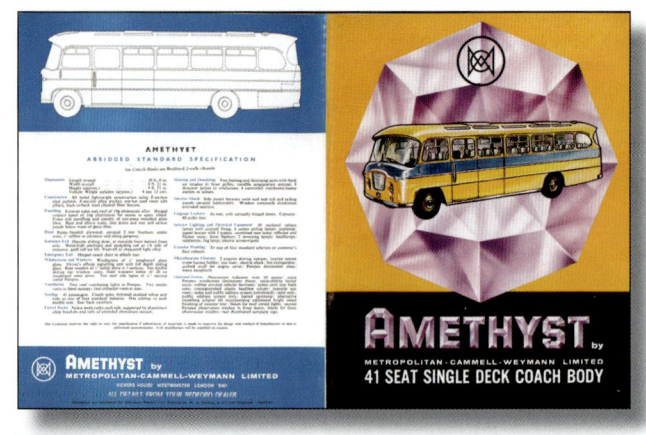

An attempt was made in 1962 to break into the lightweight coach market, one which was already well served, but needs must and so a body was designed for the Bedford SB3 chassis (which was familiar in the factory in its military form) seen here in the paintshop and then in the yard, lettered ready for the Commercial Motor Show. M303 served as a 41-seat Bedford demonstrator from September 1962 until sale to Leybourne Grange Hospital of West Malling after being repainted in a smart overall dark blue colour scheme and registered 144 YKR. The body was named Amethyst and its frontal body styling reappeared on one VAL in 1965, see page 185, the last of the six in a second and final unsuccessful bid to expand the coaching side of the business. Salford's elusive Fanfare coach can just be seen in the corner of the paintshop view. (PG both)

Another one-off on display at the Show was this Dodge single-deck bus, M671, 2498 UK, shown on that manufacturer's stand, but this time it is Norman Froggatt's turn to pose for the record shot. We are grateful to Shirley Moon, Chief Inspector George Page's daughter, for sending the tilt pictures which her father had kept and which in some cases, as here, provide the only record of a particular vehicle or even group of vehicles. It also verified that some batches had indeed been built at Station Road, for Elmdon did not use London Transport's Chiswick facilities for tilt testing. It is believed to have been sold on by Dodge, and John Davies, who left Weymann's and went to work for Dodge, recalls seeing the bus there but not knowing who owned it.

Lagos took nine of these Leyland Tigers in 1961, body numbers M290-8. The chassis used was the export OPS4/5 which had a wheelbase of 21ft 6in, carrying dual-door bodies as seen. In *The Leyland Bus* Doug Jack records that the model was very popular in Africa and over 300 chassis were sold to that continent, apparently many bodied locally, before the model was withdrawn from production. (PG)

In addition to its famous Motorway coaches Ribble also took 20 Atlanteans with less well appointed bodies for local express services such as those between Manchester and the Lake District. Here we see M342 from the batch M336-55 delivered between May and July 1962. They had seats for 59 passengers and were fitted with toilets. (JAS)

When Leeds changed its bus livery from light blue and cream to two shades of green the result was a rather drab outcome. The livery was later amended to produce a more attractive scheme by reversing the colours and a later example is seen alongside this rather gaunt looking 70-seat Orion, M162, from a batch of ten delivered in September and October 1962. (STA)

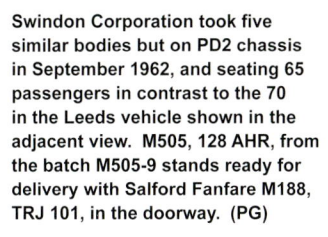

Swindon Corporation took five similar bodies but on PD2 chassis in September 1962, and seating 65 passengers in contrast to the 70 in the Leeds vehicle shown in the adjacent view. M505, 128 AHR, from the batch M505-9 stands ready for delivery with Salford Fanfare M188, TRJ 101, in the doorway. (PG)

171

Fishwicks took six Olympians in 1959 and here 526 CTF, LW52, is seen as built in the operator's yard, standing alongside Orion M7831. In response to a need for more comfortable vehicles for excursion and medium-distance express work after purchase of the Singleton business, two of the Olympians were sent to Duple Northern (formerly Burlingham, see page 160) in Blackpool for refurbishment and fitment of coach seats for their new role in 1963. LW49 is seen below after this treatment. (AEJ; KWS)

After giving sterling service with their original owner all the vehicles found new homes and here 521 CTF, LW 47, the first of the batch, is seen below left operating for independent Green Bus, Warstone of Great Wyrley. This was not one which had been refurbished, as is apparent, and it has now been preserved and restored to as-new condition in Fishwick's distinctive livery. (AEJ)

Below: King Alfred Motor Services of Winchester took three Tiger Cubs in 1959, M9187-9, and the bodies sported the deep metal moulding which Edinburgh had specified for its fleet. (JAS)

172

BET subsidiary Potteries Motor Traction, based in Stoke-on-Trent, took Leyland, AEC and Albion chassis to be fitted with Hermes bodies finished in the same livery style as North Western's. Here 736 CVT, one of PMT's Albion Aberdonians, is seen before delivery. In the relentless ongoing drive to reduce unladen weights some of these buses were fitted with single rear wheels bringing them well below 5 tons with 44 seats, but when a spate of groundings occurred due to nearside wheels dropping in steep-sided gutters, and the offside wheels being off the ground, PMT's General Manager declared them a step too far. Fifteen were bodied by Weymann's, M8322-36, and a further 15 by Willowbrook, in 1958, following an initial four from Station Road in 1957.

Posed by the operator, Albion Aberdonian 734 CVT clearly shows how the Hermes body was virtually identical on the various chassis makes and models taken by Weymann's customers. Aberdonians also entered service with North Western in 1957. They tipped the scales at just under five tons.

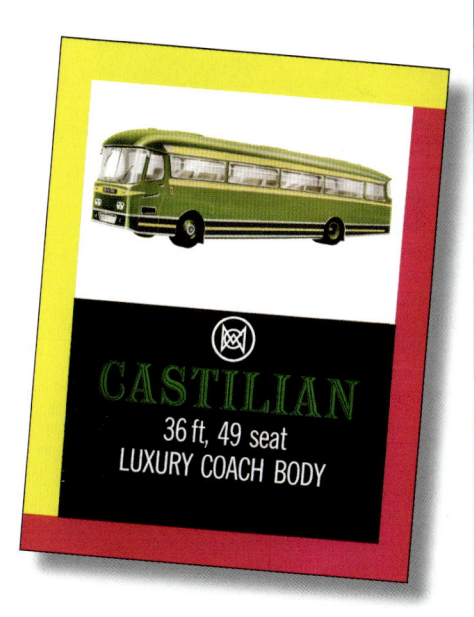

When the Construction & Use Regulations allowed single-deck buses and coaches to be up to 36ft long Southdown approached Weymann's to produce a stretched Fanfare coach to the new dimensions. The result was the Castilian, with M648 seen here, and first shown at the 1962 Commercial Motor Show. Mounted on Leyland Leopard chassis the 15 examples produced for Southdown – M648-62 – represented the extent of the model's production with delivery of the balance of 14 effected between March and May 1963. There was an enquiry from Timpsons for a small number but nothing came from it.

173

CHAPTER 14 – 1963-66

Sell Out; Walk Out; Time Out

Nineteen-sixty-three was a year which those who lived and worked through it are unlikely to forget in a hurry. The blizzard conditions which took the country by storm at the beginning of January lasted until April in some parts of the country, with deep snowdrifts and temperatures lower than they had been since 1947. Nevertheless, work continued, and the blue single-deckers from the big export order for 250 Royal Tiger Worldmasters for AMDET in Montevideo, Uruguay continued to flow out of the Station Road factory and into the yard at the rate of four per week before moving to Newport, South Wales, for shipment. Also going through at the same time were silver and blue Worldmasters for CUTSCA, the other major operator in that South American country. Domestic orders were on a much smaller scale and included seven forward-entrance Leyland Titans for Brighton Corporation, with the balance of a further seven not being delivered until late in 1965, while other small municipal contracts were for Rotherham and Stockton, the latter on Daimler chassis. These were going down the lines alongside a large batch of rear-engined Atlanteans for Maidstone & District, a contrast in types and colours.

An unusual order completed at the very beginning of the year was one for 25 Leopards for Midland Red, an operator which built many of its own vehicles and when it did outsource had not previously used Weymann's. The balance of the order, for a further 25, was later completed at Elmdon. The 15 new Castilian coaches – stretched Fanfares – for Southdown were in build but would remain unique to that operator. This mix of operators, and chassis make and types, seemed to indicate that things had settled down after the upheaval of the fire in 1961, and although the workforce was now smaller there seemed plenty to keep them busy.

There was, however, a subtle warning contained in this activity, for the proportion of export business which was coming through the association between Leyland and MCW now accounted for just over half of the Addlestone firm's output. When the contracts ran out, or if matters should take a downward turn at Leyland, Weymann's could be left dangerously exposed. Output for 1963 was later recorded as 530 buses, of which some 270 had been for export.

In the event the first serious jolt occurred from a different set of circumstances, for after years of refusing to agree to any form of closer amalgamation or buyout the Birmingham arm of MCW suddenly changed its mind. The reason for the change of heart at this particular time was not recorded but clearly Metropolitan-Cammell must also have been acutely aware of the potential downturn in future business once these huge overseas contracts were completed.

During 1963 a policy of looking for more accident repair work brought a selection of unfortunate examples into Station Road, mainly for local operators including Aldershot & District, Southdown and King Alfred Motor Services, but a replacement roof for a lowbridge victim from Western Welsh was also seen in the works. A Fanfare coach awaiting its turn can be seen on page 177.

It was unusual for A&D to be rebodying but they they decided to have a batch of Reliances so treated by Weymann's with the earlier BET style body when their original centre-entrance Strachan bodywork made them unsuitable for downgrading to o-m-o duties. Although the preparatory work was carried out in Weymann's drawing office, they were actually rebodied in Birmingham in 1966 after the Addlestone closure. MOR 581 survives in preservation. (JAS)

The start of the big freeze in January 1963 with two buses for South America standing in the Addlestone snow. Much more bad weather was soon to follow. (PG)

When MCCW finally agreed to purchase Weymann's from United Molasses, in June 1963, the Profumo Affair was in full swing, and the change of company ownership, confirmed when UM received a cheque for £957,697 13s 0d in July, seems to have been largely unnoticed in the local press, very much a small parochial matter when compared to the salacious details of the sex scandal splashed across the national newspapers. Only weeks later, in August, the Great Train Robbery took place and again people's attention was focussed elsewhere, particularly with some of the robbers being local men and a nearby caravan park being a short-term hideout. If ever there was a good time to bury bad news MCCW had been given it on a plate – twice. As has been mentioned earlier the first attempts by UM to divest itself of the bus building concern went back as far as 1947, with further attempts more recently in 1960/1.

In the factory it was a very different matter. The news needed to be disseminated quickly, accurately, and effectively. Heads of department and union representatives would be given this task, but quite what the overall reaction was remains unknown. Did everyone realise just how easy it would be for everything to be changed in future? Certainly the management would have been aware . . .

From now on the key decisions would be made in Birmingham, and doubtless one of the very first would be to scrap the *Joint Sales Agreement*, that instrument which had so irritated United Molasses over the last few years and which would by now have been superfluous since MCCW would also have been holding or acquiring all the MCW shareholding. Those formerly belonging to Homfray Davies had already come into their possession from UM through circumstances described earlier. Who built what, where, and for whom was now a matter for expediency rather than the 60:40 formula dating back to the MCW shareholdings of 1933, or its 1949 revised version. The effect was almost immediate, as the body records clearly show.

The body number sequence, allocated when orders were confirmed, was virtually continuous from the beginning of post-war production except where orders were cancelled, and remained so again from M1, the start of the new series after the fire in 1961, until Nos. 558-60, an order incorrectly recorded as cancelled by Rotherham around September 1963. More significantly, after the next block built at Station Road, M561-74, regular breaks occur where the entry records that the missing numbers are accounted for by vehicles built in Birmingham. The first occasion, numerically, was when 16 Atlanteans for Devon General – Weymann's numbers M575-90 – were reallocated to Birmingham and dual-numbered official prints in the archive confirm the 'double identity'. Thereafter the practice was commonplace and between autumn 1963 and closure it appears that approaching 300 vehicles were so affected.

Chief Inspector Page is well wrapped up in this view of one of Rotherham's three Daimlers, M558-60, 2147 ET, passing its tilt test in the bitterly cold open-ended shed at Chiswick in 1963.

Spring sunshine makes a pleasant contrast to the icy view opposite as one of Southdown's Castilian coaches from the batch of 15, M648-62, awaits collection. The first of the batch had been displayed at the 1962 Motor Show as recorded earlier.

Standing alongside in its distinctive and attractive darker green livery is Maidstone & District's full-height 77-seat Atlantean body number M542 from the batch M511-57, delivered between January and May 1963 and dating this around April time. (PG)

175

Western Welsh had already taken 76 Atlanteans by the time this forward-entrance PD2, M1033, 911 DBO, and one of a batch of 21 was delivered in July 1963. Body numbers M1026-1046 were PD2A/27 models and delivery was effected between June and November 1963. (AEJ)

Halifax Corporation were taking small buses as well as their 30ft long Auroras – in 1965 they took ten Albion Nimbuses with 31-seat bodywork, M830-9, and M834, RJX 253, is seen above. (RMC)

It would be understandable if this arrangement had occurred after the major strike (see below) where, following the numbers of men who were either made redundant before the walk out, or left because of it, there may well have been shortages of skilled men in some areas, but the fact that it occurred *before* the strike must relate to adjustments by Birmingham to regulate matters better, and doubtless in their favour.

It appears that possibly the second decision affecting Addlestone's work force was to scrap the New Bonus Scheme, introduced at Station Road only the previous year. Then came the serious matter of assessing the order book and deciding how much business was available and how many man hours would be required to fulfill those orders. It would not have been a pleasant occupation, certainly as far as Weymann's were to be concerned.

Output for 1963 was good at 530 buses and 18 taxis, over 100 up on 1962 (437 + 14), but the big contract for 250 Leyland Royal Tigers for AMDET in Montevideo was due to be completed in February or March 1964, (it would be the last export order). There had been previous large Leyland orders for British bus bodymakers, the most notable being one in 1951 for 620 Royal Tigers for Cuba bodied by Saunders Roe of Anglesey. Cuba was a somewhat sensitive market at the time, and it seemed jinxed when a fire followed by a massive explosion on a French ammunition ship in Havana caused severe damage to the content of one delivery and then, even more spectacularly because it happened 'at home' when a Japanese freighter, the *Yama Maru*, collided in thick fog in the Thames with the East German vessel the *Magdeburg*, outward bound from Dagenham and taking 23 of the buses to Cuba in October 1964 (see page 181). The *Magdeburg* capsized and lay on its side with some of the buses still on deck making for an eye-catching item in next day's *Daily Mail*. Rumours of a CIA-arranged plot were routinely dismissed. Despite the capsized vessel then being struck by a tanker, some of the vehicles survived to be repaired – at Addlestone and elsewhere – whilst others, recovered from the bottom of the river, were less fortunate. Some

Missing or damaged components would sometimes delay delivery to the customer. Here a Portsmouth Leopard awaits the driver's side window assembly before it can be released. M678 was one of a batch of seven fitted with dual-door bodywork, seats for 41 and space for 16 standees and seen in April 1963. One of Newcastle Corporation's Atlanteans stands alongside. (PG)

176

A sorry mix of chassis stuck in the field behind the factory during the strike with a completed Aldershot Loline and a Fanfare coach in for repair also trapped. (PG)

Below: How the *Surrey Herald* reported matters.

were rebuilt, some were rebodied, some were dismantled for spares. And with the exception of 50 Dennis Loline double-deckers to be supplied to Aldershot & District beginning in January 1964, the only other business was for relatively small numbers of vehicles amounting to perhaps no more than a further 100 units in total.

Clearly, there was a considerable shortfall, for although the annual bus build figures had been dropping steadily year-on-year since 1949 (with the exception of 1956 and 1960), this was far more serious. The likely output for 1964 could be as low as 150-200, less than half the previous year's figure. Municipal orders were steady, but in the main for small numbers. The former big orders from BET were reducing as that organisation was spreading its net wider. Marshalls, Willowbrook and Alexanders of Falkirk were all now taking more of the business which in earlier years could have gone to Weymann's when the Hermes body reigned supreme. North Western, as one example, had not been supplied with a single vehicle from Station Road since 25 dual-purpose Reliances in 1958, M8186-8210.

To what extent this dilution of BET business reflected the earlier loss through the forced resignation of Jack Davies (who had, like Bill Black before him, sought refuge at Beadles until they ceased bus and coach construction in early 1958, but later and more significantly in 1960 took charge of sales at Marshalls) and the departure of ace salesman Homfray Davies in 1956 to go into waste disposal, can only be a matter for conjecture now but coupled with the more vigorous approach from Marshalls and the revitalised Scottish Alexander concern, none of these factors would appear to have been likely to have helped Weymann's cause.

Returning to the situation in autumn 1963, the lack of orders meant that there would have to be another round of redundancies at Addlestone in 1964. Whether by accident or design two shop stewards in the finishing department, both considered by the management to be known agitators, were among those selected to be paid off. The immediate result was entirely predictable, the longer term effects were devastating. Eighty-five men in the finishing area walked out on strike, 200 more were forced to be laid off, and 160 left to find work elsewhere. For 21 weeks between March and August nothing moved and pickets ensured no vehicles or chassis went in or out of the factory or its grounds.

The strike was unofficial and various parties attempted to bring it to a close but it was not until the NUVB ordered the men back to work in July/August that the matter was brought to a close. For its

---

MARCH 20 1964

WEYMANN'S: 200 MEN LAID OFF 'DUE TO STRIKE'

ABOUT 200 men from various departments were laid off last Friday by Weymann's Ltd., Addlestone, due to production difficulties caused by the four-week strike of 85 finishing shop employees.

A spokesman for the management said the action had been forced on them because of the strike.

Saying that they had kept the men employed as long as was possible, he commented: "We have about 160 men left in the factory. I would not like to say how long we can keep them here."

Of the strike itself, which was caused by a dispute over redundancy notices, the spokesman said: "We cannot see the dispute coming to an end at the moment."

The strike was declared official last week by the National Union of Vehicle Builders.

This week Addlestone and District Trades Council announced plans to hold a mass demonstration and march tomorrow (Saturday) in support of the men.

The march starts at 11 a.m. at Victory Park, Addlestone, and will be followed by a mass meeting outside Weymann's works in Station Road. Following a special meeting of the local Trades Council to discuss the dispute, Mr G. Elliott (President) said "If the Weymann's management choose to remain adamant and to allow their policy to prejudice the future livelihood of some 600 local workpeople then the public must show their indignation".

He added that, with further men laid off, the future looked very uncertain and it was obviously a case which called for "urgent action."

MAY 8th 1964

Weymann's: No sign of settlement

There is still no sign of a settlement in the dispute at Weymann's Ltd., Addlestone. Twelve weeks ago 85 men from the firm's finishing department walked out after claiming that two men included in redundancy notices had been victimised.

The men's union, the National Union of Vehicle Builders, declared the strike official on March 9.

On Wednesday Mr. L. J. Cowlard (N.U.V.B. Area Organiser) said: "There are no signs of a settlement. At present informal discussions are taking place between top officials of the N.U.V.B. and representatives of Weymann's management."

He said the two sides had met on Tuesday, and it was hoped they would be meeting again later in the week.

A spokesman for Weymann's said: "There is nothing really concrete which we can say."

The firm is continuing to employ a number of workers, but the spokesman added: "I don't know how long we can continue to do this."

21-week strike is over

Seventy-one employees of Weymann's Addlestone, Surrey, returned to work yesterday after a 21-week strike over alleged victimisation of two men included in redundancy notices.

The men, who work on bus bodies, were ordered back by the National Union of Vehicle Builders national executive.

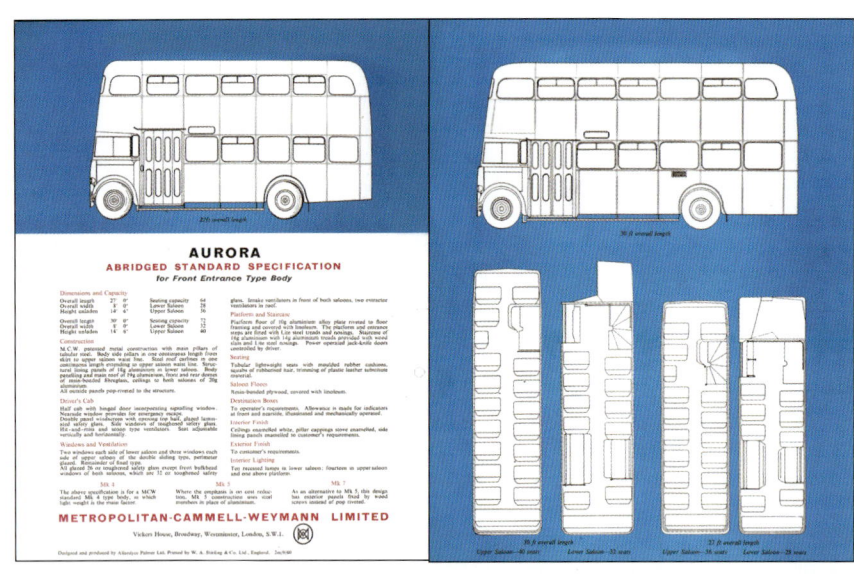

The Aurora name was dusted off and reappeared for the forward-entrance version of the full-height Orion body in 1960. It was available in two lengths, 27ft and 30ft, as shown in the accompanying leaflet. Halifax, Brighton and Southport were amongst those who took it into their fleets and one of Brighton's examples is seen below in the lingering snow in the spring of 1963.

Brighton's 27ft long Leyland Titan vehicles seated 64 and were allocated body numbers M561-7 and M568-74. The first tranche were delivered between January and July 1963, carrying registration numbers 21-4 ACD and 25-7 CCD. The balance of the order was not completed until 1965, being spread between February and November of that year, and carrying the later registrations BUF 528-30C and DCD 17C-20C. The final ones would be amongst the very last vehicles out of the factory. Note that these vehicles incorporated a two-piece folding door in contrast to the single sliding unit fitted to the Wolverhampton vehicles shown on the facing page. (STA)

In contrast South Wales took nine Regent V models with 72-seat 30ft long bodies, and these were delivered after the strike in October 1964. M1467 is shown here in restored condition at a rally in 2011. (JAS)

Wolverhampton Corporation was not normally a Weymann's customer but in October 1963 it was building a batch of 50 Guy Arab V 30ft long models, M757-806 of which M798, 7101 UK, is seen in the above and lower illustrations. The contract was completed early in 1965. Wolverhampton had taken similar bodies built in Birmingham but not on Guy chassis. (PG all)

part the Company had been obliged to agree to reinstate the two men, but on the strict condition that they took no further part in Union activities for the next three years.

The enormous damage done to the Company was shown in the annual production figures, 172 buses and 17 taxis representing the dismal total. Customers had been let down and Weymann's had become a dirty word amongst many operators.

Infinitely worse, perhaps, was the human relations aspect. In a company where family members of perhaps three generations worked side by side, or in different departments, feelings ran high. The smaller number taking the side of the two stewards had effectively held everyone else to ransom. Wages had been lost, suppliers and local traders had suffered, and MCCW had been reminded very clearly that Weymann's reputation for poor industrial relations was unchanged. The local paper reported problems when Weymann's cricket team was playing and some members would refuse to talk to others, even family members in some instances.

If MCCW had spent almost £1million buying Weymann's to maintain output and profits these events must have given rise to serious concerns. If their intention was, as it surely must have been, to close the factory, the militants were playing directly into their hands.

Either way, patience and sympathy must have been in short supply in Birmingham, and from now on it seems quite clear that charity began at home. Analysis of the body records reveals that beginning at number 557, the last of a batch of Atlanteans for Maidstone & District, orders cancelled by customers together with those moved to Birmingham, lost Addlestone some 293 vehicles between 1963 and closure.

179

AMDET based in Montevideo, Uruguay, numbered its Worldmasters 1001-1250, Weymann's body numbers M1047-1296 and the first examples were completed at the end of 1962, with construction proceeding through the whole of 1963 and being completed after the strike in 1964. The specially posed picture above shows one week's output, number 1064 below right shows the offside aspect, whilst the picture at Newport docks reminds us of the days before roll-on-roll-off ferries could be used for such work. It was a 6,000 mile journey to Montevideo. (PG two; STA two)

Lower right: The AMDET body design was used in differing configurations for orders for 120 vehicles for Madrid, of which one from MCCW was shown at the 1960 Motor Show, and also for the 180 'super-standee' buses for Belgrade supplied between October 1961 and May 1962, one of which is seen on page 165. Although the AMDET contract was to be the last to see vehicles being exported from Addlestone, the drawing office staff were still working on specifications for Israel and Helsinki in addition to enquiries for further anticipated business from Africa and South America. Such business as came from this preparatory work went to Elmdon.

DAILY MAIL, Wednesday, October 28, 1964

Buses for Cuba end up in the Thames

A SHIP lies on her side half submerged after a collision in thick fog in the Thames yesterday.

And buses bound for Cuba cling perilously to her decks, some half-submerged, others completely submerged.

Two passengers and the crew of 54—including three young stewardesses — were rescued when the East German ship Magdeburg (9,656 tons) sank on her side at Broadness Point, Kent.

The Magdeburg, outward bound from Dagenham with 23 buses for Cuba, was in collision with the 10,466-ton Japanese cargo ship, Yama Maru.

Not all overseas shipments went smoothly, though few were as catastrophic and headline making as the one above. When exports to Cuba were extremely sensitive, with worries over Russian influence in that country, the last thing anyone wanted was the sinking in the Thames of a boatload of Cuban buses from Leyland and MCW. Seemingly just to make doubly sure, the stricken vessel was rammed for a second time, by another ship, in the thick fog on the river. The *coup-de-grace* was delivered when the damaged vessel was being towed to a shipbreaker in Greece. It sank in a violent storm in the Bay of Biscay taking the remaining buses with it.

By contrast, sending vehicles to Maidstone and Newcastle was plain sailing although there were many in the company who remembered a brand new double-decker bus returning to the works within the hour needing to have a new top deck fitted after going home the wrong way and under a low railway bridge after leaving the factory. As Victor Meldrew might have said of both events "I simply don't believe it." (PG)

This figure does not include those partially constructed shells or bodies sent to Birmingham for completion after closure was announced and represents more than a year's production by this time in the company's unfortunate history.

If patience was running out when the strike began it had certainly run out before it finished. Keith Barkham and Maurice Bullivant, in the offices and at the sharp end of the customers' wrath, described the situation to the Author as a complete nightmare. When it was all over, and men returned to work in August, picking up the threads where they had left off was another nightmare. Many tradesmen had left, others were still not on speaking terms with their workmates, and everyone was clamouring to get their buses completed and delivered.

From the records we can see that amongst the last orders to be delivered in February 1964 were five Fleetlines for Rochdale, the first of Aldershot & District's 50 Lolines, then nine Albion Lowlanders for Yorkshire Woollen in February and the balance of five in March. Nine completed Fleetlines for Birkenhead were unable to leave, and were held until August whilst the long run of Royal Tigers for AMDET was temporarily halted along with everything else.

First out when work resumed appear to have been the nine Birkenhead buses, followed by the rest of the Lolines for A&D, Atlanteans and Fleetlines for Tyneside and Tynemouth, Regents for South Wales, Atlanteans for Bournemouth, a couple of Regents for Hebble and then the start of a run of Leopards for Ribble, though, as someone famously once remarked, not necessarily in quite that order. The AMDET Royal Tigers would have to wait until their contract was finished to make another boat load from Newport.

Over the years Weymann's craftsmen in the setting out department had produced some very fine models and this Bournemouth Fleetline of November 1964 was no exception. Based on body M1528 it is believed to have been displayed at the 1964 Motor Show though this has not been confirmed. There had earlier been a one-eighth scale model of an Olympic, detailed even down to hand-made rivets. Where are they now we wonder?

The approaching 1964 Motor Show must have caused some headaches. The MCW-branded stand displayed four vehicles, three from Birmingham and just one from Addlestone. Weymann's contribution was what Alan Townsin, writing in *Buses Illustrated* magazine in his review of the Show, considered 'must qualify as one of the most attractive versions of the basic Orion breed'. It was, of course, M1358, one of the Aldershot & District Lolines which had been held up by the strike. It was fortuitous that the contract was one of Station Road's more interesting ones and that finding a suitable vehicle for the Show was thus quite easy! MCCW displayed an Atlantean for Salford City Transport, also in a handsome green livery, and two export single-deckers, one for CUTSCA and the other for a Swedish operator in Helsinki. There must have been much placating of disenchanted customers to do during the time of that Show. It would be the last such event for Weymann's.

It was at this show that Leyland caught up with Daimler so far as the Atlantean was concerned. The unveiling of the Atlantean PDR1/2 in 1964, with three examples on stands other than MCW, showed the ability to reduce overall height to 13ft 4in thanks to the adoption of a drop-centre rear axle, as used on the Daimler Fleetline, but none were to be bodied at Addlestone.

The year end figures could only be disastrous, and, of course, they were. The effects of the 21-week strike and its aftermath had not been helped by the introduction of the 41 hour week that year. Only 172 buses and 17 taxis had been built, the lowest peacetime figure since 1935. It gave an average of 3.52 buses built per week, a very sad reflection of the heady days in 1948 when the average had been 19.44 per week.

During the first six months of 1965 momentum gradually returned to the firm, with some 240 buses being completed during spring and early summer, including 61 Reliances, 93 Leopards and a mixture of double-deck models. But it must have

Walter Healy started in the wages department in October 1940, moving to the buying office after army service and remaining there until being made redundant on New Year's Day 1966. Another staunch member of the darts team he married his wife Marcelle in August 1958 and they were regulars at the reunions until Walter's death in December 2010. Walter's father Tim had been mechanic to racing driver Sir Henry Segrave, and, after the latter's tragic death, chauffeur to Mr EG Izod.

Rochdale came into the rear engine era when they took five Fleetlines in March 1964. M1297, 6325 DK, is seen in the usual spot passing its tilt test.

The two men who maintained the high standard of the paintwork on Weymann's vehicles are seen here – Cyril Hutchins on the left and Dick Higgins to his right. Both men had spent many years at Station Road, joining the Company in the 1930s. (BB both)

182

Peter Gascoine, who took many of the photographs in this section of the book, worked for Aldershot & District in Aldershot as did his friend Bob Rowe, seen admiring the vehicle. It was one of these fine buses – M1358 – which became Weymann's last ever Motor Show exhibit. Here Dennis Loline III M1353, the first of the batch of 50 lowheight vehicles from the Guildford factory, is seen. Bob recalls that it was the only one to leave the factory before the pickets stopped any further movement until the strike was over. Aldershot & District were only one of many very angry customers. (PG)

The contract was not completed until June 1965 and the official photographer had to wait until the dust had settled before he could get into the factory to catch up on recording any completed vehicles. Here M1354 from the batch of 50 Lolines is seen in October 1964. Note that A&D used the sliding door which could be lethal if left open in hot weather and then slid closed in response to sharp braking if the locking mechanism failed to hold it securely.

Here we see AEC's answer to the lowheight question, but Nottingham had its own ideas about bus design – one of its later 'Standard' bodies is seen behind this distinctive if not particularly attractive Weymann's product. It is one of 35 AEC Renowns – M1472-1506 – delivered between February and June 1965, the lower build of the chassis enabling the low window line in the lower deck and same size glasses for upper and lower decks. The vehicle has not benefitted from the brightwork of the AEC grille being overpainted in black and thus being hardly visible in this reproduction. Only one other operator ordered Renowns to be bodied by Weymann's, Wolverhampton Corporation, and their five carried the final Station Road body numbers, M1962-6. Unfortunately, they were amongst the vehicles unfinished when closure came, and the framed chassis duly joined the sorry trek north to Birmingham. It was a sad irony that the very last body number should confirm the year of closure. (AEJ)

183

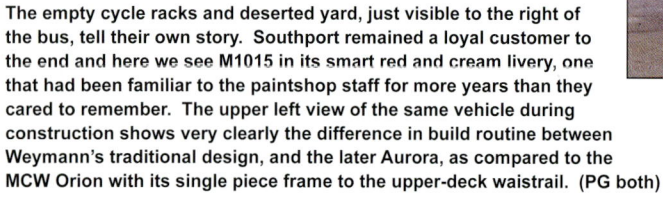

The empty cycle racks and deserted yard, just visible to the right of the bus, tell their own story. Southport remained a loyal customer to the end and here we see M1015 in its smart red and cream livery, one that had been familiar to the paintshop staff for more years than they cared to remember. The upper left view of the same vehicle during construction shows very clearly the difference in build routine between Weymann's traditional design, and the later Aurora, as compared to the MCW Orion with its single piece frame to the upper-deck waistrail. (PG both)

Leeds were taking ten Atlanteans as the closure was announced, with delivery being made between June and August 1965, although M1518, the last of the batch, was actually completed in Birmingham but not until October 1966. M1509, CUB 331C, has been preserved and this rear view of it below shows the engine shrouds specified by the Yorkshire operator. A further 15 similar vehicles, allocated Weymann's body numbers M1878-1892, were built entirely at Elmdon. (JAS)

184

The earlier attempts at trying to break into the coach market on a lightweight Bedford chassis with the Amethyst body had not been a success and only one such body was built. By 1965 Weymann's were desperate to find new markets to improve the output and so they once again approached Vauxhall, but this time to take six of the VAL 14 chassis with their distinctive twin front axle arrangement. The body created for this model was christened Topaz, being based on the 1962 Amethyst stretched for the longer chassis, as seen in the brochure below left, but it was destined to be no more successful than its predecessor. It is perhaps not too unkind to say that the design was hardly a world-beater. MCW then went on to produce the Topaz II publicity brochure, below right, using an imaginative version of the body shown in the two photographs below. First we see M1567, wrongly registered SAX 8C instead of FAX 8C, and then M1568, FAX 314C, from the batch M1566-71 and finished between April and June 1965. (PG colour view)

become obvious that things would never be the same again and the new owners in Birmingham would have been counting the cost of the 1964 disruption, and assessing the orders for 1965/6. There could only be one outcome, and the bombshell came when, in June 1965, the closure was announced and Notices were posted to that effect.

For all the woes the year was actually quite productive, with 279 buses and 11 taxis going out through the gates and there had been some last ditch attempts to turn things round including the construction of a half-section full-size model of a prototype taxi which bore an uncanny resemblance to the modern people carriers of today. Sadly, it was not acceptable to the taxi owners. Another last gasp concerned the bodying of a small group of six Bedford VAL 14 chassis, the famous twin front axle model, with two distinctly different versions of a coach body named Topaz. The VAL was not the easiest chassis on which to create an elegant design and it would not be unfair to say that Weymann's version was never going to win any gold medals. John Davies, working on the designs in the drawing office, recalls that there were also two Bedford VAM chassis being bodied, but that they were taken to Elmdon before much progress was made. Curiously, they do not appear to feature in either company's lists. In addition to doing detail work on Bournemouth's open top Fleetlines, M1917-26, John was also involved in the contract for 15 Atlanteans for BOAC, fitted with coach seats and a large luggage pen, for the service from London Airport to the West London Air terminal. These vehicles also ended up being built at Elmdon after Weymann's closed.

Heavyweight chassis from Leyland and AEC continued to be where the bread and butter work lay and examples moved down the lines right to the very end. The last six months saw vehicles for some of Weymann's long-standing BET and municipal customers, and also long-standing independents such as Fishwick and Brindle of Leyland. From the announcement of closure to the end of December when the last of the tradesmen left some 107 buses had been completed, taken into the yard, and driven away. Some had gone to Elmdon for completion, others had gone there as bare chassis, but either way they had gone and there would be no more.

185

The final contracts included dual-purpose vehicles for BET subsidiaries Ribble, PMT and Northern. Ribble's ten, M1751-60 delivered in spring, were on Leopard chassis, whilst PMT took five on Reliances, M1780-4 delivered in July, and Northern took eight, M1801-8, on the same chassis in the same month. Southdown, like Ribble, stayed faithful to Leyland, taking 20 buses on Leopards; these were destined to be the very last complete vehicles out of the factory and the picture below shows the Southdown drivers ready to take them away. The gates were locked for the very last time on 31st March 1966 as far as Weymann's were concerned. Arthur Musselwhite and Toddy Bubb look on, the former having been the Company's transport manager. (JAS; AEJ; AEJ; STA)

The Notice of Sale recorded everything in the factory from the largest presses down to typewriters and adding machines. In the sepia view alongside a group including Norman Froggatt (eighth from left) watch from the balcony as the removal men load up the final items to be delivered to their new owners. (STA; BB)

By Order of Weymanns Limited
ADDLESTONE, SURREY

IMPORTANT SALE OF
PUBLIC SERVICE VEHICLE BODYBUILDING PLANT

Machine Tools, Press Brakes and Presses to 200 tons
PEARSON 12 ft. x ¼ in. ELECTRO-HYDRAULIC GUILLOTINE
Spot and Arc Welders, Smiths Plant
1963 HILMOR MSA1, AUTOMATIC TUBE BENDER
Sheet Metal Rolls, Folders, Wheeling Machines
1961 ECKOLD METAL STRETCHER & SHRINKER
Waterwash Spraybooths, Stoving Ovens, Maintenance Equipment, Air Compressors
1962 WOOD MILL PLANT
Saws, Routers, Spindle Moulders etc.
Stocks of Metal Sheet Section, Tube, Timber and Trimmers Upholstery, Vehicle Fittings and Engineers Stores
1960 NATIONAL ACCOUNTING MACHINES
Calculators, Adders, Typewriters and Furniture, Canteen and Kitchen Equipment

LEOPOLD FARMER & SONS

Will Sell the above BY AUCTION in lots at the works
STATION ROAD, ADDLESTONE
TUESDAY, 1st MARCH, 1966 and following days
at 11 a.m. each day
On View 23rd to 25th Inclusive and 28th February and Mornings of Sale

Catalogues (price 2/- each) of:
Messrs. LEOPOLD FARMER & SONS, Industrial Property, Plant & Machinery Auctioneers,
Tel.: MONarch 3422 (8 lines)   Surveyors and Valuers, 46 Gresham Street, London, E.C.2

CHAPTER 15 – A QUESTION

Was Closure Really Inevitable?

We have seen in the earlier chapters that over the 20 years or so that Weymann's had been in United Molasses' ownership there had been periodic attempts to sell the company, but that none had been successful. The Addlestone company was a large one, a major force in the British bodybuilding industry with a capacity to build up to 20 bodies per week, and few of its competitors would have been in a position to make such a move, particularly when, in the late '40s and early '50s, the company was still profitable and would have been very valuable as a going concern.

Nevertheless, with the end of the war in 1945 United Molasses could be excused for wanting to dispose of this small (by their standards) company which offered little return on capital (again by their standards) in order to allow them to get on with what they did as their main business — moving molasses over water.

The logical first place to begin was with Metro-Cammell, the Birmingham arm of the joint Sales Company. Accordingly, in December 1947 UM's Board received a report that 'discussions were taking place with a view to creating a merger between the two companies'. The result was not favourable, though the reasons are not given.

No time was lost in seeking an alternative solution and Park Royal, the major London competitor, was next approached, in January 1948. Whilst the first tranche of the big London RT3 split contract was going through both company's factories, discussions between Keilberg of UM and Bill Black of Park Royal continued for nearly five months before being 'abandoned for the time being'. Park Royal must have seemed the best bet to Keilberg, but Bill Black was still digesting the purchase the previous July of Charles H Roe of Leeds, a very much smaller concern than Weymann's but nonetheless one which would have absorbed time and energy to integrate it into PRV routines. Once again United Molasses were to be disappointed.

Duple, then still in north London and builders of luxury coaches, had a large factory complex capable of extension so were not likely to be a contender for both reasons. AEC, with whom Weymann's then still had good working relationships, were not into bodybuilding. Thus in terms of southern England, there were, realistically, probably no other prospects. Doubtless those at Metro-Cammell noted and digested this rather significant piece of information, filing it for future reference.

At this time Weymann's order book was full, and the factory would continue operating profitably, with both 1952 and 1953 being reported as 'satisfactory'. The following year saw a change for, as the big RT contract came to an end the Board Minute records that 'Due to intensive competition conditions proved difficult; profits showed a substantial reduction on 1953'. Things were not destined to improve. In 1955 the Board Minutes record 'Difficult conditions in the industry; profits showed substantial reduction on previous years'.

This was even worse than it first appears, for between 1950 and 1955 several of the key competitors had pulled out of bus building, or gone out of business altogether: Brush Coachworks in 1950; Northern Coachbuilders in 1950; Leyland Motors in 1954; and Saunders Roe in 1955. Their combined weekly output would have been some hundred bodies and yet, even with that volume removed from the overall capacity, the remaining UK manufacturers were still facing very difficult times.

United Molasses must have mused that moving sticky black stuff by sea around the globe, to and from countries where English was hardly spoken, was easy compared to trying to make money building buses back home in Surrey. Some members of the Board might have thought privately that it was as well that Weymann's purchase in 1942 had been masterminded by the Chairman!

Thus, as the years passed United Molasses' options had diminished. The only one which seemed to hold out any hope, and also must have still seemed to them to make good sense, was Metro-Cammell but that concern was resolutely not interested. A significant factor may well have been that the Birmingham Directors and management were well aware of Weymann's track record where industrial relations problems were concerned, and would have wanted nothing to do with any arrangement which might well jeopardise their own factory's output. Another would be that having realised that United Molasses attempts to off-load the Addlestone plant had met with no success they were making sure that, when the time came, United Molasses were sellers rather than Metro-Cammell being buyers, as the expression goes.

Metro-Cammell were also aware through their involvement in MCW and elsewhere that the market was still shrinking. What has been described as the 'Golden Age' – the late 'forties to early 'fifties – had seen a massive replacement of the country's bus stock. Now, with the longer lives of the replacement vehicles and the rapid and ever-increasing decline in bus usage as more people became car-owners in Harold MacMillan's 'never-had-it-so-good' years, there would be over-capacity in the industry for decades to come. In addition to the major bus builders mentioned above, many small builders of coaches, new to the industry in the immediate post-war years, had or would soon cease to manufacture. In effect the bus-building bubble had burst.

United Molasses' Board Minutes, regrettably from our point of view, are routinely brief, but nevertheless the monthly report from James Don, the Director responsible for Weymann's, makes consistently depressing reading. 'Difficult conditions in the industry; but satisfactory profit. Prospects difficult for coming year; reasonable rate of production should be maintained for first half; engineering industry strikes effect not accurately determined tho' Weymann's staff not directly engaged in the strike. Supply of chassis delayed, interfering with production.' [1956]. 'Difficult conditions in the industry; but reasonable production and small profit. Reduction in labour force during autumn, reduced production rate in 1958'. [1957]. The UM asset was losing value year-on-year now. 'First 9 months reasonably satisfactory profit. Further curtailment of demand in autumn'. 'Forced curtailment' in 1961 involved considerable redundancies. 'Sales Company has numerous enquiries but difficult to assess with accuracy which are likely to accrue.' [1960].

Apparently, at this time, the huge Leyland overseas orders which would come MCW's way were not in the bag, though what effect they might have had on the future relationship between the two companies is conjectural. The MCW sales team must have been aware of the potential order size, since they would have quoted for the bodybuilding content. It was big enough to keep both factories busy for several months but United Molasses confirm they considered 'Production still unsatisfactory due to lack of orders.'

By July 1961 the export buses were being built but there then followed a surprise – a tentative approach from Birmingham with a view to Metro-Cammell (MCCW) taking over. The UM Board welcomed the approach but agreed that if no progress was made 'then notice be given to MCCW to terminate *Joint Sales Agreement* since Weymann's Ltd would not be in a worse position operating on its own . . . and there would at least be some saving in not maintaining the separate joint sales company'.

Metro-Cammell were now facing up to some unpleasant truths in their future production planning. Whether Leyland's Donald Stokes could find more export orders of this latest size must have seemed doubtful and if so they had overcapacity with their three factories. There was, of course, one major difference between the two situations – salvation for the Birmingham factories could have been through its huge railway business, something Addlestone could not look to.

All went quiet again after the 1961 approach but then the first steps in a major rationalisation took place when MCCW closed their Saltley works in 1962 and concentrated group adminstration at the Washwood Heath factory's offices. Then, in 1963, there was a positive move from Birmingham regarding Weymann's, and on 11th June of that year UM minutes confirm that agreement had been reached concerning an offer from Metro-Cammell to purchase Weymann's Ltd. At its next meeting, 12 days later, it was confirmed that Metro-Cammell's cheque had been received for the purchase of the 390,897 shares which United Molasses held.

At what point the change of ownership became common knowledge is not yet clear but it seems certain that the purchase was for one reason only, to enable closure of the plant when apposite, and thus remove further excess capacity from the industry. If Metro-Cammell ever had ideas of keeping Weymann's in existence the disastrous 21-week strike in 1964 at Addlestone, by then under their ownership, would surely have settled the matter otherwise. More immediately, however, since

Keith Barkham smiles for the camera but there was really precious little to smile about in the last few months. Keith was to end up back in this same office in his job with Plessey. The various press cuttings in this book came from his files. He was later awarded the MBE. (BB)

Reports from the local paper in 1965, below and opposite, make sad reading. The figure of 550 must have been the total workforce with some 400 being prepared to put their redundancy money into a new venture. At that stage MCCW had apparently not precluded sale of the premises for bus work – apparently they soon put that omission right.

1965
BUS BUILDERS TO LOSE JOBS

MORE than 550 workers of a firm which once built buses for Cuba were told yesterday that they will lose their jobs at the end of the year.

They are employed by Weymann's Ltd., at Addlestone, Surrey.

Two years ago, Metropolitan-Cammell took over the firm and now want to centralise production at their Birmingham works.

A management spokesman said: "The factory will close completely on December 31. This decision has been brought about by the drop in the demand for buses. Everyone seems to travel in a car these days."

Redundant workers to advertise for a new boss 13/8/65

THE 400 redundancy threatened bus body workers at Weymann's Ltd., Addlestone, this week decided to advertise for a new boss!

They instructed their works committeee to send an advertisement to two national newspapers asking for a new management to replace the Metropolitan-Cammell Company who are closing the factory at the end of the year.

REJECTED

But Mr. Charlie Sims (Works Committee Secretary) said on Wednesday that the advertisement—which begins "Unique situation for the right personnel"—had already been turned down by one of the papers because of legal difficulties.

"We may reword it to try and make it acceptable," he said.

The company itself has had the premises up for sale for about a week.

A management spokesman said on Wednesday: "I do not know if there have been any inquiries from prospective buyers, and I do not know the price asked."

There is no stipulation that the factory may not be sold to another bus body company.

Metro-Cammell now owned both factories it was possible to tear up the *Joint Sales Agreement*, that instrument which for so long had been a thorn in United Molasses side. Birmingham could now call all the shots as to what was built where, when, by whom and for whom.

The events concerning that fatal dispute have been recorded in the previous chapter but the damage done by such a long strike was enormous. Customer relations were stretched and loyalties were put aside as operators made whatever arrangements they could to solve their vehicle shortages; in many cases their chassis were parked in the field behind the factory at Addlestone but could not be recovered from behind the picket lines to be sent elsewhere. Maurice Bullivant and Keith Barkham, involved in Purchasing and Contracts respectively, remembered the period as one long nightmare.

Nevertheless, it was not until June 1965 that the decision to close the factory was made public. Predictably, throughout this period industrial problems had continued unabated and Maurice Bullivant claimed that even after the 'For Sale' notices went up outside the factory, after the Closure Notices had been posted in September, the more intransigent of the rate fixers and union agitators were still claiming that the factory closure story was just a bluff to keep their piece rates down.

A last-ditch attempt to raise capital to mount an employee-buy-out was doomed to failure. Although over 400 persons pledged financial support, and they even advertised for a General Manager to run the new organisation, this was not sufficient response, especially with Metro-Cammell being hardly likely to welcome or assist such a notion when their reason for closing the plant was to safeguard jobs in Birmingham. Furthermore, many of the workforce had already had enough and decided to seek work elsewhere. The growing Heathrow airport and the ever-present Vickers offered two of several options, and both were reasonably local for many of Weymann's workforce. Inevitably, the skilled men left first, and as these people moved away the problems in completing orders became increasingly apparent. Some contracts were cancelled; others were transferred to Birmingham. Some part-completed buses were driven to Birmingham to be completed, some waited patiently for some progress.

Friday 28th January saw the last of the employees leaving the premises, save for those still working in the offices and a handful looking after security and the collection of the remaining vehicles still parked in the yard.

On the following Sunday, 30th January 1966, the last of the batch of Southdown

M1895, TTE 642D, in service below, was one of three Leyland semi-lowheight Atlanteans for Fishwicks which had been part-completed at Weymann's before being taken for a draughty ride on trade plates to be completed at Elmdon later in 1966. It was 'intercepted' near the factory and in this fascinating view the untrimmed one-piece grp assembly which formed the complete upper deck first bay can be seen with much other body constructional detail. (PG; STA)

Leyland Leopard single-deckers was driven out of the yard by the Brighton company's driver, watched out onto Station Road by Arthur Musselwhite and Toddy Bubb, and Weymann's bus production was no more.

The *Surrey Herald* carried a picture of this event, and reported that of the final 400 workers who had been employed at the plant most had already found new jobs, mainly in their own trades. Seventy-five or so had been found new jobs by the Weybridge Employment Exchange, with another 40 or so 'still on the books but expecting to be placed within the next two weeks'.

More significant was the story behind the adjacent paragraph, recording that a former chargehand had been unsuccessful in his appeal claiming severance pay. He had seen the closure notice posted at the factory in September 1965 announcing closure at the end of December of that year and duly found another job. He had subsequently attempted to claim under the then new Redundancy Payments Act, 1965 but his appeal failed because he had not been continuously employed by the company, having in effect jumped the gun.

What was significant was the date of the Act. It came into force on 6th December 1965, one month before it had been intended to be launched in January 1966 as part of the Labour Government's employment legislation. Weymann's shop stewards apparently had sufficient pull with Labour MPs that they were able to have this Act put into force in time for the firm's employees to be the first in the country to benefit from its provisions. By good fortune Marcelle Healy kept her statutory notice and it duly recorded that she was entitled to one week's pay for each of the ten years she had worked in the Station Road factory.

Maurice Bullivant soon found that Keith had been wise to stay away from MCCW and returned to Surrey after six months or so, reluctantly leaving Jack Guarnori to be the sole survivor. (BB)

During February, after most people had gone, the final vehicles were driven up to Birmingham as chassis or part-completed shells for finishing until there were no longer any buses in the yard. Leopold Farmer & Sons, Auctioneers from London, then moved in and started to catalogue the plant and fittings. 'Lot Number' signs appeared everywhere and viewing took place from 23rd February, with the actual mammoth sale beginning on Tuesday 1st March.

Bunny Beaver, busy with his camera as ever, recorded the demise, as cranes and lorries removed the various items of equipment, until the factory was an untidy empty shell. Keith Barkham closed the gates and Edna Bubb locked them, and it was all over, the good times and the bad. Sadly, the days of walk-outs, strikes and other unrest had finally come home to roost, playing into the hands of the Birmingham management.

It was subsequently sold to Brixton Estates who let a part of the site – the 1947 'new' paintshop – to a small firm of bodybuilders, but later Plessey purchased the whole complex and the buildings began to be converted for their new use. Local historian JH Rowe produced a book entitled *Air, Road and Sea* which records the history of the site from the construction of the aircraft hangar in the summer of 1916 to allow Blériot's SPAD planes to be built, through Weymann's years, to Plessey and later GEC/Marconi days. In 2002 the site was razed to the ground and a new business park created on the land. The site stood empty for several years.

Tenant is found for empty offices
At last! Aviator set to take off

FIRST LETTING: Aviator Park in Addlestone

By Dan Murdoch
surreynewspapers@trinitysouth.co.uk

A BUSINESS park that has lain empty since it was built two and a half years ago, has finally attracted its first tenant.

Juniper Networks, an international networking and IT company, is expected to begin fitting out the top floor of the larger of the two buildings at Aviator Park, Addlestone, in June.

The business is expected to bring around 150 new workers into Addlestone.

Addlestone Chamber of Commerce chairwoman Peggy Broadhead said: "I'm absolutely delighted. Hopefully this will open the floodgates and they will let them all.

"We had high hopes when they built the park that it would bring that it hasn't worked out but hopefully this will be the start of something big."

Construction was completed at Aviator Park in Station Road in 2003.

At the time, residents hoped that

'Hopefully this will open the floodgates and they will let them all'

Peggy Broadhead

the large glazed office buildings would help revitalise Addlestone. But the buildings have remained empty shells ever since.

James Brounges, of the letting agents CB Richard Ellis, said: "The problem that speculative developers have is that it takes a couple of years from deciding to go ahead with a pro- dict the market conditions two years down the line, which is a very risky business.

"Back in 2000, when Aviator Park was conceived, the economy was gripped by the IT bubble and office space was in high demand.

"But that bubble burst and demand fell away. As an illustration of that, the volume of good quality office space let in 2000 was three times the amount let in 2005.

"But the economy has picked up, the market is getting stronger in the South East, and the excess office space is now being filled."

He added: "The fact that we have let one floor will create more interest and there are a number of companies that are potentially interested."

Aviator Park was originally developed by Brixton in 2003, but the company sold the site to Delancey six months ago as part

190

CHAPTER 16 – AN AFTERLIFE OF SORTS

Metro-Cammell-Weymann's Frimley Office

At the time of the closure there was a shortage of skilled draughtsmen in the bus industry and Metro-Cammell attempted to persuade many of Weymann's drawing office staff to move to the Birmingham factory. There was little or no enthusiasm for such a move, the west midlands being seen as less attractive than Surrey, and in any case many of those concerned were past the stage of wanting to uproot and start making a new home far away from family and friends. There was also the not inconsiderable matter of security. What guarantee had they that this wouldn't happen again, and then where would they be?

A compromise was struck, and a satellite drawing office was created at Frimley, just outside Camberley in Surrey, where the Weymann's team took on, amongst other projects, the detail design work for the London Transport Red Arrow single-deckers which would be built in Birmingham. Those working in the Frimley office included Moss Nelson, Cecil Fleming, Joe Allen, Bunny Beaver, Frank Wright, Robert Fleming, Eric Banham, Fred Smith, Tommy Thomson, Arthur Herring, Johnny Mitson and Reginald Swain with Edna Bubb looking after the administration and paper work. The office functioned for some two years and when it was finally closed it was decided that a get-together should take place the following year. From that first meeting has come the Annual Reunion, still being held, and to which the Author has been privileged to be a guest on several occasions since 1999.

Only three people were actually scheduled to move north – Jack Guarnori, Maurice Bullivant and Keith Barkham. Jack was wanted for his engineering prowess, Maurice for his purchasing knowledge and contacts and Keith for his expertise in preparing contracts. The experience of these three would, sadly, bear out the concerns that the others had expressed.

Jack, with his years of experience as a hands-on engineer, and track record of running his own factory in the RT days of J-Building, was put onto work-study. He soon became a disillusioned man, not welcome and not wanted by the workforce and not recognised for his enormous potential by the new management regime in Metro-Cammell. At a time when the Birmingham factory was heading for catastrophe here at least was one person whose experience ought to have been invaluable yet who was to be ignored. Having bought a new house in the area, and with an ailing wife and handicapped son, Jack's options were few and he had to stick it out until he retired, sad, lonely and perhaps not a little bitter.

There was to be some joy for him, however, for after the death of his wife he re-established contact with June Buckell (née Didcot) who had been his progress chaser in J-Building in happier times, and in 1976 they married. They had 24 happy years together before sadly Jack died in 1999, but June lived on in the house he had had built and his Royal Scot hand-built 'O' gauge locomotive still had pride of place in her lounge when the Author met her.

Maurice, on the other hand, soon decided that the set-up was not to his liking and, after around six months in lodgings with Jack whilst the latter's new house was being built, returned to his beloved Surrey. He took a position with Stone Magnet before joining Dennis Bros, in Guildford, and remained there until retirement.

Keith's experience was even more unsatisfactory. In August 1965 he accepted a position in the Birmingham sales office and although transferred to the MCCW payroll was asked to remain at Addlestone until the site closed. A reorganisation took place at MCCW at the end of the year but it was not until March, shortly before transfer, that Keith became aware that a totally different job was now on offer and so, not surprisingly, he turned it down and accepted redundancy. After one year with Racal he returned to the old Weymann's site, working for Plessey, and by a quirk of fate found himself back in his old office!

The full story of the Metro-Cammell saga remains to be told but this can hardly have been one of their brightest moments. Having apparently misread all the signs, and having nicely disposed of Weymann's and all its skilled, if somewhat mutinous,

One of the younger members of the team outside the Frimley office. The sign confirms that MCW's Design Office is located on the second floor. It closed around 1967/8. (BB)

Cecil Fleming joined in 1928/9, went to Vickers 1930-3, returned to Weymann's 1933 and was Chief Draughtsman at the time of closure. His daughter Gillian and son Robert also worked for Weymann's. (BB)

191

workforce, they suddenly found themselves totally overwhelmed by orders; only a few months after Weymann's closed, unable to cope, they were forced to sub-contract work to Strachans, Alexanders and others. Like other approaching fiascos in the British transport manufacturing industry, particularly those in the Leyland empire in years to come, it was just beyond belief. Or had it all been cleverly planned?

One million pounds to eliminate a competitor, with the Government putting up the severance pay commitment, and the development value of the land to look forward to, not to mention some useful tax losses from previous years trading, must have seemed like a good day's work. When the Leyland empire collapsed it was said that no-one there had the wit to have planned such a situation; were Metro-Cammell that bit sharper?

In later years CG Allott, one-time Weymann's Chairman but, by then, back with United Molasses and the man who brokered this final deal, defended his position and refuted the charge that he had let Weymann's go too cheaply by saying that "he didn't mind the other party getting a bargain so long as he made a profit".

Whilst there was genuine sadness in the industry some years later when Metro-Cammell Carriage and Wagon, having closed Elmdon in 1970, closed down the bus building division completely to concentrate on its railway business, there were some who remembered this period in its history and were glad that they had chosen not to be part of it. Some of them will be readers of this book.

Gordon Whindle joined the Drawing Office around 1934 but his sister had already been with the Company since 1927 as recorded in Volume 1. Gordon was not one who moved to Frimley, working from home on planning applications before his eventual retirement. (BB)

The cars on the frontage no longer belong to the bus builders – now another set of builders have taken over. (BB)

One of London Transport's RLH lowbridge Regents is carefully posed to show the change of ownership of the factory. (PG)

INDEX

Entries in Italics indicate illustrations

Aberdeen Corporation 51, 52, 81
ACV Group 66, 119, 167
Addlestone Factory (see also Factory Views) *12, 13, 17, 62, 192*
AEC 82
AEC
  Demonstrators
  Regal IV *106, 107*
  Reliance 130
  Renown 183
  RF 107, *107,*124, *129*
  RLH *89, 97, 116, 192*
  Routemaster *4,* 139
  RT *2, 51,* 78-89
  RTL *87*
Aircraft Industry 35, 67, 119
Air Travel 119, 130, 143
Albion 153, 167, 169
  Aberdonian *173*
  Nimbus *176*
Aldershot & District Traction Co *91, 148, 150, 177, 183*
Alexander Coachbuilders Ltd 66, 133
Allen, Joe 26
Allen, Reg 16
Allen, WG 107
Allott, CG 138
Amalgamation with MCCW 54, 174, 175, 187, 188
AMDET, Montevideo 174, *180*, 181
Annual Reunions 4
Argentina *112, 113*
Arthur, Don 16
Atkinson 101, 106, 107, *108*
Attlee, Clement 27, 112
Auckland Transport Board (NZ) *55, 57*

Barbados *110*
Barkham, Keith MBE 100, 158, 181, *188,* 189
Baroth, Charles 56
Barrett, Ron 16, 100
Beadle, JC Ltd (Dartford) 10, 133, *142,* 177
Beardmore Taxis 65, *69,* 143, 158, *162*
Beaver, Norman (Bunny) 26, *Front End Paper*
Beaverbrook, Lord 22
Bedford
  Green Goddess Fire Engine *119,* 133
  SB3, 164, 170
  VAL 14, 185
  VAM 185
BEF, Federation Body Design 39, 40
Belgrade 160, *165*
Bernhard Scholle & Co Ltd 159
BET 109, 112
BET and Tilling Share Exchange 18, 72
BET Contracts 23,
Biggs, George 26, *26*
Birkenhead Corporation *136*
Birmingham Corporation *101, 102*

Black, William (Later Sir William; Later Lord Black) 9, 13, 20, 39, *66,* 119, 177, 187
Bleriot, Louis 9
Blue Bus Service *161*
Boat Building *163,* 164, 167, *167*
Body Construction Illustration *11*
Body Numbers Allocation *69, 89,* 175, 179
Bournemouth Corporation *70, 74, 90, 93, 146, 154, 162, 167, 182*
Boyd, AJ 123
Bradbury, Tom 26
Bradford Corporation *24, 59, 71, 95*
Brighton Corporation *14, 31, 32, 54, 146, 178*
Brighton Hove & District Transport Co 32, 74
Bristol Bus Production 25, 53, 56, 72, 107
Bristol Tramways & Carriage Company 107
Brunton, Philip 99, 124
Brush Coachwork Ltd 99, 106, 187
Bubb, Edna 13, 16, 99, 133, 189
Bubb, Toddy 190
Buenos Aires 112
Bullivant, Maurice 16, 100, 133, 181, 189 *190*
Burlingham, HV Ltd 22, 160
Burton, Brian MBE 35, 133, *140*
Bury Corporation *1, 2, 62, 135, 144, 147*
Bus Bodies (SA) Ltd 53, *123*
BUT (British United Traction) 36, 65, 118

Canteen *64*
Cape Electric Tramways Ltd *36, 77*
Carman, John 26
Carris Museum, Lisbon *75*
Carter, Stan 68
Central Electricity Generating Board 65, 72
Central Mining & Investment Corp 9, 13, 36, 159
Ceylon 112, *114*, 118, 153
Charitable Work 100
Chatfield, WCS 26, 34
Cheesley, AT 34
Cheltenham & District Traction Co Ltd *16, 53*
Cherry, David 136
Cherry, George 136
Chesson, Godfrey 99, 158, *158*
Chesterfield Corporation *46, 147, 162*
Chile 109, *110*, 130
Chiswick Works 49, 78, *92*
Christmas Parties *64*
Churchill, Winston 27
City Oxford Motor Services Ltd *115, 146, 164*
Closure of Addlestone 185, *188, 189*
Coachbuilt (Timber Frame) Bodies 37, 67, *75*
Cole, RM (Bon) 25, 34, 36, 39, 99, 112, *112*
Collective Bonus Scheme 36
Commercial Motor Shows 37, 55, 59, 91, *92,* 101, *103,* 106, 107, *120, 124, 128,* 130, 131, 132, *134, 136,* 138, 143, *143,* 152, 160, *160, 162,* 182

Commer-Beadle, Rochester Coach *142*
Commer-Karrier 10
Common Market 139
Company Chauffeur 26
Composite Bodywork 31, 39
Construction and Use Regulations 30, 102, 153, 166, 173
Cook, Harold 26, 34, 36, 37, 39, *93,* 110, 116, 119, 133 *133,* 164
Council of The National Federation of Vehicle Trades 20
Cox, Edgley 81, 87
Crossley Motors Ltd 25, 37, 57, 132
Crosville Motor Services 68, 72, *94*
Cuba 176, *181*
Cumberland Motor Services Ltd *11*
Cunard Motor & Carriage Co Ltd 9
CUTSCA, Montevideo *149,* 174

Daimler 109, 158
  Demonstrators *11, 161*
  Fleetline 160, 182
  Wartime Chassis 21
Damascus 110
Darts Team 16 *64,* 132
Davies, CH 34
Davies, Jack 34, 37, *93,* 99,, 100, 116, 119, 132, 133, *133, 142,* 177
Davies, John 4 *4,* 185
Decompression Chambers
Dennis Bros 177
Derby Corporation 15
Devaluation of Sterling 99
Devon General Omnibus & Touring Co Ltd *37, 38, 51,* 81, *120,* 130
Didcot, June 26
Dimensions of Vehicles 22, 24, 35, 81, 101, 102, 119, 128, 138
Dixon, Don 26
Docker's Strike 27, 39
Dodge *170*
Dodsworth, Walter 26, 34, 37, 100, 116, 133, 138
Don, James 26, 112, *112,* 116, 119, 133, 158, 188
Drawing Office, Frimley 4, *191*
Driver, HS 101, 107
Dundee Corporation *107*
Duple Motor Bodies Ltd 68, 130, 160, 172, 187
Durban Transport

Earls Court Exhibition Centre *55*
Eastbourne Corporation *8, 52*
Eastern Coach Works 29, 56, 72, 107
East Kent Road Car Company *25, 132*
East Midland Motor Services Ltd *38, 39, 151*
East Yorkshire Motor Services Ltd *41*
Edinburgh Corporation *28, 69, 105, 159*
Edwards, HN 34
Electric Car Project 18
Ellis, Monty 26
Employee Buyout – Failed Attempt 189, *189*
English Steel Corporation 26
Essential Works Orders 34
Exeter Corporation *5, 41, 145*
European Recovery Programme 54

Factory Closure and Auction 185, *186*, 187, *188*, 188, *189*, 190
Factory Fire 162, 163, *163*, 174
Factory and Factory Views 11, *12, 13, 17, 62, 192*
Family Relationships 26
Festival of Britain 100, *117*
Fibreglass (GRP) 99, 124, *126*
Financing of Weymann's 9
Fishwicks 104, *105, 147, 172, 189*
Fitzpayne, ERL 167
Fleming, Cecil 4, 26, *191*
Fleming, Gillian
Fleming, Robert
Flexible Patent Bodywork 6, 10, *11,* 29
Ford, Henry 100
Formby, Captain 39
Freak Winter 29
Frimley Drawing Office *191*
Froggatt, Arthur Thomas MBE 13, *17, 19,* 26, 36, 39, 90, 99, *100,* 116
Froggatt, Mrs Beryl 117, *117*
Froggatt, Norman 19, 26, 34, 117, *117,* 158
Fuel Duty 107

Gardner Engines 22, 25, 107
Gascoine, Peter 69
Ghana 167, *169, 170*
Gimson PH 66
Glasgow Corporation *93, 97, 99, 135, 144*
Gordon Boys School 100
Green Bus Service, Warstone *172*
Green Goddess Fire Engines 119, 133
Green Line; Green Line Coaches Ltd *9*
General Working Agreement 133
Grey Cars *142*
Gray, Ivor 161, 165
Gray, WH 13, 34, 99
Guarnori, Jack (John) 26, 80, 104, 138
Guy Motors, 21, 22, 37, 108, 109, *109, 114, 126, 145, 179*

Halifax Corporation, Halifax JOC *168, 176*
Hall, Lewis Coachworks (See also Park Royal) 34
Harmonisation of European Traffic Standards 35
Harringtons Ltd 33
Hastings Tramway Company *30, 31,* 39, *44*
Healy, Mrs Marcelle 26, 100, *115,* 190
Healy, Tim 26
Healy, Walter 13, 26, 100
Heath Row (Later Heathrow) 35, 189
Hebble Motor Services Ltd *42, 106*
Higgins, Dick *182*
Hoggard, Jackson 35
Hoggard, Richard 35
Home Guard 17
Homfray Davies, Baden Rhys Aubrey 26, 36, 123 133, *133,* 138, 175, 177
Humber Cars 10
Humphrey, Dave *64,* 132
Humpidge, CT 95
Hutchins, Cyril *182*

International Monetary Fund 30
Institute of British Carriage and Automobile Manufacturers 39, 91, 100
Isle of Man Road Services Ltd *103*
Izod, Edwin Gilbert 9, *17,* 26, 36, 92

Jack, AD 165
Jaguar 158
Jamaica Omnibus Services 110, *111,* 128, *161*
James, Ammanford (Lewis & James) *164*
James, WT 165
J Building 31, *78-89,* 119, 138
Jennings *101*
Joint Sales Organisation and Agreements 10, 25, 54, 65, 84, 85, 175, 188, 189
Jones Bros, Aberbeeg *154, 168*

Kampala *139*
Keilberg, Sir Michael 187
Kemp, WP 36
Kennedy, Stanley *66*
King Alfred Motor Services *172*
Kingston upon Hull Corporation 32, *44, 49,* 149
Knight, Jim 26
Kuwait 110

Lagos *170*
Lahore 114
Lambert, HR 39, 101, 107
Lancashire United Transport & Power Co Ltd 27, 45, 49, 52, 70, *109*
Lawrence, Bill 26, 164
Leeds City Tramways & Transport Dept *118, 171, 184*
Leicester Corporation *151*
Leyland
  Atlantean 138, *138,* 143, 152, *152, 155, 156, 157, 182*
  Comet *161*
  Demonstrators *92,* 106, 124, *125, 134,* 154
  Olympian 130,*134, 150, 172*
  Olympic 91, *92,* 101, *101, 103, 104, 105,* 110, *117, 123,* 124, 130, 134, 167
  Royal Tiger *104, 106, 109,* 110, 124, 167, 176
  Royal Tiger Worldmaster *144,* 149, 167
  Tiger Cub 107, 124, *125,* 130, *125*
Leyland Motors 29, 33, 37, 39, 115, 123, 133, 187
Light, Henry 10
Lighting Regulations for Trolleybuses 30
Lindon, Jim 26
Lisbon Tramways 33, *55, 75, 76, 128, 159*
Liverpool Corporation *47, 63, 72*
Lough Swilly 149
London Aircraft Production Group (LAP) 22, 79
London Transport *2, 4,* 31, *33,* 33, 34, 39, *78-89,* 97, 107, 116,118, *129, 139, 192*
Lydney Coachworks *53,* 68

Maddocks, Freddie 26
Madrid *110, 180*

Maidstone Corporation *70*
Maidstone & District Motor Services Ltd *37, 55, 61, 96, 151, 153, 155, 166, 175, 181*
Manchester Corporation 11, 23
Mann, Egerton 10
Mansfield District Traction Co Ltd 22, *94*
Markland, Stanley 124
Marshalls of Cambridge 133, 167
Mason, Frank 132
Massey Bros 149
Maudslay Motor Co Ltd 57
MCW 21st Anniversary 123, *128, 129*
MCW Body Designs 124
  Amethyst *170*
  Atlantean 138, *138,* 152, *152, 153, 157, 160*
  Apollo *111*
  Arcadian 132, 138, *143*
  Aurora *120,* 124, 160, *169, 178*
  Castilian 153, *173,* 174, *175*
  Fanfare *131,* 132, 138, *142, 150, 153, 166*
  Hermes 102, *106,* 111, *125, 128,* 132, 141
  Jason *111,* 124
  Olympian *134,* 130, *150*
  Olympic 92, 101, *101, 103, 104,* 110, *117, 123,* 130, 143, 167
  Olympic Series 2 *111*
  Orion *121, 123,* 124, 128, 133, 136, *137, 146, 184*
  Topaz *185*
MCW Exports 27
Merthyr Tydfil Corporation *21, 154*
Metal-Framed Bodywork 11, 31. *63*
Metropolitan Cammell Carriage & Wagon Company 10, 26, 175, 187
Metropolitan Cammell Carriage & Wagon Company – Factory Closures 188
Metropolitan Cammell Carriage & Wagon Company – Purchase of Weymann's 175, 188

Metropolitan-Cammell-Weymann 7,10
Mexborough & Swinton Traction Co Ltd *148*
Midland General Omnibus Co Ltd *62*
Midland Red 32, 49, 101, *169,* 174
Military Contracts 133
Miner's Strike 29
Ministry of Supply 19, 23, 119, 158, 164
Ministry of War Transport 19, 22, 27
Morecambe & Heysham Corporation *10,* 94
Morter, RM 114
Motor Export Group 23
Motorway Coaches 143, *156, 166*
Mr Cube 67
Mumfords *18,* 34, 68
Museum of Transport, Clapham *74*
Musselwhite, Arthur *3,* 190

Nationalisation 28, 36, 39, 65, 67, 72, 114, 138
Napier, Sir Joseph 13
Nash, Miss Hilda C 26
National Federation of Vehicle Trades 20